01/14
78.00

D0154613

INTRODUCTION TO
Adobe® Photoshop® CS6

Complete Coverage of the Adobe® Certified Associate Exam:
Visual Communication using Adobe® Photoshop® CS6

AUTHOR	Jennifer Smith
ADDITIONAL WRITING	Chad Chelius
PROJECT MANAGER	Cheri White
VIDEO PRODUCTION	Chris Leavey
VP & EXECUTIVE PUBLISHER	Don Fowley
EDITOR	Bryan Gambrel
DIRECTOR OF SALES	Mitchell Beaton
EXECUTIVE MARKETING MANAGER	Chris Ruel
ASSISTANT MARKETING MANAGER	Debbie Martin
EDITORIAL PROGRAM ASSISTANT	Jennifer Lartz
SENIOR PRODUCTION MANAGER	Janis Soo
ASSOCIATE PRODUCTION MANAGER	Joel Balbin
CREATIVE DIRECTOR	Harry Nolan
COVER DESIGNER	Georgina Smith
TECHNOLOGY & MEDIA	Tom Kulesa, Wendy Ashenberg
TECHNICAL EDITORS	Cathy Auclair, Kate Erikson
ART DIRECTOR	Jennifer Smith

This book was set in Bembo by Spoke & Wheel with production and development services provided by American Graphics Institute. It was printed and bound by Courier Kendallville. The covers were printed by Lehigh Phoenix.

ISBN 978-1-118-39408-3

Printed in the United States of America

10 9 8 7 6 5 4 3 2 1

Preface

Welcome to *Introduction to Adobe Photoshop CS6*. Part of Wiley's Adobe courseware series, this book is designed as a complete introduction to Adobe Photoshop for Creative Suite 6. With this series, we've set out to produce a series of textbooks that deliver compelling and innovative teaching solutions to instructors and superior learning experiences for students. Infused and informed by in-depth knowledge from Adobe Certified Experts and Photoshop professionals who have created many official training titles for Adobe Systems, and crafted by a publisher known worldwide for the pedagogical quality of its products, these textbooks maximize skills transfer in minimum time. Students are challenged to reach their potential by using their new technical skills as highly productive members of the workforce. This courseware was designed to ensure you receive the topical coverage that is most relevant to your personal and professional success.

Wiley's Adobe courseware Program

Wiley's Adobe courseware series is a complete program for instructors and institutions to prepare and deliver great courses on Adobe software technologies. With this courseware series, we recognize that—because of the rapid pace of change in the technology and curriculum developed by Adobe—there is an ongoing set of needs beyond classroom instruction tools for an instructor to be ready to teach the course. This courseware program endeavors to provide solutions for all these needs in a systematic manner in order to ensure a successful and rewarding course experience for both instructor and student via technical and curriculum training for instructor readiness with new software releases and a great set of tools for delivering instruction in the classroom and lab. All are important to the smooth delivery of a course on Adobe software, and all are provided with Wiley's Adobe courseware program. We think about this model as a gauge for ensuring that we completely support you in your goal of teaching a great course.

VIDEO TUTORIALS

Your *Introduction to Adobe Photoshop CS6* textbook comes with access to approximately 2 hours of online video tutorials. The video tutorials are designed to supplement each lesson in the book. These video tutorials are created and presented by the authors and demonstrate topics covered in each lesson or related topics that enhance your understanding of each lesson.

Illustrated Book Tour

Pedagogical Features

The Wiley Adobe courseware and textbooks for Adobe Creative Suite 6 are designed as complete introductory textbooks on a particular Adobe software product. The books are also designed to cover all the learning objectives for that product's related Adobe Certified Associate (ACA) exam. The ACA exam is industry-recognized and identifies skills and topics expected for entry-level positions. Each ACA exam item is referred to as an exam objective, and these objectives are highlighted throughout the textbooks. Many pedagogical features have been developed specifically for this courseware. Unique features of our task-based approach include a Lesson Skill Matrix that correlates skills taught in each lesson to the ACA objectives; Certification Ready sidebars; Step-by-Step exercises; and two levels of increasingly rigorous lesson-ending activities—Competency Assessment and Proficiency Assessment.

Presenting the extensive procedural information and technical concepts woven throughout the textbook raises challenges for the student and instructor alike. The Illustrated Book Tour that follows provides a guide to the rich features contributing to Wiley's Adobe courseware pedagogical plan. Following is a list of key features in each lesson designed to prepare students for success on the certification exams and in the workplace:

- Each lesson begins with a **Lesson Skill Matrix**. More than a standard list of learning objectives, the skill matrix correlates each software skill covered in the lesson to the specific ACA exam objective.

- Each lesson features a real-world **Business Case** scenario that places the software skills and knowledge to be acquired in a real-world setting.

- Concise and frequent **Step-by-Step** instructions teach students new features and provide an opportunity for hands-on practice. Numbered steps give detailed instructions to help students learn software skills. The steps also show results and screen images to match what students should see on their computer screens.

- **Illustrations** provide visual feedback as students work through the exercises. The images reinforce key concepts, provide visual clues about the steps, and allow students to check their progress.

- When the text instructs a student to use a particular tool, **tool images** are shown within the text.

- Important technical vocabulary is listed in the **Key Terms** section at the beginning of the lesson. When these terms are used later in the lesson, they appear in bold italic type and are defined. The Glossary contains all of the key terms and their definitions.

- Engaging point-of-use **Reader Aids** located throughout the lessons tell students why this topic is relevant (*The Bottom Line*) and provide students with helpful hints (identified with the words *Take Note*) or ways to expand their skills (identified using the text *Learning More*). Reader aids also provide additional relevant or background information that adds value to the lesson.

- **Certification Ready** features throughout the text signal students where a specific certification objective is covered. They provide students with a chance to check their understanding of that particular ACA exam objective and, if necessary, review the section of the lesson where it is covered. This courseware provides complete preparation for ACA certification.

- Each lesson ends with a **Skill Summary**, recapping the ACA exam skills covered in the lesson.
- Accompanying **video tutorials** for each lesson provide a visual way to see selected content from the each lesson presented by the authors.
- The **Knowledge Assessment** section provides a total of 20 questions from a mix of True/False and Multiple Choice, testing students on concepts learned in the lesson.
- **Competency Assessment** and **Proficiency Assessment** sections provide progressively more challenging lesson-ending activities.
- Integrated **Circling Back** projects provide students with an opportunity to renew and practice skills learned in previous lessons.
- The student companion website contains the **online files** needed for each lesson.

Illustrated Book Tour

Key Terms ——

Lesson Skill Matrix ——

Business Case ——

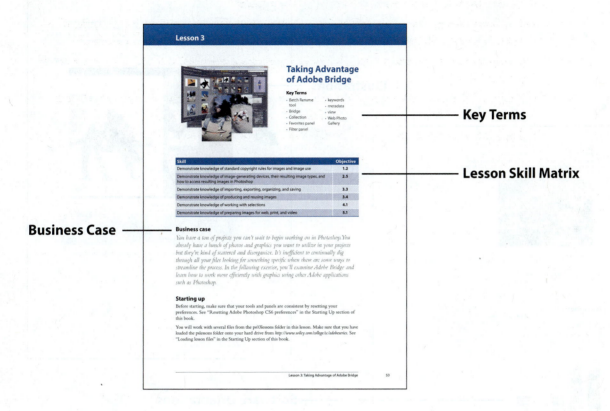

Certification Ready ——

Step-by-Step ——

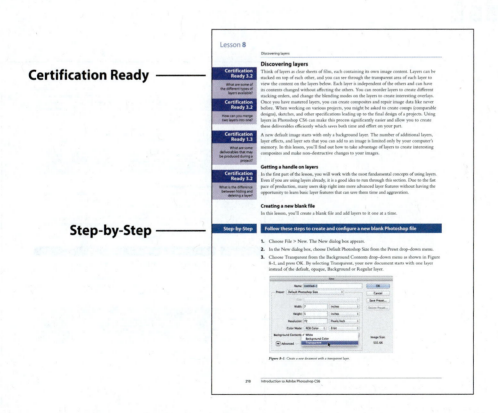

Illustrated Book Tour

Illustrations ———

Software Orientations ———

Take Note ———

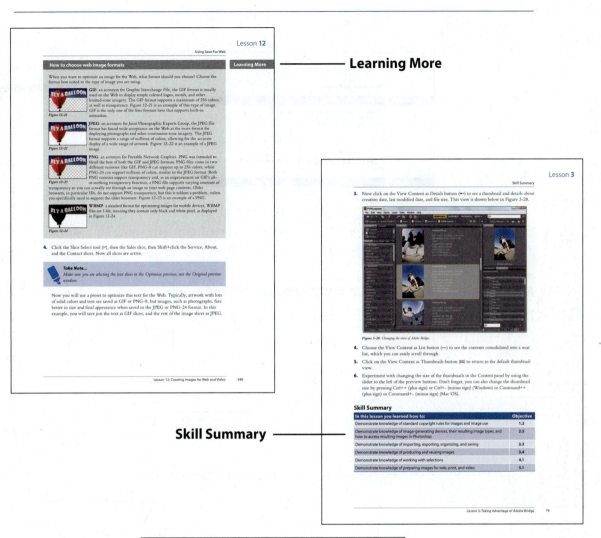

Learning More

Skill Summary

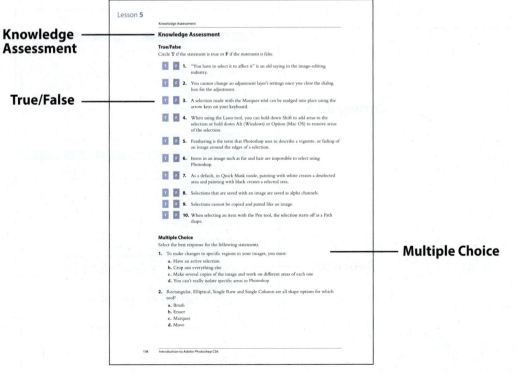

Knowledge Assessment

True/False

Multiple Choice

Illustrated Book Tour

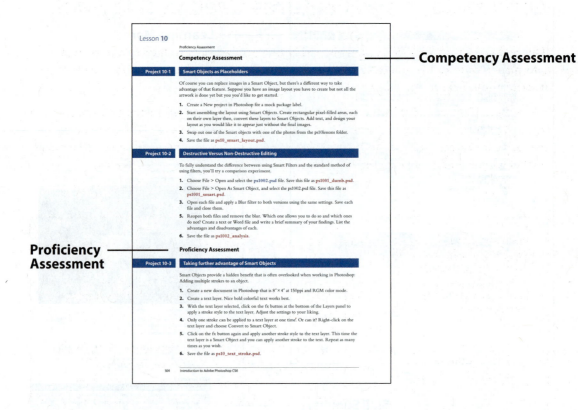

Competency Assessment

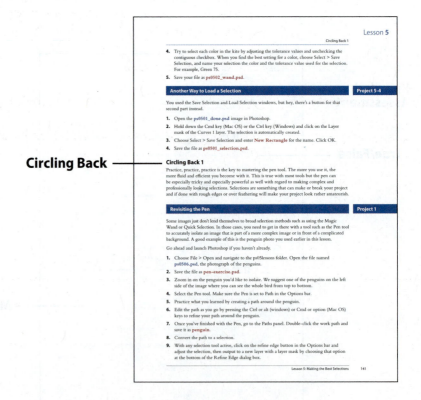

Proficiency Assessment

Circling Back

Conventions and Features Used in This Book

This book uses particular fonts, symbols, and heading conventions to highlight important information or to call your attention to special steps. For more information about the features in each lesson, refer to the Illustrated Book Tour section.

File > Open Text separated by the greater than symbol (>) indicates instructions for using a menu to perform a task—with the first item indicating the menu to use and the second item indicating the menu choice. If the menu includes additional choices, more than one greater than symbol will be used to indicate the additional choices, such as File > Open > Recent

Certification Ready 3.1 What are the different parts of the Photoshop workspace?	This feature signals the point in the text where a specific certification objective is covered. It provides you with a chance to check your understanding of that particular ACA objective and, if necessary, review the section of the lesson where it is covered.
 *Take Note...*	Take Note reader aids provide helpful hints related to particular tasks or topics. These notes, set in green shaded boxes, provide pointers to information discussed elsewhere in the textbook or describe interesting features that are not directly addressed in the current topic or exercise.
ALT+Tab	A plus sign (+) between two key names means that you must press both keys at the same time. Keys that you are instructed to press in an exercise will appear in the font shown here.
Key Terms	Key terms appear in green.
Type My Name is	Any text you are asked to type on the keyboard appears in red.
ps0201.psd	The names of data files will appear in blue for easy identification.

Instructor Support Program

Wiley's Adobe courseware program is accompanied by a rich array of resources that incorporate the extensive textbook visuals to form a pedagogically cohesive package. These resources provide all the materials instructors need to deploy and deliver their courses. The following resources are available online for download.

- The **Instructor's Guide** contains solutions to all the textbook exercises as well as chapter summaries and lecture notes. The Instructor's Guide and Syllabi for various term lengths are available on the Instructor's Book Companion Site (*http://www.wiley.com/college/sc/adobeseries*).

- The **Solution Files** for all the projects in the book are available online on the Instructor's Book Companion Site (*http://www.wiley.com/college/sc/adobeseries*).

- A complete set of **PowerPoint Presentations** is available on the Instructor's Book Companion Site (*http://www.wiley.com/college/sc/adobeseries*) to enhance classroom presentations. Tailored to the text's topical coverage and the Lesson Skill Matrix, these presentations are designed to convey key Adobe Photoshop concepts addressed in the text.

  All images from the text are on the Instructor's Book Companion Site (*http://www.wiley.com/college/sc/adobeseries*). You can incorporate them into your PowerPoint presentations or create your own overhead transparencies and handouts.

  By using these visuals in class discussions, you can help focus students' attention on key elements of Photoshop and help them understand how to use it effectively in the workplace.

- The **Student Data Files** are available online on both the Instructor's Book Companion Site and for students on the Student Book Companion Site.

- To create a complete certification solution, this textbook can be bundled with Adobe **Certified Associate exam vouchers** and/or **ACA practice tests** from Certiport—available as a single bundle from Wiley. Providing your students with the ACA exam voucher is the ultimate workforce preparation.

- When it comes to improving the classroom experience, there is no better source of ideas and inspiration than your fellow colleagues. The **Wiley Faculty Network** connects teachers with technology, facilitates the exchange of best practices, and helps to enhance instructional efficiency and effectiveness. Faculty Network activities include technology training and tutorials, virtual seminars, peer-to-peer exchanges of experiences and ideas, personal consulting, and sharing of resources. For details, visit *www.WhereFacultyConnect.com*.

Wiley Faculty Network

VIDEO TUTORIALS

The Introduction to Photoshop CS6 textbook comes with access to approximately two hours of online video tutorials that accompany each lesson in the book. These video tutorials are designed to help your students to better understand certain topics covered within each lesson. The video tutorials do not replace the lessons and only cover select material the authors have selected to enhance the content being covered within the lesson. To obtain access to the video tutorials, go to *http://www.wiley.com/college/sc/adobeseries*.

Important Web Addresses and Phone Numbers

To locate the Wiley Higher Education Rep in your area, go to *www.wiley.com/college*, select Instructors under Resources & Events, and click on the Who's My Rep link, or call our toll-free number: 1+(888) 764-7001 (U.S. and Canada only).

Student Support Program

VIDEO TUTORIALS

Your Introduction to Photoshop CS6 textbook comes with access to approximately two hours of online video tutorials that accompany each lesson in the book. These video tutorials are accessible online and are hosted on Wiley Publishing's site. To obtain access to the video tutorials, go to *http://www.wiley.com/college/sc/adobeseries.* and search for Introduction to Photoshop. A broadband Internet connection is required to view the video tutorials.

Book Companion Website

The Students' Book Companion Site for this textbook (*http://www.wiley.com/college/sc/adobeseries*) includes any resources, exercise files, and web links that will be used in conjunction with this course.

Wiley E-Text: Powered by VitalSource

Wiley E-Texts: Powered by VitalSource are innovative, electronic versions of printed textbooks. Students buy the Wiley E-Text for 50% off the U.S. price of the printed text and get the added value of permanence and portability. Wiley E-Texts provide students with numerous additional benefits that are not available with other e-text solutions.

Wiley E-Texts are NOT subscriptions; students download the Wiley E-Text to their computer desktops. Students own the content they buy and keep it for as long as they want. Once a Wiley E-Text is downloaded to the computer desktop, students have instant access to all of the content without being online. Students can also print the sections they prefer to read in hard copy. Students also have access to fully integrated resources within their Wiley E-Text. From highlighting their e-text to taking and sharing notes, students can easily personalize their Wiley E-Text as they are reading or following along in class.

CourseSmart

CourseSmart goes beyond traditional expectations providing instant, online access to the textbooks and course materials you need at a lower cost option. You can save time and hassle with a digital version of this book. The eTextbook option allows you to search for the most relevant content at the very moment you need it. To learn more go to: *www.coursesmart.com.*

WHY ACA CERTIFICATION?

The Adobe Certified Associate (ACA) credential has been upgraded to validate skills with the Adobe Creative Suite 6 system. The ACA certifications target information workers and cover the most popular business applications.

Adobe offers four areas in which to gain certification for entry-level skills: Web Communication using Adobe Dreamweaver, Rich Media Communication using Adobe Flash, Video Communication using Adobe Premiere Pro and Visual Communication using Adobe Photoshop. To learn more about becoming an Adobe Certified Associate and exam availability, visit *www.certiport.com/adobe.*

Student Support Program

Preparing to Take an Exam

The workplace demand for digital media skills—creating, managing, integrating, and communicating information by using Adobe's dynamic multimedia, video, graphic, web, or design software—is on the rise. This new certification program will help educators effectively teach and validate digital communications skills while providing students with credentials that demonstrate real-world prowess to prospective employers.

What are the Benefits of Becoming Certified?

By certifying one's skills, individuals can validate their technical abilities and demonstrate proficiency. Adobe's associate-level certifications are based on research about digital communications skills required by industry, government, and education. The objectives reflect the foundation skills needed to be successful communicators in today's digital world.

In educational settings, industry-recognized certification programs ensure students and teachers are acquiring the knowledge and skills valued in today's workplace. For institutions seeking to keep curriculum vitalized and relevant, certification plays a critical role in bridging classroom learning to real-world application.

Preparing to Take an Exam

Unless you are a very experienced user, you will need to use a test preparation course to prepare for the test to complete it correctly and within the time allowed. Wiley's Adobe courseware is designed to prepare you with a strong knowledge of all exam topics. With some additional review and practice on your own, you should feel confident in your ability to pass the appropriate exam.

After you decide which exam to take, review the list of objectives for the exam. This list can be found in Appendix A at the back of this book. You can also easily identify tasks that are included in the objective list by locating the Lesson Skill Matrix at the start of each lesson and the Certification Ready sidebars in the margin of the lessons in this book.

To take the ACA test, visit *www.certiport.com/adobe* to locate your nearest testing center. Then call the testing center directly to schedule your test. The amount of advance notice you should provide will vary for different testing centers, and it typically depends on the number of computers available at the testing center, the number of other testers who have already been scheduled for the day on which you want to take the test, and the number of times per week that the testing center offers ACA testing. In general, you should call to schedule your test at least two weeks prior to the date on which you want to take the test.

When you arrive at the testing center, you might be asked for proof of identity. A driver's license or passport is an acceptable form of identification. If you do not have either of these items of documentation, call your testing center and ask what alternative forms of identification will be accepted. If you are retaking a test, bring your ACA identification number, which will have been given to you when you previously took the test. If you have not prepaid or if your organization has not already arranged to make payment for you, you will need to pay the test-taking fee when you arrive.

Test Format

All ACA certification tests are live, performance-based tests. There are no multiple-choice, true/false, or short-answer questions. Instructions are general: you are told the basic tasks to perform on the computer, but you aren't given any help in figuring out how to perform them. You are not permitted to use reference material other than the application's Help system.

Acknowledgments

Thank you to Nell Hurley, Tacy Trowbridge, Matt Niemitz, and Melissa Jones at Adobe for their encouragement and support in making this textbook the finest instructional materials for mastering the newest Adobe technologies for both students and instructors.

About the Author

Jennifer Smith is a designer, educator, and author. She has authored more than 20 books on digital design and creative software tools. She provides consulting and training services across a wide range of industries, including working with software developers, magazine publishers, catalog and online retailers, as well as some of the biggest names in fashion, apparel and footwear design. When not writing and consulting you'll often find her delivering professional development workshops for colleges and universities.

Jennifer also works extensively in the field of web usability and user experience design, working alongside application developers and web developers to create engaging and authentic experiences for users on mobile devices, tablets, and traditional computers. She has twice been named a Most Valuable Professional by Microsoft for her work in user experience (UX) and user interface (UI) design fields, and her leadership in educating users on how to integrate design and development skills.

Jennifer Smith's books on Photoshop, Illustrator, and the Creative Suite tools include the *Photoshop Digital Classroom*, the *Illustrator Digital Classroom*, and the *Adobe Creative Suite for Dummies*, all published by Wiley. She has also authored *Wireframing and Prototyping with Expression Blend & Sketchflow*.

Jennifer is the cofounder of the American Graphics Institute. You can find her blog and contact her at *JenniferSmith.com* and follow her on Twitter @jsmithers.

Starting up

Resetting Adobe Photoshop CS6 preferences

When you start Adobe Photoshop, it remembers certain settings along with the configuration of the workspace from the last time you used the application. It is important that you start each lesson using the default settings so that you do not see unexpected results when working with the lessons in this book. The method described in the following steps restores Photoshop back to the original setting. If you have made changes to your Colors Settings and wish to maintain them, follow the steps in the section, "Steps to reset default settings, but keep color settings."

Steps to reset Adobe Photoshop CS6 preferences

1. If Photoshop is open, choose File > Exit (Windows) or Photoshop > Quit (Mac OS).

2. Press and hold the Ctrl+Alt+Shift keys (Windows) or Command+Option+Shift keys (Mac OS) simultaneously while launching Adobe Photoshop CS6.

3. A dialog box appears verifying that you want to delete the Adobe Photoshop settings file. Release the keys then press OK.

Steps to reset default settings, but keep color settings

As you reset your preferences to the default settings, you may wish to keep your color settings. This is important if you have created specific color settings, or work in a color-calibrated environment.

Use the following steps to reset your Adobe Photoshop CS6 preferences and save your color settings.

1. Launch Adobe Photoshop CS6.

2. Choose Edit > Color Settings, and then press the Save button. The Save dialog box opens. Enter an appropriate name for your color settings, such as the date. Leave the destination and format unchanged, then press the Save button. The Color Settings Comment dialog box opens.

3. In the Color Settings Comment dialog box, enter a description for the color settings you are saving and then press OK. Press OK again in the Color Settings dialog box to close it. You have saved your color settings so they can be accessed again in the future.

4. Choose File > Quit, to exit Adobe Photoshop CS6.

5. Press and hold the Ctrl+Alt+Shift keys (Windows) or Command+Option+Shift keys (Mac OS) simultaneously when launching Adobe Photoshop CS6. A dialog box appears verifying that you want to delete the Adobe Photoshop settings file. Release the keys then press OK.

6. After Adobe Photoshop CS6 launches choose Edit > Color Settings. The Color Settings dialog box appears.

7. From the Settings drop-down menu, choose your saved color settings file. Press OK. Your color settings are restored.

A note about color warnings

Depending upon how your Color Settings are configured, there may be times when you will receive a Missing Profile or Embedded Profile Mismatch warning. Understand that if you reset your preferences before each lesson (without restoring your color settings) you should not see these color warnings. This is because the default color setting of North America General Purpose 2 has all warning check boxes unchecked.

If you do receive Missing Profile and Embedded Profile Mismatch warnings, choose the Assign working option, or Convert document's colors to the working space. What is determined to be your working space is what you have assigned in the Color Settings dialog box. Color Settings are discussed in more detail in Lesson 6, "Painting and Retouching" and in Lesson 7, "Creating a Good Image."

Missing color profile.

Mismatched color profile.

Loading lesson files

The *Introduction to Adobe Photoshop CS6* book includes files that accompany the exercises for each of the lessons. Please review the instructions below on downloading the lesson files to your desktop.

For each lesson in the book, the files are referenced by the file name of each file. The exact location of each file on your computer is not used, as you may have placed the files in a unique location on your hard drive. We suggest placing the lesson files in the My Documents folder (Windows), or at the top level of your hard drive (Mac OS), or on your desktop for easy access.

Copying the lesson files to your hard drive:

1. Use your web browser, navigate to *http://www.wiley.com/college/sc/adobeseries*. Follow the instructions on the web page to download the lesson files to your computer.

2. On your computer, navigate to the location where you downloaded the files and right-click (Windows) the .zip file you downloaded, then choose Extract All or double-click on the .zip file (Mac OS).

Brief Contents

Contents

Lesson 1: Exploring Photoshop CS6   **1**

Contents

Lesson 4: Photoshop Basics **85**

Contents

Lesson 5: Making the Best Selections   107

Lesson 6: Painting and Retouching **143**

Contents

Contents

Lesson 11: Using Adobe Photoshop Filters   **307**

Contents

Contents

Exploring Photoshop CS6

Key Terms

- brush tip
- brush stroke
- Crop tool
- Custom Shape tool
- Move tool
- Options bar
- text styles

Skill	Objective
Identify the purpose, audience, and audience needs for preparing image(s)	1.1
Demonstrate knowledge of project management tasks and responsibilities	1.3
Communicate with others (such as peers and clients) about design plans	1.4
Demonstrate knowledge of design principles, elements, and image composition	2.2
Transform images	4.3
Demonstrate knowledge of drawing and painting	4.6
Demonstrate knowledge of type	5.7

Business case

Your new client (a ski resort) is looking for an exciting image to help promote skiing. They'd like a photo of a skier to be the centerpiece but want some accentual images and some text to drive the point home. The problem is that you don't want to clutter the project so you have to figure out a way to blend everything while still getting all the pieces in place. You might be a little rusty to Photoshop or new to it, so it might be a good idea to start with the basics by following along in this lesson.

Starting up

Before starting, make sure that your tools and panels are consistent by resetting your preferences. See "Resetting Adobe Photoshop CS6 preferences" in the Starting up section of this book.

Users of all levels can follow this step-by-step exercise of new features in Photoshop CS6. However, if you are a new user, we recommend that you start with Lesson 2, "Getting to Know the Workspace," and return to this lesson when you have completed all the other lessons.

You will work with several files from the ps01lessons folder in this lesson. Make sure that you have loaded the pslessons folder onto your hard drive from *http://www.wiley.com/college/sc/adobeseries*. See "Loading lesson files" in the Starting up section of this book. Now, let's take a look at some of the new features in Photoshop CS6.

Taking a look at the final project

This project was created for a client who provided a project plan that detailed the scope of the project, the project due date, additional tasks that may be required, and identified any resource allocation that might be needed. A project plan like this will often outline the phases of the project such as planning, designing, building and testing but can vary from one project to the next.

This project plan wanted to appeal to an audience in the age range of 18-45 years of age with a college education, living or traveling in the midwest U.S. states and have a fair amount of disposable income. When creating projects using Photoshop CS6 for a client, it's always important to keep the goals of the client in mind. Paying attention to the specifications of the project details like age, occupation, gender, education, ethnicity, and computer literacy of the intended audience will help you to meet the client goals and produce a project that the client will be happy with.

When you're ready to begin the execution of a project, as you will be doing shortly, a design plan can be helpful to keep everyone on task and keep the project moving forward. It's always helpful to obtain feedback on a design plan from colleagues and clients so that everyone is aware of the direction and status of the project. Obtaining feedback can be done via meetings, phone conversations, e-mail, and even PDF distribution. Adobe Acrobat or Adobe Reader can be used to comment on PDF files providing valuable feedback to designers and authors.

In this lesson, you'll create a photocomposition that will come from several sources, allowing you to use some of the new tools and features available in Adobe Photoshop CS6.

Certification Ready 1.1

What is the target audience of the project and the goals of the client?

Step-by-Step

Certification Ready 1.3

What would be some items that you would typically see on a project plan?

Certification Ready 1.3

What are some examples of phases that could appear on a project plan?

Certification Ready 1.4

What are some methods for obtaining feedback from clients and peers on a design plan?

Follow these steps to open an image with Adobe Bridge

1. Choose File > Browse in Bridge. You will use Adobe Bridge to locate your images for this lesson. Adobe Bridge also helps you to search for, organize, and manage your documents. Refer to Lesson 3, "Taking Advantage of Adobe Bridge," to find out more about Adobe Bridge.

2. In Bridge, choose Window > Workspace > Essentials to make sure that you are viewing the entire workspace.

   If you are unfamiliar with Adobe Bridge, click the Folders tab in the upper-left corner of the workspace to navigate from one folder to another. If you saved your lesson files on the desktop, click Desktop; all the folders on your desktop appear in the Content panel.

3. Navigate to the ps01lessons folder and double-click to open the file called
ps0101_done.psd. An image of a skier appears as shown in Figure 1-1.

Figure 1-1: *The completed lesson file.*

In addition to some standard Photoshop features, some *need-to-know* new features have
been integrated into this lesson. As you can see by investigating the Layers panel for
this image, many of the new features in this lesson relate to new and exciting vector
capabilities.

4. Now that you have seen the final image, choose File > Close. If a Warning dialog box
appears, click No (Windows) or Don't Save (Mac OS).

Experimenting with new Vector capabilities

In this part of the lesson, you will learn to append custom vector shapes, apply a pattern to
them, and adjust the stroke and fill.

**Certification
Ready 4.6**

How do you create a
vector layer?

Follow these steps to create and style a vector shape

Step-by-Step

1. Choose File > Browse in Bridge. If you do not already have the contents of the ps01lessons
folder open, click the Favorites tab in the upper-left of the Bridge workspace, and then
choose Desktop. Locate the ps01lessons folder.

2. Open the ps01lessons folder and double-click to open the **ps0101.psd** file. An image of a
skier appears.

3. Choose File > Save As to open the Save As dialog box. Using the Save In drop-down
menu, navigate to the ps01lessons folder. Type **ps0101_work** in the File Name text
field and choose Photoshop from the Format drop-down menu. Then click Save. If the
Photoshop Format Options dialog box appears, click OK.

Certification Ready 4.6

What are some tools that can be used for drawing?

4. Select the Rectangle tool (▬) located directly above the Hand tool in the Tools panel, and then click and drag to create a large rectangle that covers the right half of the image (Figure 1-2). When you release the mouse, notice that a Rectangle 1 vector layer has been added in the Layers panel. Note that in addition to the Rectangle tool, you can also use the Ellipse, Rounded Rectangle, Polygon, Line, and Custom Shape tools to drow other vector shapes as well.

You will now fill this rectangle with a pattern by taking advantage of some of the new vector features that have been added to Photoshop CS6.

Figure 1-2: Click and drag to create a large rectangle across the right side of the image.

Filling a vector shape with a pattern

The vector tool capabilities that you can use in Photoshop CS6 have improved dramatically. In this section, you will learn how to fill a vector shape with a pattern but you can also use the on-screen color picker to fill the shape with a solid color as well.

Step-by-Step

Follow these steps to fill a vector shape with a pattern

1. With the Rectangle 1 vector layer still active, click Fill in the Options bar, and then click the Pattern button (Figure 1-3).

2. Select Grey Granite as the pattern (Figure 1-4) and see the result in Figure 1-5. You can learn about saving your own patterns in Lesson 9, "Taking Layers to the Max."

Figure 1-3: *Select Pattern from the Fill menu.*

Figure 1-4: *Select Grey Granite.*

Figure 1-5: *The shape is filled with the pattern.*

Take Note...

If you do not see the options for the vector layer, you may have inadvertently selected another tool. The Vector options appear only when you have selected a vector shape tool, such as the Rectangle tool.

You will now create another shape and subtract it from the rectangle.

3. Click and hold the Rectangle tool, and then select the hidden Custom Shape tool (✿) as shown in Figure 1-6. Your **Options bar** reflects the selection of this tool. You gain access to a few default shapes when you select the **Custom Shape tool**. You can also append additional custom shapes to add more to your collection as you will see in the following steps.

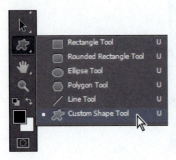

Figure 1-6: Select the hidden Custom Shape tool.

4. Click the arrow in the Shape drop-down (on the right side of the Options bar) menu to see the default shapes.

5. Click the gear icon (✿) in the upper-right of this menu and select the Nature category from the list of collections that appears.

6. When the warning dialog box appears, choose Append (Figure 1-7). Appending keeps the default shapes and adds the Nature shapes to the bottom of the list. Additional shapes are now added to your list.

Figure 1-7: Select the nature collection of shapes, and then select Append.

7. Select the shape named Snowflake 1 as shown in Figure 1-8.

Figure 1-8: Select the Snowflake 1 shape.

8. Click Path operations (⬛), which is located in the Options bar, and select Subtract Front Shape. If Subtract Front Shape is not available, make sure that you still have the Rectangle 1 vector layer selected in the Layers panel.

9. Position your mouse approximately in the middle of the left side of the Rectangle shape, and press and hold the Alt key (Windows) or Option key (Mac OS). Click and drag to create a large snowflake shape from the center. Continue dragging until the snowflake is almost as large as the square. As shown in Figure 1-9, the shape is subtracted from the Rectangle shape.

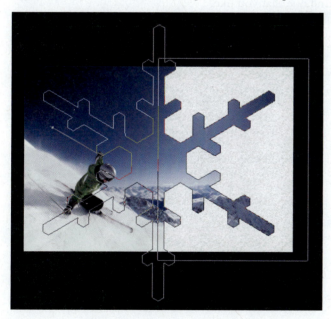

Figure 1-9: Create a large snowflake shape that subtracts from the Rectangle shape.

If you couldn't create the large snowflake, press Ctrl+Z (Windows) or Command+Z (Mac OS) to try again. You can use selection and transform tools to resize a vector shape, but it will be easier to practice creating the shape by starting over again.

10. Click the Path Selection tool (⬉) in the Tools panel, and notice that you can click and drag the snowflake and reposition it as an independent shape. Once you are finished experimenting with moving the snowflake, position it back in the center.

> **Take Note...**
>
> *If you do not like seeing the Path Selection tool, you can choose View > Show > Target Path to make it invisible. You can also toggle this view off and on by pressing Ctrl+Shift+H (Windows) or Command+Shift+H (Mac OS).*

Adding a mask to a Vector layer

In this next part of the lesson, you will add a mask to the large snowflake vector layer. Adding a mask allows you to fade the shape into the rest of the ski image.

Make sure that Rectangle 1 is still the active layer in the Layers panel, and then select the Add layer mask button (▣) at the bottom of the Layers panel. Visually, nothing happens to the image, but a mask appears to the right of the Vector layer thumbnail.

Select the Gradient tool (▬) from the Tools panel and click and drag from the right side of the snowflake toward the center. A gradient appears, but only on the mask. Layer masks allow you to cover-up parts of your image and make them transparent. Notice in Figure 1-10 that the snowflake does not appear where the gradient is black, and that it appears where the gradient is white. Using the gradient, you have faded the snowflake into transparency. If you are not satisfied with the gradient that you created, you can click and drag as many times as you want in different directions until you find one that you like.

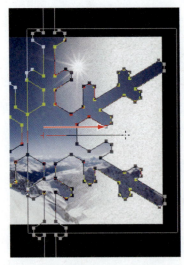

Figure 1-10: Click and drag to create a gradient mask.

Using the new brush tips

The Erodible and Airbrush tips were added to Photoshop CS6. The Erodible tip allows you to scribble, draw, and wear out your **brush tip** much like a pencil or piece of chalk. The Airbrush tip offers extra controls and settings that allow the brush to act more like a real airbrush. In this example, you will use one of the new Airbrush tips to make snow blow off the skier. Airbrushing is a painting technique that uses a stream of air to apply the paint to a surface.

Follow these steps to adjust the behavior of a Photoshop brush | **Step-by-Step**

1. Select Background in the Layers panel, press and hold the Alt (Windows) or Option (Mac OS) key, and click the Create a new layer button at the bottom of the Layers panel. This opens the New Layer dialog box so that you can immediately name the layer.

2. Type **Strokes** in the Name text field, and then click OK.

3. Select the Brush tool (✐), and then select Window > Brush; the Brush panel appears.

4. Scroll down in the Brushes panel to select the Airbrush tip labeled 80 (Figure 1-11). Once the brush is selected, you see that options specific to the selected brush tip appear at the bottom of the Brushes panel. You can experiment with the settings and see a preview of your brush stroke.

Certification Ready 4.6

How do you adjust the behavior of brushes?

Hardness: Use it to set the Airbrush tip hardness.

Distortion: Use it to set the distortion of the airbrush.

Granularity: Use it to set the granularity (particles) of the brush tip.

Spatter Size: Use it to set the airbrush spatter size.

Spatter Amount: Use it to set the spatter amount.

Spacing: Use it to adjust the space between brush applications. Spacing set at 100% will give you even spaces between applications.

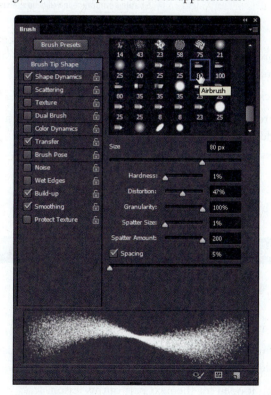

Figure 1-11: Select the 80 Airbrush tip and experiment with its settings.

5. Change settings and paint the image area to add texture. You can use any color. Experiment with different settings to see how the changes affect the **brush stroke** in the image area. Be sure to experiment with the shape dynamics, rotation, and opacity to see the effect that they have on the brush.

6. Once you are finished experimenting, choose Select > All, and then press the Delete key. You can repeat this step any time you want to paint again.

7. Reset your 80 Airbrush to the default settings by clicking the brush again in the Brush panel.

8. Enter these settings:

    Hardness: **5%**

    Distortion: **0%**

    Granularity: **45%**

    Spatter Size: **15%**

    Spatter Amount: **50%**

    Spacing Amount: **25%**

9. With the Brush tool still selected, change the following in the Options bar (Figure 1-12):

    Change the Flow to 25%. Changing this setting lessens the flow of "paint" when painting.

    Click the Enable airbrush-style build-up effects. If you hold the mouse button on one place, this feature spreads the paint much like an actual airbrush.

Figure 1-12: *Set flow and build-up options in the Options bar.*

**Certification
Ready 2.2**

What design elements
and principles can you
incorporate to improve
the aesthetics of your
artwork?

10. If your Foreground color is not white, press the letter **D** to return to the Default colors of a Black Foreground and a White Background.

11. Press **X** to swap the Foreground and Background color so that White is forward.

12. Confirm that you still have the blank Strokes layer in the Layers panel selected, and start painting snow flying behind the skier adding texture to the image. If you want to start over again, choose Select > All and press Delete.

Saving the new Brush

You can save your own customized brushes by following these steps.

Step-by-Step	Follow these steps to save a customized Photoshop brush

1. To save the Brush, click the New icon (▣) located in the bottom-right of the Brush panel. The Brush Name dialog box appears.

2. Type **MyBrush** in the Name text field, and then click OK.

3. If you want to use your brush in the future, you can find it by selecting Window > Brush Presets and scrolling to the bottom of the list. Your saved brush appears there.

4. Choose File > Save to save this file. Keep it open for the next part of this lesson. If a Photoshop options dialog box appears, click OK.

Adding strokes to vector images

In this next section, you will add a set of vector shapes and then add strokes to the shapes.

1. Select the Rectangle 1 layer.

2. Select the Custom Shape tool (✿) from the Tools panel.

3. Click the Shape drop-down menu, on the right side of the Options bar and select Snowflake 3. Notice that there are many forms to choose from in this drop-down menu that can be used as a focal point of your design to add emphasis.

4. Click the image area once. By clicking the image area, you can enter the size of the shape without first creating it. The Create Custom Shape dialog box appears.

5. Enter **60** into the width and height text fields (Figure 1-13), and click OK.

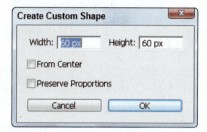

Figure 1-13: Put in exact values for your new custom shape.

As shown in Figure 1-14, the shape is created and a new Vector layer called Shape 1 has been added in the Layers panel.

Figure 1-14: A new vector layer is added.

6. With the Custom Shape tool still selected, click Fill in the Options bar and select the No Color icon as shown in Figure 1-15.

Figure 1-15: Change the Fill to No Color.

7. Click Stroke and select the 50% Grey color swatch as shown in Figure 1-16.

8. In the Options bar, change the stroke size from 3 pt to **2 pt**.

Figure 1-16: Select 50% gray for the stroke color, and change the size to 2 pt.

9. Hide the path selection by choosing View > Show > Target Path, or use the keyboard shortcut Ctrl+Shift+H (Windows) or Command+Shift+H (Mac OS).

10. Select Set shape stroke type in the Options bar, and then click More Options (Figure 1-17); the Stroke dialog box appears.

Figure 1-17: Selecting a shape stroke type using the Stroke dialog box.

Change the following:

- Select **Center** from the Align drop-down menu.

- Make sure **Round** is selected for both the Caps and Corners.

- Make sure the **Dashed Line** checkbox is checked and enter the first four values at 2.

11. Click Save to save your custom stroke (Figure 1-18), and then click OK; your new stroke is added to the Stroke Options drop-down menu.

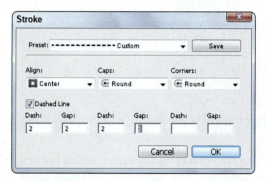

Figure 1-18: Change the stroke options and save it as a preset.

Certification Ready 1.3

What are some common problems that could occur with project management?

12 Choose File > Save to save this file. Keep it open for the next part of this lesson.

Staying on task

As you can see, Photoshop CS6 provides some powerful tools for both creating and editing content. However, be careful to stick to the project plan that was provided to you. Don't take an approach that would cause you to stray too far from the items identified in the project plan or you could experience scope creep, which could throw your project off track causing missed deadlines and an unhappy client.

Cloning your new snowflake

In this section, you will clone the snowflake several times and then merge all the new snowflake vector layers into one layer.

Follow these steps to duplicate a vector layer

Step-by-Step

1. Select the **Move tool** (✛). Position your cursor over the snowflake that you just created, and then press and hold the Alt key (Windows) or Option key (Mac OS). Notice that a double cursor appears (▸).

2. While pressing and holding the Alt/Option key, click and drag a copy of the snowflake to another location in the image area as shown in Figure 1-19. No exact location is necessary.

Figure 1-19: Press and hold the Alt/Option key and drag to clone (copy) the snowflake.

3. Position your cursor over the newly-cloned snowflake, press and hold the Alt/Option key, and duplicate that snowflake as well.

4. Repeat step 3 so that you have a total of four snowflakes on the image which creates some repetition. You have now created an additional four layers in your Layers panel (Figure 1-20). Try to balance the design by placing the snowflakes in proximity to one another but keep them grouped and leave some white space between the them.

Figure 1-20: The image with the four cloned snowflakes.

5. In the Layers panel, click the topmost layer, called Shape 1 copy 3, and then Shift+click the layer called Shape 1. This selects all four layers. Notice that your layers might have slightly different names as shown below with Figure 1-21.

Figure 1-21: *Select all the new layers.*

6. Press Ctrl+E (Windows) or Command+E (Mac OS) to merge the layers. You can also select Layers > Merge Shapes.

7. Select the Path Selection tool (▶) that is located directly beneath the Type tool in the Tools panel, and click and drag any of the snowflake shapes to reposition it. Notice that the shapes remain independent even though you have merged the layers to vector.

8. Select one snowflake and press Ctrl+T or Command+T (Mac OS); a bounding box appears. Grab a corner point to resize the snowflake down in size; no specific size is necessary. Press the Enter (Windows), or the Return (Mac OS) key when you are finished resizing to commit the change.

9. Using the Path Selection tool, select and resize several other snowflakes to random sizes.

Adding Text layers from another document

In this next section, you will add text to the image and then save the text as a style, thus allowing you to reuse the style and keep your **text styles** consistent. To save time, you will open a .psd file with the text layers already created. You will then move both layers to your **ps0101_work.psd** file.

Step-by-Step	**Follow these steps to create paragraph styles**

1. Choose File > Open, and then browse to and select **ps0102.psd**; a file opens with a transparent background and two text layers in the layers panel.

2. Click the Pure text layer, and then Shift+click the Powder text layer to select both layers as shown in Figure 1-22.

Figure 1-22: *Press Shift + click to select both layers.*

3. Right-click (Windows) or Ctrl+click (Mac OS) on the right side of either layer, and then select Duplicate Layers from the contextual menu that appears as shown below in Figure 1-23. You can also select Layer > Duplicate Layers.

Figure 1–23: Select Duplicate Layers from the contextual menu.

4. When the Duplicate Layers dialog box appears, select **ps0101_work.psd** from the Document drop-down menu in the Destination section (Figure 1-24), and click OK.

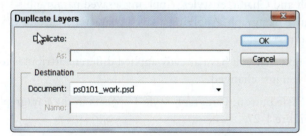

Figure 1–24: Duplicate the selected layers to an open file.

5. In the **ps0102.psd** file, choose File > Close to close the file.

6. Return to the **ps0101_work.psd** file, select the Type tool (T), and then click the text area that contains Pure to activate the cursor in that text area. Once your cursor is active, press Ctrl+A (Windows) or Command+A (Mac OS) to select all, or choose Select > All from the menu.

Certification Ready 4.7

How do you edit text in Photoshop?

Certification Ready 2.3

How can a background image affect text?

Certification Ready 2.3

How might you change the placement of text when being placed on different photographs and artwork?

Certification Ready 4.7

What is the functionality of each type panel?

7. The text is already set to Myriad Pro in the Set the font family drop-down menu. In the Set the font style drop-down menu, select Bold (Figure 1-25). This will help the text to stand out against the blue background of the image increasing its readability. The alignment of the text has been adjusted to create balance in the artwork and the text has been placed in the upper-left corner where there are no interruptions.

Now you will decrease the spacing between each letter by changing the tracking value in the text.

8. Press Alt (Windows) or Option (Mac OS)+(◄) left arrow repeatedly to decrease the spacing between the letters. Visually, decrease the size until you like the results as seen in Figure 1-26. If you want to spread the text back out, press Ctrl+(►) right arrow until you have the spacing that you want.

You can also use the Paragraph panel (Window > Paragraph) to adjust the alignment of the text to justified, align left, align right, or centered. You can use the Character panel (Window > Character), to adjust features such as kerning and tracking as well as the anti-aliasing of the text as it appears in the file.

Figure 1-25: Before tracking the text.   *Figure 1-26*: After tracking the text.

Select Window > Paragraph Styles; the Paragraph Styles panel appears. In Photoshop CS6, you can save both Paragraph and Character styles. Applying a saved paragraph style changes the style of text in an entire paragraph. Applying a saved character style allows you to change just the style of selected text.

You can easily create styles from text that you have already applied different attributes to, as you will do with the text that you just changed.

9. Click the Create new Paragraph Style button; Paragraph Style 1 appears in the Paragraph Styles panel as shown below in Figure 1-27.

Figure 1-27: Create a new paragraph style based on your text formatting.

10. Double-click Paragraph Style 1 to open the Paragraph Styles Options dialog box and view the attributes that are stored in this style.

11. Change the Style name by typing **Headline** into the Style Name text field as seen in Figure 1-28, and click OK.

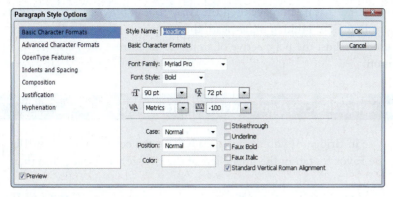

Figure 1-28: Change the style name.

12. Make sure that you are still on the Type tool, click anywhere in the Powder text area, and then click the Headline style that appears in the Paragraph Styles panel. The same text attributes are applied.

13. Click the Commit any current edits button (✔) in the Options bar to commit your style change.

Take Note...

A plus sign next to the Headline style indicates that there may have been a style manually applied. Click the Clear Overrides button (⬜) at the bottom of the Paragraph Styles panel to apply only the Headline style attributes to the text.

Updating text styles

As you can see, saving styles can help you build more consistent text content, and it can also help you edit text more quickly. In this next section, you will make a change to your Headline paragraph style.

Follow these steps to modify a paragraph style   **Step-by-Step**

1. Double-click the Headline text style in the Paragraph Styles panel to open the Paragraph Style Options dialog box.

2. Click once on the Color field at the bottom of the Paragraph Style Options dialog box; the Color Picker appears.

3. Your cursor is now an eyedropper; use it to sample a color from your image. Choose a light gray from the snow and click OK in both dialog boxes. The style has been updated.

Take Note...

If your style does not automatically update, press the Clear Overrides (⬜) button.

4. Choose File > Save and then File > Close to close this file.

Cropping an image

In this section you receive a quick overview of the Crop tool (🛱) and how to use it in Photoshop CS6. Keep in mind that if you have used the Crop tool in previous versions, it has been improved on Photoshop CS6. Hidden underneath the Crop tool is also the Perspective crop tool that can be used to adjust the perspective of an image to correct the perspective during the crop operation.

| Step-by-Step | Follow these steps to use the crop tool and modify its options |

1. Choose File > Browse in Bridge. If you do not already have the contents of the ps01lessons folder open, click the Favorites tab in the upper-left of the Bridge workspace, and then choose Desktop.

2. Open the ps01lessons folder and double-click to open the **ps0101_done.psd** file. This is a final version of the completed lesson file from the previous exercise.

3. Choose File > Save As to open the Save As dialog box. Using the Save In drop-down menu, navigate to the ps01lessons folder. Type **ps0102_work** in the File Name text field and choose Photoshop from the Format drop-down menu. Then click Save. If the Photoshop Format Options dialog box appears, click OK.

4. In the Layers panel, select the Background layer, and then hold down the Alt (Windows) or Option (Mac OS) and double-click on the Background layer. This converts the Background layer into a layer named Layer 0.

5. Select the **Crop tool**. Handles appear around the image area. You can now crop using one of three main methods:

   - Click and drag from the anchor points surrounding your image

   - Click and drag anywhere in your image to create a new crop area.

   - Enter in a fixed (Constrained) size in the textboxes in the Options bar while the Crop tool is selected.

   Since the first two methods are self-explanatory, you will experiment with the third method, entering a fixed amount for your crop area.

6. In the Options bar enter **500 px** in the first textbox, and **300 px** in the second textbox as shown in Figure 1-29 to define the aspect ratio for the final cropped size. Press the Tab key after you type in the 300 px value. The crop area immediately changes on your screen to reflect this amount.

Figure 1-29: *Enter pixel values into the Crop tool Options bar.*

7. Uncheck the Delete Cropped Pixels checkbox in the Options bar. The Options bar also provides preset aspect ratios that can be used to crop your image. You can also pick different grid layouts from the drop-down menu to help you crop your image. The ability exists to define a cropping rotation and straighten your image using the straighten tool. All of these capabilities are found in the Options bar.

8. Click and drag from the lower-right corner to see that your crop area remains proportionally correct to the values that you have entered. You can also see a crop preview in your layers panel. Click and drag to any size, making sure that you have some of the image area cropped, as indicated by the crop overlay that appears on your image in Figure 1-30. The crop area also shows a rule of thirds grid by default that can help you to frame the photo, create balance, and to redefine the field of view. Factors that can determine how you will crop your image may include foreground subjects, background subjects, color, tone, and contrast in different areas of an image. Another hidden gem of the Crop tool is the Straighten option in the Options bar that allows you to click and drag along a straight line in your image to automatically straighten it with a single click.

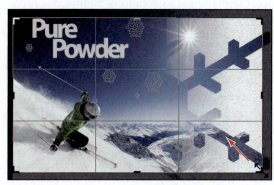

Figure 1-30: *Click and drag the crop overlay.*

9. Press the Commit current crop operation button (✔) in the far right of the Options bar to commit the crop. If you decide that you don't like the crop after commiting the crop, simply choose Edit > Undo to undo the crop.

10. Select your Move tool (⊹), and then select Layer 0. Click and drag to reposition the contents of this layer. Note that the pixels were not actually deleted; you can reposition any of the layers in this image file to show original content. Keep in mind that the cropped content of layers is saved, but not Background layers. This is why you converted the Background layer into a layer in step 4.

Skill Summary

In this lesson you learned how to:	Objective
Identify the purpose, audience, and audience needs for preparing image(s)	1.1
Demonstrate knowledge of project management tasks and responsibilities	1.3
Communicate with others (such as peers and clients) about design plans	1.4
Demonstrate knowledge of design principles, elements, and image composition	2.2
Transform images	4.3
Demonstrate knowledge of drawing and painting	4.6
Demonstrate knowledge of type	5.7

Knowledge Assessment

True/False

Circle **T** if the statement is true or **F** if the statement is false.

T F 1. The vector tool provides numerous shape options that even include a Custom Shape tool.

T F 2. The keyboard shortcut to Undo in Photoshop on the Mac OS is Ctrl+Z.

T F 3. Masks can be added to vector layers to hide portions of an image.

T F 4. You can only apply a solid line pattern to strokes when creating them.

T F 5. Photoshop will allow you to consolidate the amount of layers you have by merging them.

T F 6. You can add and stylize text as well as save that style to apply to other text later on.

T F 7. You can only save Paragraph Styles in Photoshop; you don't need Character styles like in InDesign.

T F 8. You can only create one master style to apply to text from the Paragraph Styles panel.

T F 9. Patterns as well as solid colors and gradients can all be applied to shapes.

T F 10. The Path Selection tool will allow you to select and modify shapes that you've created using the vector shape tool.

Multiple Choice

Select the best response for the following statements.

1. Which of the following categories is an option when choosing a custom shape?
   a. Animals
   b. Arrows
   c. Nature
   d. All of the above

2. Which new brush tips have just been added to Photoshop CS6?
   a. Drop Shadow and Dry Media
   b. Erodible and Airbrush
   c. Natural and Wet Media
   d. Calligraphic and Faux Finish

3. When clicking and dragging on an object, which key should you hold down to make a copy of it while dragging?

   a. Shift

   b. Control

   c. Alt (Windows) / Option (Mac OS)

   d. Space bar

4. Which of the following is not a category when setting up a Paragraph style?

   a. Basic Character Formats

   b. OpenType Features

   c. Composition

   d. Spelling and Grammar

5. Which of the following is not a category when adjusting the Airbrush tip?

   a. Hardness

   b. Flux Capacitor Pressure

   c. Granularity

   d. Spatter Size

6. Which path operation allows you to punch one shape out of another like a stencil?

   a. Subtract

   b. Blend

   c. Opacity

   d. Scale

7. Mode, Opacity, and Flow are all characteristics of which tool?

   a. Selection Tool

   b. Shape Tool

   c. Crop tool

   d. Brush tool

8. How can you open up the dialog box that has the style settings for the Paragraph styles you've applied once you've applied them?

   a. Double-click the name of the style to open it

   b. Choose Paragraph > Settings

   c. Choose Edit > Text

   d. You cannot change the settings for the style once you close the dialog window

9. Which is the correct abbreviation for pixels?

   a. pxl

   b. px

   c. pxel

   d. pix

10. Layers can be re-positioned using which tool?

    a. Move tool

    b. Selection tool

    c. Gradient tool

    d. Brush tool

Lesson 1

Competency Assessment

| Project 1-1 | **Reverse Cropping** |

So you've seen how you can crop things out, but did you know that you can use the Crop tool to add space and make an image larger as well? In this exercise, you'll learn how to expand the size of your image to create a frame type effect for a picture.

1. Open the **ps0101.psd** file on your computer. Save a copy of it as **ps0101_crop-expansion.psd** so you don't alter the original.
2. Set your background color to white.
3. Select the Crop tool.
4. Click and drag with the Crop tool around your picture.
5. Using the crop area handles, expand the crop area beyond your picture into the gray work area. Stretch out to your satisfaction and try to keep the edges proportionate.
6. Double-click or press Enter (Windows) or Return (Mac OS).

| Project 1-2 | **Experimenting with Paragraph Styles** |

You got a taste of what styles are like to work with but to gain further understanding of the benefit; it's good to try other settings to see what else can be done.

1. Create a new Photoshop file.
2. Copy and paste text from another document, from the Internet, or enter your own text. Make sure you have 2 or 3 paragraphs to work with.
3. Create a new Paragraph Style and try working with other settings such as Indents and Spacing or Justification.
4. Save the file as **ps01_text_styles.psd**.

Proficiency Assessment

| Project 1-3 | **More settings with the Airbrush and Color Panel** |

There are many more combinations to be had with the Airbrush and different color choice variations.

1. Create a new, blank document.
2. Start working with the Airbrush, different settings for the Airbrush than used in this lesson so far, and different color combinations. Create an abstract painting.
3. Save the file as **ps01_airbrush.psd**.

24   Introduction to Adobe Photoshop CS6

Creating Masks Continued

You'll want to understand how masks can be used in other ways. Using shapes to stencil each other out with masks is just another different way to create new shapes.

1. Create a new document.

2. Use the Ellipse and Polygon tools, trying the variations to the drawing settings for each. Draw multiple shapes in your document.

3. Add a Vector mask to the layer, and draw shapes in path mode on the Vector mask to mask out different areas of the background design to create new and interesting shapes.

3. Convert and Undo different mask combinations between the shapes you created.

4. Save the file as **ps01_shapes.psd**.

Getting to Know the Workspace

Key Terms

- Hand tool
- History panel
- Mini Bridge
- Mixer Brush
- panel group
- panels
- Tabbed workspace
- Tools panel
- zoom

Skill	Objective
Identify elements of the Photoshop CS6 user interface and demonstrate knowledge of their functions	3.1
Demonstrate knowledge of retouching and blending images	4.5
Demonstrate knowledge of drawing and painting	4.6

Business case

Your uncle has a nice vintage car collection. His birthday is coming up and you're wondering what to get him. Somebody suggests getting one of his photos, stylizing it and then printing it out as a present. Getting the car to stand out is a factor that's important for this project. There a number of ways to achieve this, one of which includes creating a vignette. Let's make one by hand to get more familiar with the Photoshop workspace.

Starting up

Adobe Photoshop is an image-editing program that can open an image captured by a scanner or digital camera, or downloaded from the Web. It can also open captured video images and vector illustrations. In addition, you can create new documents in Photoshop, including vector graphics, which are scalable image files (for example, the images can be enlarged or reduced in size with no loss of clarity).

Before starting, make sure that your tools and panels are consistent by resetting your preferences. See "Resetting Adobe Photoshop CS6 preferences" in the Starting up section of this book.

You will work with several files from the ps02lessons folder in this lesson. Make sure that you have loaded the pslessons folder onto your hard drive from *http://www.wiley.com/college/sc/adobeseries*. See "Loading lesson files" in the Starting up section of this book.

Starting up

Certification Ready 3.1

What are the different parts of the Photoshop workspace?

Opening an existing document in Mini Bridge

Mini Bridge works like the stand-alone Adobe Bridge application, but resides in Photoshop. You can access Mini Bridge by using the File menu, or by selecting Window > Extensions > Mini Bridge.

Step-by-Step

Follow these steps to open a document using Mini Bridge

1. Launch Adobe Photoshop CS6 and choose File > Browse in Mini Bridge or Window > Extensions > Mini Bridge; Mini Bridge appears as a panel across the bottom of the workspace. If a message displays indicating that you must launch Bridge CS6, press Launch Bridge.

   Even though you will be instructed to use Adobe Bridge throughout the lessons in this book, you can also choose to use Mini Bridge.

2. Click on Favorites and select your User Name from the drop-down menu in the navigation pod on the left side of Mini Bridge. You now see personal folders that you can navigate to, such as Desktop, Documents, and Pictures.

3. Double-click on Desktop (Figure 2-1) to see the folders on your desktop appear in the Navigation pod, including the pslessons folder. If you do not see your folder on the Desktop, verify that you didn't save your folder to the Desktop of another user.

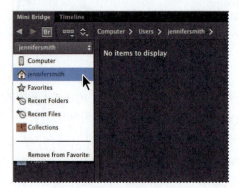

Figure 2-1: Select your user name to see the desktop folder, if it is not immediately visible.

4. Double-click the pslessons folder to reveal the contents, and then click ps02lessons. The Mini Bridge now displays three images of an antique car in the folder as shown below in Figure 2-2.

Figure 2-2: Use Mini Bridge to locate your lesson files.

5. Locate and double-click to open the file named **ps0201_done.psd**. An image of an antique car appears as shown below in Figure 2-3. This is the finished project. You may keep it open as you work or close it once you have examined the file.

Figure 2-3: *The completed lesson file.*

As you practice with the files throughout this book, you will find that you are instructed to save a work file immediately after opening the original file.

6. Open the file named **ps0201.psd**, which is the starting file used for this lesson. Choose File > Save As to open the Save as dialog box.

7. Navigate to the ps02lessons folder. In the File name textbox, type **ps0201_work**, and choose Photoshop from the Format drop-down menu. Click Save.

Discovering the Tools panel

When you start Photoshop, the **Tools panel** appears docked on the left side of the screen—by default it is not a floating Tools panel, as it was in earlier versions of Photoshop. There are four main groups of tools, separated by functionality on the Tools panel (Figure 2-4): selection, cropping, and measuring; retouching and painting; drawing and type; and navigation. At the bottom of the Tools panel you find Set foreground color and Set background color, as well as Quick Mask.

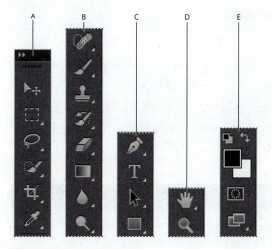

Figure 2-4

A. *Selection, cropping, and measuring tools.*
B. *Retouching and painting tools.*
C. *Drawing and type tools.*
D. *Navigation tools.*
E. *Foreground/Background and Quick Mask.*

Selection, Cropping, and Measuring Tools

Icon	Tool Name	Use
▶+	Move (V)	Moves selections or layers.
⬚	Marquee (M)	Makes rectangular, elliptical, single row, and single column selections.
⬭	Lasso (L)	Makes freehand, polygonal (straight-edged), and magnetic selections.
✎	Quick Selection (W)	Make selections by painting.
🔲	Crop (C)	Crops an image.
✎	Eyedropper (I)	Samples pixels.

Retouching and Painting Tools

Icon	Tool Name	Use
✎	Spot Healing (J)	Removes imperfections.
✦	Brush (B)	Paints the foreground color.
♣	Clone Stamp (S)	Paints with a sample of the image.
✦	History Brush (Y)	Paints with the selected state or snapshot.
◣	Eraser (E)	Erases pixels—or reverts to a saved history state.
▮	Gradient (G)	Creates a gradient.
◍	Blur (no shortcut)	Blurs pixels.
✎	Dodge (O)	Lightens pixels in an image.

Take Note...
You can create a floating Tools panel by clicking on the gray title bar at the top of the Tools panel and then dragging it to a new location. You can dock it again by dragging it back to the left side of the workspace; release when you see the blue vertical bar appear.

Drawing and Type Tools

Icon	Tool Name	Use
✎	Pen (P)	Draws a vector path.
T	Horizontal Type (T)	Creates a type layer.
▶	Path Selection (A)	Allows you to manipulate a path.
▮	Rectangle (U)	Draws vector shapes.

Navigation Tools

Icon	Tool Name	Use
	Hand (H)	Navigates the page.
🔍	Zoom (Z)	Increases and decreases the relative size of the view.

Take Note...
Can't tell the tools apart? You can view tooltips that reveal a tool's name and keyboard shortcut by positioning your cursor over the tool.

The Tools panel is in a space-saving, one-column format. Click on the double arrows in the gray title bar area above the Tools panel to bring the Tools panel into the two-column view. Click on the double arrows again to bring the Tools panel back to the default, single-column view. Keep the Tools panel set to whichever format works best for you.

Accessing tools and their options

With the selection of most tools comes the opportunity to change options. In this exercise, you will have the opportunity to use the new-and-improved Brush tool and change its options to become even more powerful.

Follow these steps to modify a tool with the Options bar	Step-by-Step

1. With the **ps0201_work.psd** image open, select the Brush tool (✏). Look in the Options bar to see a variety of options you can change as shown in Figure 2-5.

*Figure 2-5: **A.** Brush Preset Picker. **B.** Painting Mode. **C.** Opacity. **D.** Flow*

Most tools have additional options available in the Options bar at the top of the workspace.

Note that by default, your brush is loaded with black paint. The paint color is indicated at the bottom of your Tools panel in the Foreground and Background color swatches. If you have not reset preferences, you might have a different color in your foreground.

2. Click once on the foreground color to open the picker so you can select a different color (Figure 2-6).

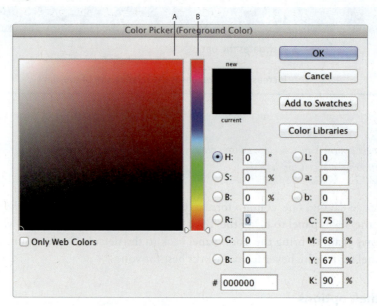

*Figure 2-6: **A.** Color Pane. **B.** Color Slider.*

Using the Color Picker, you are able to select a blue color that you will use to brighten up the sky.

3. In the Color Picker, click once on the section of the Color Slider that contains blue hues, and then choose a bright blue color from the large Color Pane as displayed in Figure 2-7. Keep in mind that, depending upon the destination of your image, you might not be able to achieve the same color of blue that you see in the screen. Lesson 6, "Painting and Retouching," discusses color, and how to use it in your images, in more detail. Click OK.

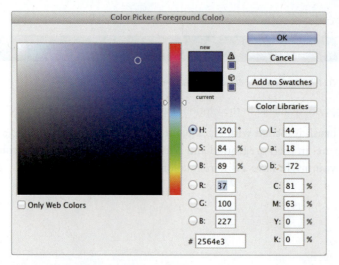

Figure 2-7: Click once in the blue section of the Color Slider, and then choose a bright blue color from the Color Pane.

Now you will change some of the Brush tool options in the Options bar at the top of the workspace.

4. Click the Brush Preset Picker to see your options for size and hardness. There are several options that you can change; for now you will focus on two.

5. Click and drag the size slider, which controls the size of the brush, to the right until you reach approximately 100 px. If the Hardness slider, which controls the hardness or softness of the brush, is not all the way to the left at 0%, slide it to the left now. This is now a large soft brush that will blend well at the edges of the strokes (Figure 2–8).

In the next step, you will paint and then undo it. This is to help you understand the concept of blending and how it can make a difference when you paint.

Figure 2–8: *Change the brush size and hardness.*

6. Click and drag anywhere in the image one time to create a brush stroke across your image. Note that you have created a large opaque streak.

7. Choose Edit > Undo Brush Tool, or use the keyboard shortcut Ctrl+Z (Windows) or Command+Z (Mac OS) to undo the paint streak.

8. Now click and hold the Painting Mode drop-down menu; you see a list of options that allow you to change how your paint interacts with the image underneath. As seen in Figure 2-9, select Color from the bottom of the list.

Figure 2–9: *Select the paint blending mode named Color.*

Certification Ready 4.5

How do you utilize the blending tools?

9. Click the arrow to the right of the Opacity option to see the slider. Click and drag the Opacity slider to the left until it reaches approximately 20%.

10. Now click and drag to paint in the upper-right corner of the image. In Figure 2-10, you see that the result is quite different and you are brightening the sky.

Figure 2-10: Click and drag to paint blue in the upper-right corner of the image.

11. Notice that you can build up the color by releasing the paint brush and painting over the same area. If you make a mistake, choose Edit > Undo, or Ctrl+Z (Windows) or Command+Z (Mac OS) to undo.

Take Note...

The Smudge, Dodge, and Burn tools can also be used to blend color by changing how the color is adjusted within the pixels of an image.

Take Note...

To go back multiple steps, choose Edit > Step Backward, or use the keyboard shortcut Ctrl+Alt+Z (Windows) or Command+Option+Z (Mac OS).

12. Choose File > Save. Keep this file open for the next part of this lesson.

Using panels

Certification Ready 3.1

What purpose do panels serve?

Much of the functionality in Photoshop resides in the **panels**, so you will learn to navigate them and quickly find the ones you need. In this section, you will learn how to resize, expand, and convert panels to icons and then back to panels again. You will also learn how to save your favorite workspaces so you don't have to set them up every time you work on a new project.

Follow these steps to arrange panels within your workspace

1. Choose Window > Workspace > Reset Essentials to put the panels back to their default locations as shown in Figure 2-11.

Figure 2-11: *The default panel locations.*

Putting the panel system to use

Photoshop has a default setting for all the panels: it's what you see when you initially launch Photoshop. There are many panels, and not all of them are needed for all projects. This is the reason Photoshop has defined workspaces, which can help you streamline your workflow. There are many prebuilt workspaces available under the Window > Workspace menu; you pick the one that helps you find the features you need for the task at hand as demonstrated in Figure 2-12.

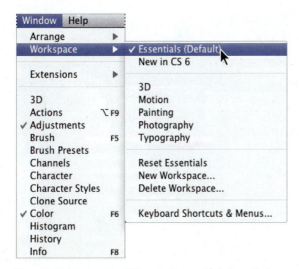

Figure 2-12: *You can select different workspaces that help you find features depending upon the task at hand.*

At this point, you have just reset the Essentials workspace. Test different workspaces by selecting Painting, and then Photography from the Window > Workspace menu. Once you have seen how panels can be collapsed and others made visible, return to Window > Workspace > Essentials.

Take Note...
Keep in mind that all these panels are accessible at all times from the Windows > Workspace menu.

To open panels that are not visible, choose the Window menu. If there is a check mark to the left of the panel listed, it means that the panel is already open. Photoshop CS6 can determine whether a panel is hidden behind another; panels that are hidden this way will not be marked as open, so you can select it in the Window menu to bring the hidden panel forward.

Step-by-Step   **Follow these steps to use the Window menu to locate a hidden panel**

1. Select the Brush tool (✓).

2. Click the Swatches tab that is hidden behind the Color panel in the docking area to the right (Figure 2-13).

Figure 2-13: Click the Swatches tab to bring it forward.

3. Click the color called Pure Red Orange in the Swatches panel. Notice that when you cross over a color, a Tooltip appears. You can also select Small List from the Swatches panel menu (·≡) in the upper-right corner (Figure 2-14).

Figure 2-14: Choose to view the Swatches panel as a list.

4. With the Brush tool selected, start painting in the upper-left of the image, adding orange to the sky as shown in Figure 2-15. If necessary, press Ctrl+Z (Windows) or Command+Z (Mac OS). Keep in mind that by masking, or selecting parts of the image, you can have much more control over where you paint in an image. Read Lesson 5, "Making the Best Selections," for more information about selective changes.

Figure 2-15: *Add orange to the sky in the upper-left part of the image.*

Choosing other panels

You will now select another panel, the History panel. The History panel allows you to undo and redo steps, as well as save versions of your image while you work. In this exercise, you will use the History panel to undo and redo steps. In Lesson 6, "Painting and Retouching," you will spend more time in the History panel.

Follow these steps to use the History panel to undo and redo steps

Step-by-Step

1. Click the History panel icon ( ) that is visible in the Essentials workspace (Figure 2-16). If you cannot locate it, choose Window > History.

Figure 2-16: *Selecting the History panel.*

Each row in the **History panel** represents a history state (or step). You can click back on earlier states to undo steps that you have taken, or redo by clicking the grayed-out history state. Keep in mind that if you step back in history and then complete a new step, all the gray history states disappear. This history default can be changed by selecting History Options from the History panel menu and checking Allow Non-Linear History.

Certification Ready 4.1

How can you selectively undo the most recent steps that you've performed?

2. Click back on the various history states to see how your steps are undone as displayed in Figure 2-17. Click forward again to see your steps redone.

Figure 2-17: Undoing a step in the History panel.

Expanding and collapsing your panels

To better manage your space, you can collapse and expand your panels. You can do this automatically with a preconfigured workspace, or you can choose to expand only the panels you want to see.

Step-by-Step | **Follow these steps to expand and collapse panels**

1. You might find that you need to reset your workspace to bring it back to its original configuration. If this is necessary, choose Window > Workspace > Reset Essentials.

2. Collapse groups of panels by double-clicking the dark gray bar (title bar) at the top of the panels (Figure 2-18). Double-click the dark gray bar again to expand them (Figure 2-19).

Figure 2-18: Collapse the panel by double-clicking on the title bar.

Figure 2-19: Expand the panels by double-clicking the title bar.

You can also collapse a panel by clicking the double-arrows in the upper-right of the panel.

3. If the History panel is no longer open, click the icon for the History panel. Click the double-arrow in the upper-right to collapse that panel back to an icon (Figure 2-20).

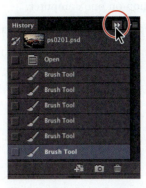

Figure 2-20: You can collapse a panel by clicking the double-arrows.

Customizing your panels

A **panel group** is made up of two or more panels that are stacked on top of each other. To view the other panels in a group, select the name on the tab of the panel. You will now learn to organize your panels according to your preferences.

Certification Ready 3.1

How can you save your panel configuration so that it is easily accessible when you need them?

Follow these steps to organize panel groups

Step-by-Step

1. If the Swatches panel is not forward, select the tab that reads Swatches; the Swatches tab is brought forward.

2. Now, select the Color tab to bring the Color panel to the front of the panel group.

3. Click the tab of the Color panel, drag it away from the panel group and into the image area (as shown in Figure 2-21), and then release the mouse—you have just removed a panel from a panel group and the docking area. Rearranging panels can help you keep frequently used panels together in one area.

Figure 2-21: The Color panel as it is dragged away from a panel group.

4. Click the tab area at the top of the Swatches panel and drag it over the Color panel. As soon as you see an outline around the Color panel, release the mouse (Figure 2-22). You have now made a panel group.

Figure 2-22: The Swatches panel dragged into the Color panel, creating a new panel group.

You'll now save a custom workspace. Saving a workspace is a good idea if you have production processes that often use the same panels. Saving workspaces is also helpful if you are in a situation where multiple users are sharing Photoshop on one computer.

5. Select Window > Workspace > New Workspace; the New Workspace dialog box appears.

6. In the Name textbox box, type **First Workspace** as shown in Figure 2-23, and then click Save.

Figure 2-23: Name your new workspace.

7. Whenever you want to reload a workspace, whether it's one that you created or one that comes standard with Photoshop, select Window > Workspace and select the desired workspace from the list.

Hidden tools

Some of the tools in the Tools panel display a small triangle at the bottom-right corner; this indicates that there are additional tools hidden under the tool.

| Step-by-Step | Follow these steps to locate hidden tools in the Tools panel |

1. Click and hold on the Brush tool to see the hidden Pencil, Color Replacement and Mixer Brush tools as seen in Figure 2-24. You can also access the hidden tools by right clicking (Windows) or Ctrl+clicking (Mac OS)

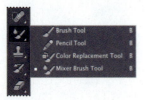

Figure 2-24: Selecting a hidden tool.

Certification Ready 4.6

Which brush tool allows you to mix and blend colors while painting?

2. Select the Mixer Brush tool (✔) and release. The Color Mixer tool is now the visible tool, and the options in the Options bar have been changed.

The **Mixer Brush** simulates realistic painting techniques, such as mixing colors on the canvas, combining colors on a brush, or varying paint wetness across a stroke.

You will now change the foreground color by selecting Set the foreground color in the Tools panel.

3. Click once on the foreground color at the bottom of the Tools panel; the Color Picker appears.

4. Position your cursor on the Color Slider (hue) to the right of the Color Pane and click and drag it up until shades of orange appear in the Color Pane.

5. Click once in the Color Pane to select an orange color. Any orange color will do for this exercise, but you can also type a value into the text fields for a more accurate selection. In this example, a color with the RGB value of R: **236**, G: **169**, B: **24** was selected (Figure 2-25).

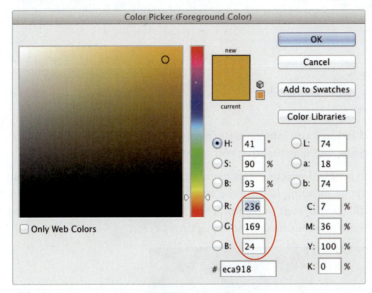

Figure 2-25: *Select an orange color from the Color Picker.*

6. Click on the Brush Preset picker button in the Options bar and set the following attributes for the Mixer Brush tool.

Size: **175 px** (This indicates the size of the brush, in this example a very large brush is indicated.)

Hardness: **20%** (A value of 100% would be a hard-edged brush.)

Leave all other settings at their defaults as shown below in Figure 2-26.

Figure 2-26: *Changing the Mixer Brush tool.*

There are many options for the Mixer Brush, but for this example, you will use a preset that will adjust all the settings to give you a smooth blended result in your image.

7. Click once on Useful mixer brush combinations drop-down menu and select the Moist, Light Mix preset as seen below in Figure 2-27.

Figure 2-27: *Change the Useful mixer brush combination to Moist, Light Mix.*

8. Press Ctrl+0 (zero) (Windows) or Command+0 (zero) (Mac OS.) This is the keyboard shortcut for Fit on Screen, and it assures that you see the entire image area.

9. With the Mixer Brush tool still selected, start painting in the upper-left area of your image to create a shade of orange blending in from the corner. Repeat this for all four corners in the image (Figure 2-28). If you want to repaint, press Ctrl+Z (Windows) or Command+Z (Mac OS) to revert to the previous image and try again.

Figure 2-28: *An orange tint is blended into the corners for an artistic effect.*

10. Choose File > Save, or use the keyboard shortcut Ctrl+S (Windows), or Command+S (Mac OS) to save your file.

Navigating the image area

Certification Ready 3.1

What features can be used to efficiently navigate a document?

To work most efficiently in Photoshop, you'll want to know how to **zoom** (magnify) in and out of your image. Changing the zoom level allows you to select and paint accurately and helps you see details that you might otherwise have overlooked. The zoom function has a range from a single pixel up to a 3200 percent enlargement, which gives you a lot of flexibility in terms of viewing your images.

You'll start by using the View menu to reduce and enlarge the document view, and end by fitting the entire document on your screen.

Step-by-Step | **Follow these steps to change the zoom level of your image**

1. Choose View > Zoom In to enlarge the display of **ps0201_work.psd**.

2. Press Ctrl+plus sign (Windows) or Command+plus sign (Mac OS) to zoom in again. This is the keyboard shortcut for the Zoom In command that you accessed previously from the View menu.

3. Press Ctrl+minus sign (Windows) or Command+minus sign (Mac OS) to zoom out. This is the keyboard shortcut for View > Zoom Out.

   Now you will fit the entire image on the screen.

4. Choose View > Fit on Screen, or use the keyboard shortcut Ctrl+0 (zero) (Windows) or Command+0 (zero) (Mac OS), to fit the document to the screen.

5. You can also display artwork at the size it will print by choosing View > Print Size.

Using the Zoom tool

When you use the Zoom tool (🔍), each click increases the view size to the next preset percentage, and centers the display of the image around the location in the image that you clicked on. By holding the Alt (Windows) or Option (Mac OS) key down (with the Zoom tool selected), you can zoom out of an image, decreasing the percentage and making the image view smaller. The magnifying glass cursor is empty when the image has reached either its maximum magnification level of 3,200 percent or the minimum size of one pixel.

Follow these steps to use the Zoom tool	Step-by-Step

1. Choose View > Fit on Screen.

2. Select the Zoom tool, and click two times on the license plate to zoom in. You can also use key modifiers to change the behavior of the Zoom tool.

3. Press Alt (Windows) or Option (Mac OS) while clicking with the Zoom tool to zoom out.

   You can accurately zoom into the exact region of an image by clicking and dragging a marquee around that area in your image. To do this, you must disable a new Zoom tool option.

4. Uncheck the Scrubby Zoom checkbox in the Zoom tool's Option bar to disable this feature as shown in Figure 2-29. The Scrubby Zoom feature allows you to click and drag to zoom immediately. In this example, you need a more predictable zoom area.

Figure 2-29: Disable the Scrubby Zoom in the Zoom tool's Option bar.

Lesson 2

5. With the Zoom tool still selected, hold down the mouse and click and drag from the top left of car's grill to the lower-right of the bumper. You are creating a rectangular marquee selection around the front of the car as displayed in Figure 2-30. Once you release the mouse, the area that was included in the marquee is now enlarged to fill the document window.

Figure 2-30: Drag a marquee over the front of the car.

6. Double-click the Zoom tool in the Tools panel to return to a 100 percent view.

   Because the Zoom tool is used so often, it would be tiresome to continually have to change from the Zoom tool back to the tool you were using. Read on to see how you can activate the Zoom tool at any time without deselecting your current tool.

7. Select the Move tool (✛) at the very top of the Tools panel.

8. Hold down Ctrl+spacebar (Windows) or Command+spacebar (Mac OS). Note that on the Mac OS you must hold down spacebar before the Command key, otherwise you trigger Spotlight; the Move tool is temporarily converted into the Zoom In tool. While still holding down Ctrl/Command+spacebar, click and drag over the front of the car again, then release. Note that although you have changed the zoom level, the Move tool is still active.

> **Take Note...**
> *You can zoom out by holding down Alt+spacebar (Windows) or Option+spacebar (Mac OS).*

9. Choose View > Fit on Screen.

Using the Hand tool

The **Hand tool** allows you to move or pan around the document. It is a lot like pushing a piece of paper around on your desk.

Step-by-Step	Follow these steps to use the Hand tool

1. Select the Zoom tool (🔍), then click and drag on an area surrounding the front of the car.

2. Select the Hand tool (✋), then click and drag to the right to push the picture to the right. Notice that when the Hand tool is active, four view buttons appear in the Options bar (at the top of the work area) that allow you to change your current view to Actual Pixels, Fit Screen, Fill Screen, and Print Size.

3. Select the Zoom tool and hold the spacebar. Notice that the cursor turns into the Hand tool. Click and drag left to view the front of the car again. By holding down the spacebar, you can access the Hand tool without deselecting the current tool.

4. Double-click the Hand tool in the Tools panel to fit the entire image on your screen. This is the same as using Ctrl+0 (zero) (Windows) or Command+0 (zero) (Mac OS).

Navigation Shortcuts	Windows	Mac OS
Zoom In	Ctrl+plus sign Ctrl+spacebar	Command+plus sign Command+spacebar
Zoom Out	Ctrl+minus sign Alt+spacebar	Command+minus sign Option+spacebar
Turn Zoom In tool into Zoom Out tool	Alt	Option
Fit on Screen	Ctrl+0 (zero) or double-click the Hand tool	Command+0 (zero) or double-click the Hand tool
Hand tool (except when Type tool is selected)	Press spacebar	Press spacebar

Tabbed windows

In Photoshop, you have control over how your windows appear in the workspace. You can work with floating image windows, or choose to tab your windows across the top of the workspace. In this section, you find out how to use the new **tabbed workspace**.

Follow these steps to work with tabbed windows	Step-by-Step

1. If the Mini Bridge is not visible, choose File > Browse in Mini Bridge. In the Navigation pod, double-click on the image named **ps0202.psd** to open it in Photoshop.

2. As shown in Figure 2-31, the image is displayed as a separate tab within Photoshop, allowing you to click on the tab to switch between active images.

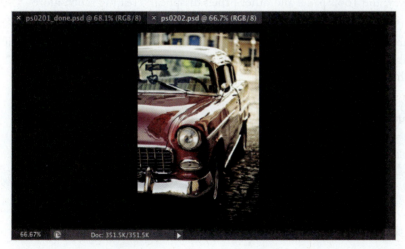

Figure 2-31: Multiple open images appear as tabs at the top of the screen.

3. Click on the **ps0202.psd** tab and then click and drag the tab away from its tabbed position and release the mouse button. The image second window is now floating.

4. Click the title bar of the floating window and drag upward until your cursor is next to the tab of the other image. When you see a blue bar appear, release the mouse button. The image is now back to being a tabbed window. You can stop a window from tabbing accidently by holding down the Ctrl (Windows) or Command (Mac OS) key while dragging the floating window.

If you would prefer not to take advantage of the tabbed window feature, you can choose Edit > Preferences (Windows) or Photoshop > Preferences (Mac OS), then choose Interface. In the Panels & Documents section, uncheck Open Documents as Tabs and press OK.

Take Note...

To quickly move all floating windows back to tabbed windows, choose Window > Arrange > Consolidate All to Tabs.

Maximizing productivity with screen modes

Now that you can zoom in and out of your document, as well as reposition it in your image window, it's time to learn how to take advantage of screen modes. You have a choice of three screen modes in which to work. Most users start and stay in the default—Standard Screen mode—unless they accidentally end up in another. Screen modes control how much space your current image occupies on your screen, and whether you can see other Photoshop documents as well. The Standard Screen mode is the default screen mode when you open Photoshop for the first time. It displays an image on a neutral gray background for easy and accurate viewing of color without distractions, and also provides a flexible work area for dealing with panels.

Step-by-Step | **Follow these steps to work with screen modes**

1. Click on the tab of the **ps0201_work.psd** image to make that image active.

2. Press the Tab key; the Tools panel and other panels disappear, creating much more workspace. Press the Tab key again to bring the Tools panel and other panels back.

3. Press Shift+Tab to hide the panel docking area while keeping the rest of the panels visible. Press Shift+Tab to bring the hidden panels back. Both the Tools panel and the panel docking area should now be visible.

Take Note...

As you position your cursor over various tools, you see a letter to the right of the tool name in the tooltip. This letter is the keyboard shortcut that you can use to access that tool. You could, in fact, work with the Tools panel closed and still have access to all the tools via your keyboard.

You will hide the panels once more so that you can take advantage of a hidden feature in Photoshop CS6.

4. Press the Tab key to hide the panels. Then position your cursor over the thin gray strip where the Tools panel had been, and pause. The Tools panel reappears. Note that the Tools panel appears only while your cursor is in the Tools panel area, and it disappears if you move your cursor out of that area. Try this with the panel docking area to the right of the screen, and watch as that also appears and disappears as your cursor moves over the gray border off to the right.

By changing the screen modes, you can locate over-extended anchor points and select more accurately up to the edge of your image. Changing modes can also help you present your image to clients in a clean workspace.

5. Press the Tab key again to display all the panels.

6. Press **F** to cycle to the next screen mode, which is Full Screen Mode With Menu Bar. This view surrounds the image out to the edge of the work area with a neutral gray (even behind the docking area) and displays only one image at a time, without tabs, and centered within the work area. You can access additional open images by choosing the image name from the bottom of the Window menu.

You can also change your screen mode by selecting View > Screen Mode.

7. Notice that the gray background area (pasteboard) now extends to fill your entire screen, and your image is centered within that area (Figure 2-32). One of the benefits of working in this mode is that it provides more area when working on images.

Figure 2-32: *The Full Screen mode with Menu bar.*

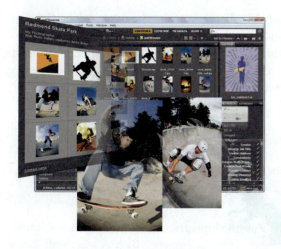

Taking Advantage of Adobe Bridge

Key Terms

- Batch Rename tool
- Bridge
- Collection
- Favorites panel
- Filter panel
- keywords
- metadata
- view
- Web Photo Gallery

Skill	Objective
Demonstrate knowledge of standard copyright rules for images and image use	**1.2**
Demonstrate knowledge of image-generating devices, their resulting image types, and how to access resulting images in Photoshop	**2.5**
Demonstrate knowledge of importing, exporting, organizing, and saving	**3.3**
Demonstrate knowledge of producing and reusing images	**3.4**
Demonstrate knowledge of working with selections	**4.1**
Demonstrate knowledge of preparing images for web, print, and video	**5.1**

Business case

You have a ton of projects you can't wait to begin working on in Photoshop. You already have a bunch of photos and graphics you want to utilize in your projects but they're kind of scattered and disorganize. It's inefficient to continually dig through all your files looking for something specific when there are some ways to streamline the process. In the following exercise, you'll examine Adobe Bridge and learn how to work more efficiently with graphics using other Adobe applications such as Photoshop.

Starting up

Before starting, make sure that your tools and panels are consistent by resetting your preferences. See "Resetting Adobe Photoshop CS6 preferences" in the Starting Up section of this book.

You will work with several files from the ps03lessons folder in this lesson. Make sure that you have loaded the pslessons folder onto your hard drive from *http://www.wiley.com/college/sc/adobeseries.* See "Loading lesson files" in the Starting Up section of this book.

What is Adobe Bridge?

Adobe Bridge is an application included with Adobe Photoshop and the other Adobe Creative Suite 6 applications. Along with application shortcuts, presets, and templates, Adobe Bridge helps you to work more efficiently. Adobe Bridge helps you locate, organize, reuse, and browse the documents you need to create print, web, video, and audio content. If you have Photoshop or any one of the Creative Suite applications, you can start Adobe Bridge by selecting File > Browse in Bridge.

> **Take Note...**
>
> *This lesson covers the functionality of the complete Bridge application, not the Mini Bridge that is available as a panel in your Photoshop workspace.*

You can use Bridge to access documents such as scanned images, digital camera images, camera RAW images, video files, text files, and even non–Adobe documents, such as Microsoft Word or Excel files. Using Adobe Bridge, you can also organize and manage images, videos, and audio files, as well as preview, search, and sort your files without opening them in their native applications.

The images that you manage using Bridge can come from a variety of different sources. Physical documents such as prints, documents and even objects can be converted to a digital image using a scanner or scanning device. Where most photos today are captured using a digital camera which digitizes the capture directly to a digital file such as a jpeg or an unprocessed format such as Camera RAW. Bridge can open files from over one hundred different file formats including psd, ai, indd, tif, pdf, jpg, gif and many more! Regardless of the format, Bridge can manage images with ease and precision.

Once you discover the capabilities of Adobe Bridge, you'll want to make it the control center for your Photoshop projects. With Bridge, you can easily locate files using the Filters panel and import images from your digital camera right into a viewing area that allows you to quickly rename and preview your files. This is why the recommended workflow throughout this book includes opening and saving files in Adobe Bridge. Reading through this lesson will help you to feel more comfortable with Adobe Bridge, and will also make you aware of some of the more advanced features that are available to you for your own projects.

>
>
> **Take Note...**
>
> *Adobe Bridge contains additional features when installed as part of one of the Creative Suites. The tools and features demonstrated in this lesson are available in both the single-product install and the Suite install, unless otherwise noted.*

Navigating through Bridge

In order to utilize Adobe Bridge effectively, you'll want to know the available tools and how to access them. Let's start navigating!

Follow these steps to learn the basics of the Adobe Bridge workspace   Step-by-Step

1. From Photoshop CS6 choose File > Browse in Bridge to launch the Adobe Bridge application. If you receive a dialog box asking if you want Adobe Bridge to launch at start-up, select Yes.

2. Click on the Favorites panel to make sure it is forward. Click on Desktop (listed in the Folders panel). You see the ps03lessons folder that you downloaded to your hard drive. Double-click on the ps03lessons folder and notice that the contents of that folder are displayed in the Content panel, in the center of the Adobe Bridge window. You can also navigate by clicking on folders listed in the Path bar that is located in the upper-left corner of the content window (Figure 3-1).

Figure 3-1: *You can view folder contents by double-clicking on a folder, or by selecting the folder in the Path bar.*

In this folder, you see a variety of file types, including Adobe Illustrator, Adobe Photoshop, Adobe Acrobat, and video files. These files came from *istockphoto.com* and many still have their default names.

You can navigate through your navigation history by clicking on the Go back and Go forward arrows in the upper-left corner of the window. Use the handy Reveal recent file or go to Reveal recent file or go to recent folder drop-down menu (🕭) to find folders and files that you recently opened. Note that there are also helpful navigational tools that allow you to quickly return to Photoshop, load photos from a camera, and flip your images.

Lesson 3

3. Click on the Go back arrow (◄) as displayed as callout A in Figure 3-2, to return to the desktop view.

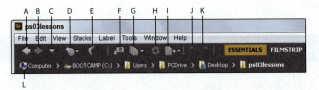

Figure 3-2

A. Go back. B. Go forward. C. Go to parent or Favorites.
D. Reveal recent file or go to recent folder. E. Return to Adobe Photoshop.
F. Get Photos From Camera. G. Refine. H. Camera Raw. I. Output.
J. Rotate 90° counterclockwise. K. Rotate 90° clockwise. L. Path bar.

 Take Note...
This example may show the file path to the ps03lessons folder differently than your example because this desktop is referencing a folder on a particular user's desktop.

4. Click on the Go forward arrow (►) to return to the last view, which is the ps03lessons folder.

Using folders in Adobe Bridge

Adobe **Bridge** is used for more than just navigating your file system. Bridge is also used to manage and organize folders and files.

Step-by-Step	**Follow these steps to use Adobe Bridge for managing folders and files**

1. Click on the tab of the Favorites panel in the upper-left corner of the Bridge window to make sure it is still forward. Then click on the arrow to the left of Desktop so that it turns downward and reveals its contents. If you are on the Mac OS, you can simply click on Desktop to reveal the contents.

2. Click on Computer to reveal its contents in the center pane of the Bridge window. Continue to double-click on items, or click on the arrows to the left of the folder names in the Folder panel, to reveal their contents (Figure 3-3).

Figure 3-3: *You can use Adobe Bridge to navigate your entire system, much as you would by using your computer's directory system.*

Managing folders

Learning More

Adobe Bridge is a great tool for organizing folders and files. It is a simple matter of dragging and dropping to reorder items on your computer. You can create folders, move folders, move files from one folder to another, and copy files and folders to other locations; any organizing task that can be performed on the computer can also be performed in Adobe Bridge. This is a great way to help keep volumes of images organized for easy accessibility, as well as easy searching. One advantage of using Adobe Bridge for these tasks is that you have bigger and better previews of images, PDF files, and movies, with much more information about those files at your fingertips.

3. Click on Desktop in the Folders panel to reveal its contents again.

4. Click on ps03lessons to view its contents. You'll now add a new folder into that lessons folder.

5. Click on the Create a New Folder icon (▣) in the upper-right corner of the Bridge window to create a new untitled folder inside the ps03lessons folder, as shown in Figure 3-4 below. Type the name **Graphics**.

Figure 3-4: Creating a new folder in Bridge.

You can use Adobe Bridge to organize images. Since you are able to see a preview of each file, you can more easily rename them, as well as relocate them to more appropriate locations in your directory system. In the next step, you will move files from one folder to the new Graphics folder you have just created.

6. Click once on the image named **boy_skateboard.ai**, and then Shift+click on the image named **flipit.ai**. Both images are selected.

Take Note...
You can easily reduce and enlarge the size of your thumbnails by pressing Ctrl+plus sign or Ctrl+minus sign in Windows or Command+plus sign or Command+minus sign in Mac OS.

7. Click and drag the selected images to the Graphics folder (Figure 3-5). When the folder becomes highlighted, release the mouse. The files have now been moved into that folder.

Figure 3-5: *You can select multiple images and organize folders directly in Adobe Bridge.*

8. Double-click on the Graphics folder to view its contents. You see the **boy_skateboard** and the **flipit** Adobe Illustrator (.ai) files that you moved.

9. Click on ps03lessons in the file path bar at the top to return to the ps03lessons folder content.

Making a Favorite

As you work in Photoshop, you will find that you frequently access the same folders. One of the many great features in Bridge is that you can designate a frequently used folder as a Favorite, allowing you to quickly and easily access it from the **Favorites panel**. This is extremely helpful, especially if the folders that you are frequently accessing are stored deep in your file hierarchy.

Follow these steps to create a favorite in Adobe Bridge	Step-by-Step

1. Select the Favorites panel in the upper-left corner of the Bridge window to bring it to the front. In the list of Favorites, click on Desktop. Double-click on the ps03lessons folder to see the skateboarding images. Since the Graphics folder is going to be used again in this lesson, you'll make it a Favorite.

2. Place your cursor over the Graphics folder in the center pane (Content), and click and drag the Graphics folder until you see a horizontal line appear in the Favorites panel as shown below in Figure 3-6. Be careful not to drag this folder into a folder (highlighted with a blue box) in the Favorites panel. When a cursor with a plus sign (⬚₊) appears, release the mouse. On the Mac OS you will see a circle with a plus sign. The folder is now listed as a Favorite.

Figure 3-6: Drag a folder to the bottom of the Favorites panel to make it easier to locate.

3. Click on the Graphics folder shown in the Favorites panel to view its contents. Note that creating a Favorite simply creates a shortcut for quick access to a folder; it does not copy the folder and its contents.

4. When you are finished looking inside the Graphics folder, press the Go back arrow to return to the ps03lessons folder.

Take Note...

If your Favorite is created from a folder on an external hard drive or server, you will need to have the hard drive or server mounted in order to access it.

Creating and locating metadata

Metadata is information that can be stored with images. This information travels with the file, and makes it easy to search for and identify the file. In this section, you are going to find out how to locate and create metadata. Metadata is particularly useful for both photographers and designers. For photographers, metadata is a way that they can add copyright information to an image letting users of the image know who owns the image, and it's a way that users can identify if the image is copyrighted as well. This is not the only way that an image can be identified as copyrighted. Sometimes you'll see this information in the credit for the photo or by looking at the date of publication as well. When in doubt, assume that an image is copyrighted and that you will need to obtain permission to use the image as these images are intellectual property owned by artist who created them. Even in cases of derivative work where the new artwork utilizes portions of an original image, copyright can still be a concern. One exception to this could be projects that relate to news reporting, research and teaching where users may be granted permission to use an image under the fair use doctrine.

Certification Ready 1.2

What methods are used to indicate that images are copyrighted?

Certification Ready 1.2

What copyright rules apply when using an image to create a review of a product?

Certification Ready 1.2

What should you do if you're not sure if an image is copyrighted?

Follow these steps to work with metadata in Adobe Bridge

Step-by-Step

1. Make sure that you are viewing the contents of the ps03lessons folder in the center pane of Adobe Bridge. If not, navigate to that folder now.

2. Choose Window > Workspace > Reset Standard Workspaces (Figure 3-7). This ensures that you are in the Essentials view and that all the default panels for Adobe Bridge are visible. Alternatively, you can click Essentials in the Application bar at the top-right of the Bridge workspace. You may need to maximize your Bridge window after you reset the workspace.

    Note that if you click on the arrow to the right of the workspace presets, you can choose other workspaces, and even save your own custom workspace.

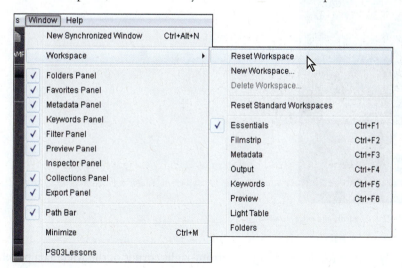

Figure 3-7: *Resetting the workspace using the Workspace drop-down menu.*

3. Click once on **iStock_1771975.jpg**, and look for the Metadata and Keywords panels in the lower-right area of the Adobe Bridge workspace.

4. If the Metadata panel is not visible, click on the Metadata panel tab. In this panel, you see the image data that is stored with the file. Take a few moments to scroll through the data and view the information that was imported from the digital camera which was used to take the photo.

> **Take Note...**
> *Click and drag the bar to the left of the Metadata panel farther to the left if you need to open up the window.*

5. If necessary, click on the arrow to the left of IPTC Core to reveal its contents. IPTC Core is the schema for XMP that provides a smooth and explicit transfer of metadata. Adobe's Extensible Metadata Platform (XMP) is a labeling technology that allows you to embed data about a file, known as metadata, into the file itself. With XMP, desktop applications and back-end publishing systems gain a common method for capturing and sharing, valuable metadata.

6. On the right side of this list, notice a series of pencil icons. The pencil icons indicate that you can enter information in these fields. Some of the information about the creator has already been included, such as the creator's name and his location. You will add additional information.

7. Scroll down until you can see Description Writer, and click on the pencil next to it. All editable fields are highlighted, and a cursor appears in the Description Writer field.

8. Type your name, or type **Student**.

9. Scroll up to locate the Description text field. Click on the Pencil icon to the right and type **Skateboarder catching air**, to add a description for the image as shown below in Figure 3–8.

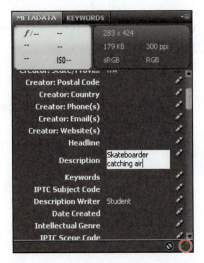

Figure 3–8: Reveal the IPTC contents and enter metadata information.

10. Click on the Apply button (✔), located in the bottom-right corner of the Metadata panel, to apply your changes. You have now edited metadata that is attached to the image, information that will appear whenever someone opens your image in Bridge or views the image information in Adobe Photoshop, using File > File Info.

Using keywords

Keywords can reduce the amount of time it takes to find an image on a computer, by using logical words to help users locate images more quickly.

Follow these steps to add keywords to images in Adobe Bridge	Step-by-Step

1. Click on the Keywords tab, which appears behind the Metadata panel. A list of commonly used keywords appears.

2. Click on the New Keyword button (⊕) at the bottom of the Keywords panel. Type **Skateboarder** into the active text field, and then press Enter (Windows) or Return (Mac OS).

3. Check the empty checkbox to the left of the Skateboarder keyword. This adds the Skateboarder keyword to the selected image.

4. With the Skateboarder keyword still selected, click on the New Sub Keyword button (⊕). Type **Male** into the active text field, then press Enter (Windows) or Return (Mac OS).

5. Check the empty checkbox to the left of the Male keyword. You have now assigned a keyword and a sub keyword to the **iStock_1771975.jpg** image.

6. Select the Skateboarder keyword, and then click on the New Keyword button (⊕) at the bottom of the Keywords panel; a blank text field appears. Type **Sunset** and press Enter (Windows) or Return (Mac OS). Then check the checkbox next to Sunset to assign the keyword to this image.

7. Right-click (Windows) or Ctrl+click (Mac OS) on the Sunset keyword, and choose the option Rename. When the text field becomes highlighted, type **Orange**, press Enter (Windows) or Return (Mac OS). As shown in Figure 3-9, make sure the Orange checkbox remains checked.

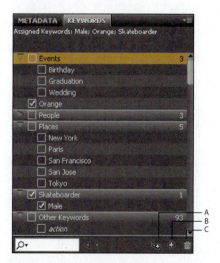

Figure 3-9: *A. New Sub Keyword.*
B. New Keyword. C. Delete Keyword.

 Take Note...
You can also enter information directly into the image by opening the image in Adobe Photoshop, and then choosing File > File Info. The categories that appear on the top include Description, Camera Data, IPTC, and IPTC Extension, among others. Once it is entered in the File Info dialog box, the information is visible in Adobe Bridge.

Creating a Metadata Template

Once you have added metadata to an image, you can easily apply it to more by creating a metadata template. In this exercise, you apply the metadata template from the **iStock_1771975.jpg** image to some others in the same folder.

Follow these steps to create a metadata template in Adobe Bridge

1. Make sure that **iStock_1771975.jpg** is selected in Adobe Bridge.

2. Choose Tools > Create Metadata Template. The Create Metadata Template window appears.

3. In the Template Name text field (at the top), type **Sunset Skateboarders**.

   In the Create Metadata Template window, you can choose the information that you want to build into a template. In this exercise, we will choose information that already exists in the selected file, but if you wanted to, you could add or edit information at this point.

4. As shown in Figure 3-10, check the Checkboxes to the left of the following categories; Creator, Creator: City, Creator: State/Province, Description, Keywords, and Description Writer, then press Save.

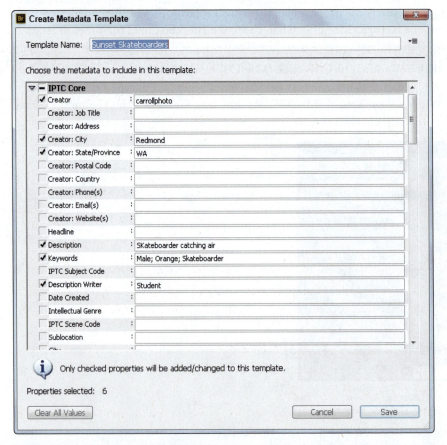

Figure 3-10: Select a file and check the information you want to save into a metadata template.

You have just saved a template. Next, you will apply it to the other two sunset images in this folder.

5. Select the **iStock_1771975.jpg** image, press and hold the Ctrl (Windows) or Command (Mac OS) key, and select the **iStock_10135568.jpg** image. Both images are selected.

6. Choose Tools > Append Metadata and select Sunset Skateboarders (Figure 3-11). Note that you can also choose Replace Metadata if you want to eliminate existing metadata. The same metadata has now been applied to all the images at once.

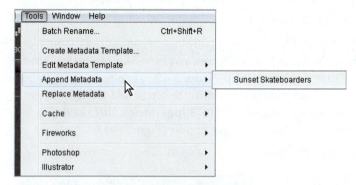

Figure 3-11: *Choose the metadata template you want to use to add metadata to an image or images.*

Opening a file from Adobe Bridge

Opening files from Adobe Bridge is a great way to begin the work process in Adobe Photoshop. Not only is it very visual, but important data stored with the files also makes it easier to locate the correct file.

Follow these steps to open a file from Adobe Bridge	Step-by-Step

1. In the ps03lessons folder double-click on **iStock_10138490.jpg** to open the file in Adobe Photoshop.

> **Take Note...**
> *Sometimes you will find that double-clicking on a file opens it in a different application than expected. This can happen if you are working in generic file formats such as JPEG and GIF. To avoid this problem, you can right-click (Windows) or Ctrl+click (Mac OS) on the image, and choose Open With to select the appropriate application.*

2. Choose File > Close and then select File > Browse in Bridge to return to Adobe Bridge.

3. You can also click once to select an image and then choose File > Open, or use the keyboard shortcut Ctrl+O (Windows) or Command+O (Mac OS).

Searching for files using Adobe Bridge

Find the files that you want quickly and easily by using the Search tools built directly into Adobe Bridge, and taking advantage of the Filter panel.

In this example, you have a limited number of files to search within, but you will have the opportunity to see how helpful these search features can be.

Searching by name or keyword

What's the benefit of adding all this metadata if you can't use it to find your files later? Using the Find dialog box in Adobe Bridge, you can narrow your criteria down to make it easy to find your files when needed.

Follow these steps to use the Find feature of Adobe Bridge

1. Make sure that you are still viewing the content in the ps03lessons folder.

2. Choose Edit > Find, or use the keyboard shortcut, Ctrl+F (Windows) or Command+F (Mac OS). The Find dialog box appears.

3. Select Keywords from the Criteria drop-down menu, and type **Skateboarder** into the third text field (replacing Enter Text) as show in Figure 3-12. Then press Enter (Windows) or Return (Mac OS). Because you are looking within the active folder only, you get a result immediately. The image files **iStock_1771975.jpg**, **iStock_10138490.jpg**, **iStock_10138506.jpg** and **iStock_10135568.jpg**, appear (Figure 3-13).

Figure 3-12: *Search for the keyword Skateboarder.*

Figure 3-13: *The images that contain the word Skateboarder in the metadata appear.*

4. Clear the search by pressing the X icon (⊗) to the right of the New Search icon at the top of the results pane.

Using the Filter panel

If you have ever been in the position where you knew you put a file into a folder, but just couldn't seem to find it, you will love the Filter panel.

Using the **Filter panel**, you can look at attributes such as file type, keywords, and date created or modified, in order to narrow down the files that appear in the content window of Adobe Bridge.

Follow these steps to use the Filter feature in Adobe Bridge

1. Make sure that you are still viewing the content of the ps03lessons folder. Notice that the Filter panel collects the information from the active folder, indicating the keywords that are being used, as well as modification dates and more.

2. Click to turn down the arrow next to Keywords in the Filter panel, and select Skateboarder from the list to see that only images with the Skateboarder keyword applied are visible (Figure 3-14). Click on Skateboarder again to deselect it and view all the images.

Figure 3-14: *Find files quickly by selecting different criteria in the Filters panel.*

3. Click the Clear filter button (◎) in the lower-right of the Filter panel to turn off any filters.

4. Experiment with investigating file types as well. Only file types that exist in the selected folder appear in the list. If you are looking for an Adobe Illustrator file, you may see that there are none located in this folder, but you will see a QuickTime video file in Figure 3-15 that you can select and preview right in Adobe Bridge.

Figure 3-15: *You can select File Types from the Filter panel to locate them easily.*

5. Again, click the Clear filter button (◎) in the lower-right of the Filter panel to turn off any filters.

Saving a Collection

If you like using Favorites, you'll love using Collections. A **Collection** allows you to take images from multiple locations and access them in one central location. Understand that Adobe Bridge essentially creates a shortcut (or alias) to your files and does not physically relocate them or copy them to a different location.

Step-by-Step	Follow these steps to use the Collections feature in Adobe Bridge

1. If your Collections tab is not visible, Choose Window > Collections Panel or click on the tab next to Filter. The Collections panel comes forward.

2. Click the gray area in the content pane to make sure that nothing is selected, and then click the New Collection button in the lower-right of the Collections panel. Type **Redmond Skateboarding** into the new collection text field as displayed in Figure 3-16. Press Return or Enter to confirm your new collection.

Figure 3-16: *Create a new Redmond Skateboarding collection.*

3. Navigate back to the ps03lessons folder, and then take two random skateboarding images and drag them to the Redmond Skateboarding collection. In this example, the two images of the girl skateboarding were selected.

4. Click on the Redmond Skateboarding collection folder to see that even though you can easily access the files that you added to the collection, the files remain intact in their original location (Figure 3-17).

Figure 3-17: *A collection helps you to organize files without moving them to new locations.*

Automation tools in Adobe Bridge

Adobe Bridge provides many tools to help you automate tasks. In this section, you will learn how to batch-process some images. In addition to this type of automation, you can also use Photoshop to create actions and droplets that will further assist in automating repetitive tasks when working in Photoshop.

Certification Ready 4.1

What are some batch-processing techniques?

Batch renaming your files

You may have noticed that in the ps03lessons file there are many files that contain iStock in the filename. These images were downloaded from *iStockphoto.com*, and instead of changing the names immediately we have opted to change them simultaneously using the **Batch Rename tool** in Adobe Bridge.

Follow these steps to rename multiple files at one time	Step-by-Step

1. Press the Go back arrow (◄) in the upper-left of the Adobe Bridge window to go back to the ps03lessons folder.

2. Choose Edit > Select All, or press Ctrl+A (Windows) or Command+A (Mac OS.) All the images are selected. Don't worry if the Graphics folder is selected; the files inside will not be affected.

3. Choose Tools > Batch Rename. The Batch Rename dialog box appears.

   In this instance we want a simple uncomplicated name. If you look in the Preview section at the bottom of the Batch Rename dialog box, you can see that the Current filename and New filename are pretty long strings of text and numbers. You will simplify this by eliminating some of text from the filenames.

4. In the New Filenames section, type **Skateboard** in the text field to the right of default criteria of Text.

5. In the Sequence Number row, verify that it is set to Two Digits.

6. Confirm that the sequence number is starting at 1. You can start it anywhere if you are adding additional images to a folder later.

7. If there is any other criteria, click on the Minus sign button (⊟) (Remove this text from the file names) to remove them. As you can see in Figure 3-18, the New filename in the Preview section becomes significantly shorter.

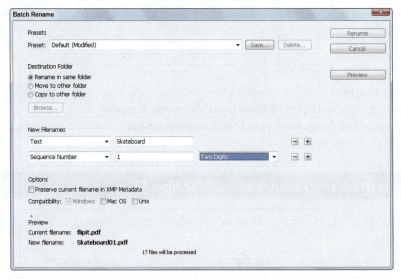

Figure 3-18: *You can change multiple files names simultaneously in Adobe Bridge.*

If you look in the Preview section at the bottom of the dialog box, you can see that the new filename is a very simple **Skateboard01.jpg** now. Press the Rename button. As you can see in Figure 3-19, all the selected files automatically have their name changed.

Figure 3-19: *The content pane after the images were renamed.*

Additional Photoshop Tools

Adobe Bridge comes with a variety of Photoshop tools that you can use in Bridge as well. In this example, you will select three images that you want to incorporate into one composited image. Instead of opening all three images and cutting and pasting or dragging them into one file, you will use the Load Files into Photoshop layers feature.

Make sure that you are still in the ps03lessons folder; select the **Skateboard03.jpg**, and then Shift+click the **Skateboard05.jpg** image. All three images are selected.

Select the Tools menu item and then select Photoshop. Note that there are many tools that you can use in this menu item; for this example, select the Load Files into Photoshop Layers option as shown in Figure 3-20. A script immediately launches Photoshop (if it is not already open) and a new layered file is created from the selected images (Figure 3-21).

Take Note...
You should ensure that your selected images are approximately the same pixel dimensions before running this script; otherwise, you may have to make some transformation adjustments in Photoshop. In this example, the images are approximately the same size.

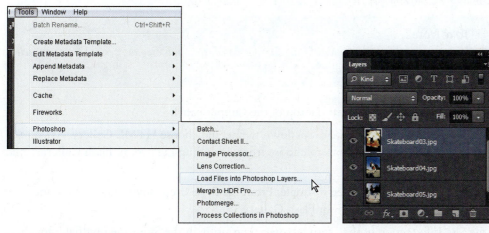

Figure 3-20: *Select multiple files in Adobe Bridge and open them in one layered file.*

Figure 3-21: *The result is three layers in one Photoshop file.*

Lesson 3

Automated tools for Photoshop: Web Photo Gallery

Certification Ready 5.1

How do you create a Web Photo Gallery in Photoshop?

If you want to share images online, you can use the **Web Photo Gallery**, which creates a website that features a home page with thumbnail images and gallery pages with full-size images. You select the images you want to include in the site and Adobe Bridge does the rest, from automatically creating navigation images, like arrows, links, and buttons, to creating Flash files. This is a fun feature that you can take advantage of quickly, even if you have no coding experience. If you have coding experience, or if you want to edit the pages further, you can open the pages in Adobe Dreamweaver or any other HTML editor to customize them.

Step-by-Step

Follow these steps to create a Web Photo Gallery using Adobe Bridge

1. Make sure that you are viewing the contents of the ps03lessons folder, and press Ctrl+A (Windows) or Command+A (Mac OS) to select all the images.

   You can leave the Graphics folder selected, you will receive a warning that some of the selected files are not supported image files, but it will not cause any errors.

2. Click and hold down on the Output drop-down menu located in the upper-right of the Application bar, and choose Output; the workspace changes to reveal an Output panel on the right.

Take Note...

If you cannot see all the options in the Output panel, click and drag the vertical bar to the left of the panel to increase its size.

3. Press the Web Gallery button at the top of the Output panel.
4. Click and hold on the Template drop-down menu, and choose HTML Gallery. As you can see, there are a lot of options to choose from, including Lightroom Flash Galleries, and Airtight viewers.
5. For this example, you will keep it simple. From the Style drop-down menu, if it's not already visible, choose Lightroom Flash Gallery.
6. In the Site Info section of the Output panel, type a title in the Site Title text field; for this example, you can type **Redmond Skate Park**.
7. You can also add photograph captions if you like, as well as text in the Collection Description text field, to include more information. In this example, those are left at their defaults.

8. Using the scroll bar to the right of the Site Info section, click and drag to scroll down through the rest of the options. Note that you can add additional contact information, and define colors that you want to use for different objects on the page, including text (Figure 3-22).

Figure 3-22: Select the template and any other customized options in the Output panel.

9. Press the Preview in Browser button that is located in the upper-half of the Output panel; your website is automatically created.

Note that because the Graphics folder and a video are selected, you will get a warning that some of the files are not supported image types; press OK. You may also receive an ActiveX warning; instruct the browser to Allow blocked content so your browser can preview your website as shown in Figure 3-23.

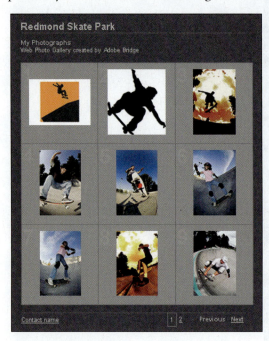

Figure 3-23: The completed website, using Web Gallery.

10. The preview is in a browser window. Close the browser before you move to the next part of this lesson.

Saving or uploading your Web Gallery

So now you have an incredible Web Gallery, but what do you do with it? The Web Photo Gallery feature creates an index page, individual gallery pages, and images, and so you need someplace to put them. You have a couple options available if you click the scroll bar to the right of Site Info and drag down until you see the option under Create Gallery for Gallery Name. Note that you can choose to save your Gallery to a location on your hard drive, or input the FTP login information directly in Adobe Bridge to upload your file directly to a server. In this example, you will save the Web Gallery to your ps03lessons folder.

Follow these steps to save or upload a Web Photo Gallery in Adobe Bridge	Step-by-Step

1. Scroll down in the Output panel until you see the Create Gallery section.

   Click the Browse button to the right of Save Location. Navigate to the ps03lessons folder on your desktop, and click OK (Figure 3-24).

Figure 3-24: *Choose where you want to save your web gallery.*

2. Click on the Save button at the bottom of the Output panel. A dialog box appears, indicating that you have successfully created a Gallery; press OK.

You have successfully saved your Web Gallery. Use Adobe Bridge to navigate and open the contents of the Adobe Web Gallery folder that was created in the ps03lessons folder. Open the contents to see that your components are neatly organized so that you can open them in your web editor and customize them, or send them to your web site administrator for uploading as shown in Figure 3-25.

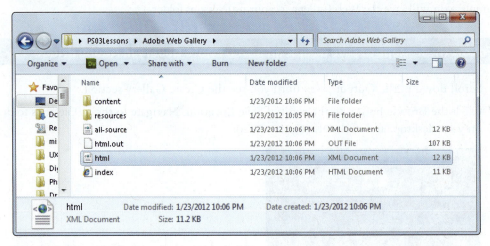

Figure 3-25: *The completed website, when saved to the hard drive.*

Automated tools for Photoshop: PDF contact sheet

By creating a PDF contact sheet, you can assemble a series of images into one file for such purposes as client approval and summaries of folders.

| Step-by-Step | Follow these steps to create a PDF contact sheet |

1. To make it easy to select just the images you want, click on Essentials to change the Adobe Bridge workspace back to the defaults. If you do not see the contents of the ps03lessons folder in the content window in Bridge, click on Desktop, and then double-click on the ps03lessons folder. If you stored the lesson files elsewhere, use the navigation tools in Bridge to locate your lesson files.

2. Click on the first skateboarder image you see and then Shift+click on the last, selecting all the skateboarding images, but none of the folders inside the ps03lessons folder.

3. Select Output from the upper-right of the Adobe Bridge workspace.

4. In the Output panel, click on the PDF button, then from the Template drop-down menu, choose 5*8 Contact Sheet.

Figure 3-26: *Choose to create a PDF contact sheet from the Template drop-down menu.*

5. In the Document section of the Output panel, choose U.S. Paper from the Page Preset drop-down menu as shown above in Figure 3-26.

Scroll down and notice that you have options for final size, document quality, and even security in the Output panel. You will leave these items at the default and scroll down to the Playback section of this panel. The Playback section allows you to set the initial view of the PDF when it is opened, as well as set the timing and transitions between pages of your PDF.

6. At the bottom of the Output panel check the checkbox to View PDF After Save; then press the Save button. The Save As dialog box appears.

7. In the Save As dialog box, type **contact**, and then browse to save the file in your ps03lessons folder; press Save.

A Generate PDF Contact Sheet dialog box may appear; press OK. The **contact.pdf** file is saved in your ps03lessons folder and your contact sheet is launched in Adobe Acrobat for you to view.

8. After examining your contact sheet in Adobe Acrobat (as shown in Figure 3-27), choose File > Close to close the **contact.pdf** file, and return to Adobe Bridge.

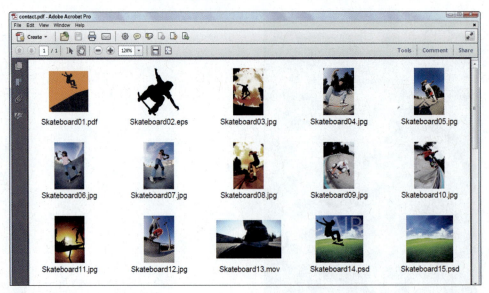

Figure 3-27: The completed PDF contact sheet.

Changing the view

You can work the way you like by adjusting the look and feel of Adobe Bridge. Changing the **view** can help you focus on what is important to see in the Content section of the Bridge workspace. Whether you need to focus on content or thumbnails, there is a view that can help you.

Step-by-Step	Follow these steps to customize the views in Adobe Bridge

1. Before experimenting with the views, make sure that you are in the Essentials workspace by selecting the Essentials button located in the upper-right of the Bridge workspace.

2. Click on the Click to Lock to Thumbnail Grid button (⊞) in the lower-right corner of the Bridge workspace. The images are organized into a grid.

3. Now click on the View Content as Details button (⬛▪) to see a thumbnail and details about creation date, last modified date, and file size. This view is shown below in Figure 3-28.

Figure 3-28: *Changing the view of Adobe Bridge.*

4. Choose the View Content as List button (▬) to see the contents consolidated into a neat list, which you can easily scroll through.

5. Click on the View Content as Thumbnails button (⣿) to return to the default thumbnail view.

6. Experiment with changing the size of the thumbnails in the Content panel by using the slider to the left of the preview buttons. Don't forget, you can also change the thumbnail size by pressing Ctrl++ (plus sign) or Ctrl+- (minus sign) (Windows) or Command++ (plus sign) or Command+- (minus sign) (Mac OS).

Skill Summary

In this lesson you learned how to:	Objective
Demonstrate knowledge of standard copyright rules for images and image use	**1.2**
Demonstrate knowledge of image-generating devices, their resulting image types, and how to access resulting images in Photoshop	**2.5**
Demonstrate knowledge of importing, exporting, organizing, and saving	**3.3**
Demonstrate knowledge of producing and reusing images	**3.4**
Demonstrate knowledge of working with selections	**4.1**
Demonstrate knowledge of preparing images for web, print, and video	**5.1**

Knowledge Assessment

True/False

Circle **T** if the statement is true or **F** if the statement is false.

T F **1.** You can access Bridge from Photoshop by choosing File > Browse in Bridge.

T F **2.** Bridge can be used to preview images, organize them, and even rename them.

T F **3.** To make something a favorite in Bridge, you can simply drag the item into the Favorites panel.

T F **4.** Keywords can only use numbers and the file name for the information that's displayed as the keyword.

T F **5.** Keywords can reduce the amount of time it takes to find an image on a computer.

T F **6.** Another way to access metadata directly in Photoshop is by choosing File > File Info.

T F **7.** Metadata can only be attached to one image. It cannot be transferred from image to image.

T F **8.** Keywords are not one of the available criteria when using the Find dialog box.

T F **9.** You can only rename one file at a time in Bridge.

T F **10.** Bridge allows automated tool functions, even the ability to create web photo galleries.

Multiple Choice

Select the best response for the following statements.

1. What program is included with the Creative Suite that allows you to locate, organize and browse files on your computer?

    a. Flash

    b. Media Encoder

    c. Bridge

    d. Dreamweaver

2. Which of the following functions are available through Adobe Bridge?

    a. Go back and forward

    b. Get Photos From Camera

    c. Refine

    d. All of the above

3. What is the name of the information that is stored inherently within an image itself?

   a. Data
   b. Metadata
   c. RAM
   d. ROM

4. Keywords, Headline, Description, and Date Created are all characteristics of which panel in Bridge?

   a. Keywords
   b. Preview
   c. Metadata
   d. Output

5. Which of the following is not a default category in the Keywords panel?

   a. Stuff
   b. Events
   c. People
   d. Places

6. Which panel allows you to choose attributes like file type, keywords and date in order to narrow down the files that appear in the content window?

   a. Filter
   b. Favorites
   c. Folders
   d. Collections

7. What Photoshop feature is available through Bridge?

   a. Contact Sheet II
   b. Lens Correction
   c. Photomerge
   d. All of the above

8. The Output panel provides output access to which two formats?

   a. PDF and Powerpoint slideshows
   b. PDF and Web Gallery
   c. Web Gallery and Flash
   d. Powerpoint and Image Segments

9. Which option is recommended for assembling a series of images into one file for purposes such as client approval?

   a. Web Gallery
   b. PDF contact sheet
   c. JPEG Sequence
   d. TIFF Sequence

Lesson 3

10. What is the name of the workspace in Bridge that will display creation date, last modified date, and file size?

    a. Essentials

    b. Details

    c. List

    d. None of the above

Competency Assessment

Project 3-1 **Entering Metadata Through the File Info Window**

Through Bridge you have plenty of great options for managing metadata and more. But, you may not have Bridge launched and still want to enter metadata but want to do it a bit more on the fly...

1. Open the **Skateboard06.jpg** image in Photoshop. If you didn't perform the batch rename Step-by-step, this file is **iStock_2411686.jpg**.

2. Choose File > File Info.

3. Enter whatever metadata you feel is appropriate in the Description and IPTC categories. Click OK, then choose File > Save As and name the file **iStock_lesson3**.

4. If you want to see how it translates in Bridge, browse for this file in Bridge and view the information in the Metadata panel.

Project 3-2 **Understanding Bridge's Mechanics**

Did you ever wonder how Bridge knows which program to open when you double-click a file? Do you have files that open in the wrong program when double-clicking on them in the Bridge?

1. Open Bridge.

2. Choose Edit > Preferences (Windows) or Bridge > Preferences (Mac OS).

3. Select File Type Associations and explore from there. This area allows you to control which application is launched when certain file types are opened in Bridge.

Proficiency Assessment

Project 3-3 **Using Bridge to Make a Back-Up of Your Files**

Renaming files is just one way to use the Batch Rename function. There's also a way to back up all your work as well.

1. Open Bridge and navigate to the ps03lessons folder. You'll make a backup of the items in this folder.

2. Go into the folder and select all of the files. You can use the shortcut Ctrl+A (Windows) or Cmd+A (Mac OS).

3. Choose Tools > Batch Rename.

4. Under Destination Folder, choose Copy to other folder and create a folder on your desktop called **ps03lessons_backup**.

5. Leave the new filename at the default. Compress this folder and submit to your instructor.

Trying More Automated Functions

Bridge is a great way to create a contact sheet of files on your computer.

1. Open Bridge and navigate to the ps03lessons folder.

2. Select all of the photos in this folder and choose Tools > Photoshop > Contact Sheet II. Configure the settings to your taste and create a contact sheet.

3. Save the contact sheet as **ps03_contact_sheet.psd** to submit to your instructor.

Photoshop Basics

Key Terms

- EPS
- file formats
- GIF
- Image Size dialog box
- JPEG
- layers
- PDF
- PNG
- resampling
- resolution
- TIFF

Skill	Objective
Demonstrate knowledge of image resolution, image size, and image file format for web, video, and print	2.1
Demonstrate knowledge of typography	2.3
Demonstrate knowledge of color correction using Photoshop CS6	2.4
Understand key terminology of digital images	2.6
Demonstrate knowledge of importing, exporting, organizing, and saving	3.3
Transform images	4.3
Demonstrate knowledge of preparing images for web, print, and video	5.1

Business case

Among the basic operations of Photoshop is the ability to combine different images together to form a composite image. Your boss would like to see how your skills are developing so he provided some files to practice with to formulate a mock postcard project. Once it's finished, you'll need to show that you can remove a white background from an image as well as layer multiple images together. Even though it's a print piece, your boss would prefer a PDF for proofing purposes.

Starting up

Before starting, make sure that your tools and panels are consistent by resetting your preferences. See "Resetting Adobe Photoshop CS6 preferences" in the Starting up section of this book.

You will work with several files from the ps04lessons folder in this lesson. Make sure that you have loaded the pslessons folder onto your hard drive from *http://www.wiley.com/college/sc/adobeseries*. See "Loading lesson files" in the Starting up section of this book.

In this lesson, you'll use multiple images to create a composite image that you will then save for both print and online use. While this lesson covers some basic information about working with files for online distribution, you can learn even more about saving files for the web in Lesson 12, "Creating Images for Web and Video."

A look at the finished project

In this lesson, you will develop a composite using several images, while addressing issues such as resolution, resizing, and choosing the right file format.

To see the finished document:

Step-by-Step | **Follow these steps to reveal or conceal a layer**

1. Choose File > Browse in Bridge to bring Adobe Bridge forward. Using Adobe Bridge, navigate to the pslessons folder on your hard drive and open the ps04lessons folder.

2. Double-click on the **ps04_done.psd** file, and the completed image is displayed in Photoshop as shown below in Figure 4-1.

Figure 4-1: *The completed lesson file.*

3. Make sure that the Layers panel is active by choosing Window > Layers.

4. Click on the visibility icon (👁) to the left of the cow layer to hide the layer. Click the box where the visibility icon used to be to make the layer visible again.

   Layers allow you to combine different elements into a single file while retaining the ability to move and modify each layer independently of the others. In this chapter, you'll be creating multiple layers in Photoshop just like the ones in this finished file.

5. You can keep this file open for reference, or choose File > Close to close the file. If a Photoshop warning box appears, choose Don't Save.

Opening an existing document

Now you will assemble all the images that are part of the final combined image.

Step-by-Step | **Follow these steps to open multiple images**

1. Return to Adobe Bridge by choosing File > Browse in Bridge.

2. Navigate to the pslessons folder you copied onto your system, and open the ps04lessons folder.

3. From the ps04lessons folder, select the file named **ps0401.psd**. Hold down the Ctrl key (Windows) or Command key (Mac OS), and also select the **ps0402.psd** and **ps0403.psd** files. Choose File > Open or double-click any one of the selected files. All the selected images open in Adobe Photoshop.

Take Note...

If you receive an Embedded Profile Mismatch warning when opening the images, you may have forgotten to reset your preferences using the instructions on page 3. If you receive the warning, choose the Use Embedded Profile option, and then click OK.

Understanding Photoshop images

Photoshop is a pixel or raster-based application. Every file that you will work with in Photoshop is composed of small square pieces of information called pixels (also referred to as rasters or bitmaps). Although Photoshop has tools that can create vector-based objects composed of paths, they almost always will be rendered as pixels or rasterized to produce the final artwork.

In this section, you will move images from one file to another to create your mock-up. Before you combine the images, you need to be familiar with each document's unique attributes, such as size, resolution, and color mode. Moving layers between documents that have different resolutions may create unexpected results, such as causing the images to appear out of proportion.

Certification Ready 2.6

What is the difference between a raster-based file and a vector-based file?

Certification Ready 4.3

How do you resample to a larger or smaller image?

Viewing an image's size and resolution

Follow these steps to view an image's size and resolution

Step-by-Step

1. Click on the tab of the image of the barn, **ps0401.psd**, to make it active. Press Alt (Windows) or Option (Mac OS) and click the file information area in the status bar, located in the lower-left corner of the document window. As shown in Figure 4-2, the dimensions of the barn image is displayed as 885 pixels wide by 542 pixels tall and the Resolution is 72 pixels/inch.

Figure 4-2: Image size and resolution information.

2. If the picture of the rooster, **ps0402.psd**, is not visible, choose Window > **ps0402.psd** or click on the tab for that image at the top of the screen to make it the active window. After confirming that this is the active document, select Image > Image Size to open the Image Size dialog box.

The Image Size dialog box appears (Figure 4-3).

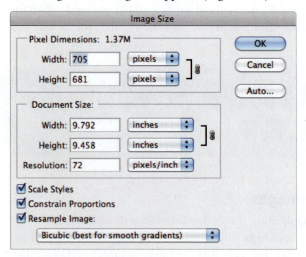

Figure 4-3: Image size plays an important role when combining images.

Certification Ready 2.1

What is the difference between image size measured in pixels and document size measured in inches?

Certification Ready 2.1

How does image resolution change after being manipulated?

Certification Ready 2.1

What is the difference between printed images and onscreen images?

The **Image Size dialog box** is divided into two main areas: Pixel Dimensions and Document Size. Pixel Dimensions shows the number of pixels that make up the image. For web graphics, the pixel dimensions are more relevant than the document's actual printing size. Document Size shows the resolution information, as well as the actual physical size of the image. The bottom portion of the Image Size dialog box allows you to Scale any Styles applied in your image and allows you to choose the interpolation method (how pixels are mapped during transformation). Pick the interpolation method that best matches the transformation that you are applying.

> **Take Note...**
>
> *The most important factors for size and resolution of web images are the pixel dimensions and the pixels per inch (ppi). If you are designing content for the Web, you should reference the top (Pixel Dimensions) section of the Image Size dialog box. As a print designer, you should reference the bottom (Document Size) section of the Image Size dialog box.*
>
> *It's common to confuse terms such as ppi (pixels per inch), dpi (used to measure ink dots on a desktop printer), and line screen frequency (used to measure dot size on a printing press. In Photoshop, we measure resolution using ppi (pixels per inch) to determine the resolution of a file. Always remember that the ppi of an image can change during manipulation of an image such as cropping and resizing.*

3. The image size of the rooster is 705 pixels by 681 pixels. At this size, the rooster is taller than the barn, which would be apparent when you combine the two files. While this might work for an *Attack of the Roosters* horror movie, you're interested in making the rooster smaller.

4. Make sure that the Resample Image and Constrain Proportions checkboxes are both selected. In the Image Size dialog box, type **200** pixels for height in the Pixel Dimensions portion at the top half of the dialog box. Press OK to apply the transformation and close the Image Size dialog box.

5. The rooster is now an appropriate size to combine with the barn image.

Combining the images

For this project, you'll use several methods to combine the images.

Using Copy and Paste

Follow these steps to copy and paste an image **Step-by-Step**

1. If necessary, click the tab of the rooster image, **ps0402.psd**, to make it active.

> ***Take Note...***
> *You can have many documents open at once in Photoshop, but only one of them is active at any given time.*

2. Choose Select > All to select the entire image. This creates a selection marquee around the outside edge of the image. You can learn more about selections in Lesson 5, "Making the Best Selections."

3. Choose Edit > Copy to copy the selected image area. The image is now in your computer's clipboard, ready to be pasted into another document.

4. Select the tab of the barn picture, **ps0401.psd**, to make it the active document. Choose Edit > Paste to place the image of the rooster into the picture of the barn.

   As you can see in Figure 4-4, the rooster appears on top of the barn, and the background surrounding the rooster blocks part of the image. Both these items will be addressed in future steps in this lesson.

Figure 4-4: *The image of the rooster is now in the middle of the barn.*

5. Select the tab of the rooster image, **ps0402.psd**, and choose File > Close to close the file. Do not save any changes.

Dragging and dropping to copy an image

In this section, you'll drag and drop one image into another.

Follow these steps to drag and drop to copy an image **Step-by-Step**

1. Choose Window > Arrange > 2-up Vertical to view both the cow (**ps0403.psd**) and the barn (**ps0401.psd**) pictures at the same time. The Arrange features allow you to determine how windows are displayed on your monitor. The Tile features allow you to see all the open images.

Combining the images

2. Select the Move tool (⊹), and then select the picture of the cow, which is the **ps0403.psd** image. Click and drag the cow image over to the barn image (Figure 4-5). When your cursor is positioned over the picture of the barn, release your mouse. The cow picture is placed into the barn picture on a new layer.

Like using the Copy and Paste command, you can use the Move tool to copy images from one document to another.

Figure 4-5: Click and drag the cow image into the picture of the barn.

> **Take Note...**
> *You do not have to position images beside each other to move them from one image file to another. You can also drag and drop an image to the document tab of another image, and then drag down into the image area.*

3. Select the tab of **ps0403.psd** and choose File > Close to close the file containing the picture of the cow. Do not save any changes to the file.

4. With the composite image of the barn, rooster, and cow active, choose View > Fit on Screen, or use the keyboard shortcut Ctrl+0 (zero) (Windows) or Command+0 (zero) (Mac OS). This fits the entire image into your document window as shown in Figure 4-6. You can also see in Figure 4-7 that you have three layers in this document.

Figure 4-6: *The barn picture combined with the other images.*

Figure 4-7: *The images are now layers.*

5. Choose File > Save As to save this file. When the Save As dialog box appears, navigate to the ps04lessons folder and type **ps0401_work** in the Name text field. Choose Photoshop from the format drop-down menu and press Save. If the Photoshop Format Options dialog box appears, press OK.

Transforming and editing combined images

Although you have combined three images together, they still require some work. The background remains in the two imported images, and the picture of the cow is out of proportion when compared with the barn.

> **Take Note...**
> *In order to use the transform options, the affected area must reside on a layer. Layers act as clear overlays on your image and can be used in many ways. Find out more about layers in Lesson 8, "Getting to Know Layers," and Lesson 9, "Taking Layers to the Max."*

In this section, you will do the following:

• View the stacking order of the layers that were automatically created when you combined the images;

• Remove the background from the copied images;

• Refine the edges of the combined images;

• Name the layers to organize them.

Changing the size of a placed image

While you could have adjusted the image size prior to dragging and dropping it into the barn picture, you can also make adjustments to layers and the objects that reside on the layers. Here you will adjust the size and position of the placed images.

Follow these steps to transform an image

1. Make sure the Layers panel is visible. If you do not see the Layers panel, choose Window > Layers.

2. Double-click the words Layer 1, to the right of the image thumbnail of the rooster in the Layers panel. When the text field becomes highlighted, type **rooster**, and then press Enter (Windows) or Return (Mac OS) to accept the change. Repeat this process to rename Layer 2, typing the name **cow**. You can see the result of this step in Figure 4-8.

Figure 4-8: The layers renamed.

3. With the cow layer selected in the Layers panel, choose Edit > Free Transform, or use the keyboard shortcut Ctrl+T (Windows) or Command+T (Mac OS). Handles appear around the edges of the cow. Keep the cow selected. If you do not see handles, press Ctrl+0 (zero) (Windows) or Command+0 (zero) (Mac OS) to fit the image into the window.

4. Press and hold Alt+Shift (Windows) or Option+Shift (Mac OS), and then click and drag any one of the handles on the outside corner edges of the cow toward the center. The image size is reduced as shown in Figure 4-9.

Notice that the scale percentages in the Options bar change as you scale the image. Reduce the size of the cow image to approximately 50 percent of its original size. Holding the Shift key maintains the proportions as you scale, while the Alt or Option key scales the image toward its center.

Figure 4-9: The cow layer being reduced in size, using the Free Transform command.

5. In the Options bar, click the Commit Transform button (✔) located on the right side, or press Enter (Windows) or Return (Mac OS), to accept the changes.

6. If you do not see the Rooster image, use the Move tool to reposition the cow to reveal it. In the Layers panel, click to activate the rooster layer, and then choose Edit > Free Transform.

7. Press and hold Alt+Shift (Windows) or Option+Shift (Mac OS) and reduce the size of the rooster to approximately 60 percent, using the Options bar as a guide to the scaling you are performing. Click the Commit Transform button, or press Enter (Windows) or Return (Mac OS), to accept the changes.

Removing a background

Photoshop makes it easy to remove the background of an image. Here you'll use a method that works well with solid backgrounds, such as the white behind the cow and rooster.

Follow these steps to use the Magic Eraser tool to remove a background	**Step-by-Step**

1. Select the cow layer in the Layers panel.

2. In the Tools panel, click to select the Magic Eraser tool (✍). You may need to click and hold on the Eraser tool to access the Magic Eraser tool.

3. Position the Magic Eraser tool over the white area behind the cow, and click once to remove the white background (Figure 4-10).

Figure 4-10: *Use the Magic Eraser tool to remove the background behind the cow.*

4. In the Layers panel, click to activate the rooster layer.

5. Position the cursor over the white area adjacent to the rooster, and click once to remove the white background. Just as the Eraser and Background Eraser tools can be used to remove pixels in an image. The Paint Bucket tool can be used to add pixels to an image.

Understanding the stacking order of layers

Layers are much like pieces of clear film that you could place on a table. The layers themselves are clear, but anything placed on one of the layers will be positioned on top of the layers that are located beneath it.

Step-by-Step	Follow these steps to reposition layers

1. Confirm that the rooster layer remains selected. Click to select the Move tool (⊕) from the Tools panel.

2. Position the Move tool over the rooster image in the document window, and drag the rooster so your cursor is positioned over the head of the cow. Notice that the rooster image is positioned under the cow. This is because the cow layer above the rooster layer in the Layers panel.

3. In the Layers panel, click and hold the rooster layer as demonstrated in Figure 4-11. Drag the layer up so it is positioned on top of the cow layer. Notice in the document window how the stacking order of the layers affects the stacking order of the objects in the image.

Figure 4-11: *Click and drag the rooster layer up to place it on top of the cow layer.*

4. Using the Move tool, click and drag the rooster to position it in the lower-left corner of the image, in front of the fence and along the side of the barn. If your image seems to *jump* when you are trying to position the image, choose View > Snap to prevent the edge of the image from snapping to the edge of the document.

5. Click to activate the cow layer, and then, continuing to use the Move tool, click and drag the cow to position it in the lower-right corner of the image. Position the cow so it appears to be grazing on the grass without hanging outside the image area.

6. Choose File > Save. Keep the file open for the next part of this lesson.

Refining the edges of copied images

When the images were copied, they maintained very hard edges, making it very clear where the picture of the cow or rooster stops and the original image starts. This hard edge makes the images look contrived. You will blend the images so they look more natural together.

| Follow these steps to use Defringe to refine the edges of an image | Step-by-Step |

1. Click to select the cow layer in the Layers panel. Choose the Zoom tool (🔍) from the Tools panel.

2. If necessary, uncheck Scrubby Zoom from the options panel, and then click and drag to create a zoom area around the entire cow. The cow is magnified to fill the entire display area (Figure 4-12).

3. Choose Layer > Matting > Defringe. The Defringe dialog box opens.

4. In the Defringe dialog box, maintain the default setting of 1 pixel, then click OK. The Defringe command blends the edges of the layer into the background, making it appear more natural as shown in Figure 4-13.

Figure 4-12: The cow before it is defringed.   *Figure 4-13: The cow after it is defringed.*

5. Press **H** on the keyboard to choose the Hand tool (✋). Using the Hand tool, click and drag the window to the right to reveal the content positioned on the left side of the image. Stop dragging when the rooster is visible.

6. In the Layers panel, click to activate the rooster layer, then choose Layer > Matting > Defringe. The Defringe dialog box opens.

7. In the Defringe dialog box, once again maintain the default setting of 1 pixel, and then click OK. The Defringe command affects only the selected layer.

Notice that both the rooster and the cow now look more naturally blended into the background.

8. Press Ctrl+Z (Windows) or Command+Z (Mac OS) to undo the application of the Defringe command. Notice the hard edge around the perimeter of the rooster. Press Ctrl+Z or Command+Z again to re-apply the Defringe command.

9. Double-click the Hand tool in the Tools panel to fit the entire image in the document window. This can be easier than choosing View > Fit on Screen, yet it achieves the same result.

10. Choose File > Save.

Adding text

**Certification
Ready 2.3**

What would be
another appropriate
font, size, and color for
the text added?

The type tool in Photoshop allows you to create text using the available fonts on your system as well format text size, color and other styles such as bold and italic. You will now add text to this image.

Step-by-Step

Follow these steps to add text with the Type tool

1. With the **ps0401_work** file still open, click to select the rooster layer in the Layers panel.

2. In the Tools panel, click to select the Type tool (T) and click in the upper-left corner of the image, just above the roof of the barn. Notice that a layer appears on top of the rooster layer in the Layers panel.

3. In the Options bar, select the following as displayed in Figure 4-14:

    • From the font family drop-down menu, choose Myriad Pro. If you do not have this font, you can choose another.

    • From the font style drop-down menu, choose Bold Italic.

    • From the font size drop-down menu, choose 72.

Figure 4-14: Choose font attributes in the Options bar.

4. Click once on the Set the text color swatch (■) in the Options bar. The text Color Picker appears. Click on white or any light color that appears in the upper-left corner of the color pane, then press OK to close the Color Picker window.

5. Type **Big Red Barn**; the text appears above the roof of the barn. When you are finished typing, click on the Commit checkbox (✔) in the Options bar to confirm the text.

6. With the text layer still active, click the Add a Layer Style button (*fx*) at the bottom of the Layers panel, and choose Stroke. The Layer Style dialog box opens, with the Stroke options visible; click on the color box and choose a red color. Press OK to accept the color, and then click OK again to apply the stroke. A stroke is added to the border of the text.

7. Choose File > Save. Keep the file open for the next part of this lesson.

Saving files

Adobe Photoshop allows you to save your files in a variety of file formats, which makes it possible to use your images in many different ways. You can save images to allow for additional editing of things such as layers and effects you have applied in Photoshop, or save images for sharing with users who need only the finished file for use on the Web or for printing. In all, Photoshop allows you to save your file in more than a dozen unique file formats.

As you work on images, it is best to save them using the default Photoshop format, which uses the .PSD extension at the end of the filename. This is the native Photoshop file format, and retains the most usable data without a loss in image quality. Because the Photoshop format was developed by Adobe, many non–Adobe software applications do not recognize the PSD format.

Additionally, the PSD format may contain more information than you need, and may be a larger file size than is appropriate for sharing through e-mail or posting on a web site. While you may create copies of images for sharing, it is a good idea to keep an original version in the PSD format as a master file that you can access if necessary. This is especially important because some file formats are considered to be *lossy* formats, which means that they remove image data in order to reduce the size of the file.

Understanding file formats

While Photoshop can be used to create files for all sorts of media, the three most common uses for image files are web, print, and video production. Following is a list of the most common **file formats** and how they are used. Unless specified otherwise in the format descriptions, the RGB color mode is used for web and video production formats, and the CMYK color mode is used for Print Production formats.

Certification Ready 2.1

What would be the appropriate image format for web, video, photos, photos, print PowerPoint or Word?

Certification Ready 2.4

Which color modes are used for web, video, and print production?

Web Production Formats	
JPEG (Joint Photographic Experts Group)	This is a common format for digital camera photographs and the primary format for full-color images shared on the web. **JPEG** images use lossy compression, which degrades the quality of images and discards color and pixel data. Once the image data is lost, it cannot be recovered.
GIF (Graphic Interchange Format)	**GIF** files are used to display limited (indexed) color graphics on the Web. It is a compressed format that reduces the file size of images, but it only supports a limited number of colors and is thus more appropriate for logos and artwork than photographs. GIF files support transparency.
PNG (Portable Network Graphics)	**PNG** was developed as an alternative to GIF for displaying images on the Web. It uses lossless compression and supports transparency.

Print Production Formats	
PSD (Photoshop document)	The Photoshop format (PSD) is the default file format and the only format, besides the Large Document Format (PSB), that supports most Photoshop features. Files saved as PSD can be used in other Adobe applications, such as Adobe Illustrator, Adobe InDesign, Adobe Premiere, and others. The programs can directly import PSD files and access many Photoshop features, such as layers.
TIFF or TIF (Tagged Image File Format)	**TIFF** is a common bitmap image format. Most image-editing software and page-layout applications support TIFF images up to 2GB in file size. TIFF supports most color modes and can save images with alpha channels. While Photoshop can also include layers in a TIFF file, most other applications cannot use these extended features and see only the combined (flattened) image.

Print Production Formats (continued)	
EPS (Encapsulated PostScript)	**EPS** files may contain both vector and bitmap data. Because it is a common file format used in print production, most graphics software programs support the EPS format for importing or placing images. EPS is a subset of the PostScript format. Some software applications cannot preview the high-resolution information contained within an EPS file, so Photoshop allows you to save a special preview file for use with these programs, using either the EPS TIFF or EPS PICT option. EPS supports most color modes, as well as clipping paths, which are commonly used to silhouette images and remove backgrounds.
Photoshop PDF	Photoshop **PDF** files are extremely versatile, as they may contain bitmap and vector data. Images saved in the Photoshop PDF format can maintain the editing capabilities of most Photoshop features, such as vector objects, text, and layers, and most color spaces are supported. Photoshop PDF files can also be shared with other graphics applications, as most of the current versions of graphics software are able to import or manipulate PDF files. Photoshop PDF files can even be opened by users with the free Adobe Reader software.
Video Production Formats	
TIFF or TIF	*See Print Production Formats, above.*
TARGA (Truevision Advanced Raster Graphics Adapter)	This legacy file format is used for video production. The TARGA format supports millions of colors, along with alpha channels.

Choosing a file format

Certification Ready 3.3

How do you import, export, and save files?

In this section, you will save your file to share online and for printing. You will use two common formats, JPEG and Photoshop PDF.

Saving a JPEG file

To save a copy of your image for sharing online, whether on a web site or to send through e-mail, you will save it using the JPEG file format. In this lesson, you will use the Save menu, but in Lesson 12, "Creating Images for Web and Video," you will discover additional features when saving files for use online, including how to use the Save for Web feature in Photoshop.

Step-by-Step

Follow these steps to save an image as a JPEG

1. Choose File > Save As.

2. In the Save As dialog box, type **farm** in the File name text field. From the Format drop-down menu, choose JPEG. If necessary, navigate to the ps04lessons folder so the file is saved in this location, then press the Save button. The JPEG Options dialog box appears.

3. In the JPEG Options dialog box, confirm the quality is set to maximum, and leave the format options set to their defaults. Press OK. This completes the Save process for your file.

4. Choose File > Close to close the file and click Save when prompted.

> **Take Note...**
> *Because JPEG is supported by web browsers, you can check your file by opening it using any web browser, such as Firefox, Internet Explorer, or Safari. Open the browser and choose File > Open, which may appear as Open File or Open Location, depending upon the application. Navigate to the ps04lessons folder and double-click to open the file you saved.*

Saving for print

In this part of the lesson, you will change the color settings to choose a color profile more suitable for print to help you preview and prepare your file for printing. You will change the resolution of the image before saving it.

The color models for images on your monitor are different than the color models used for print. Images used for print end up being reproduced with ink and this needs to be accounted for.

Changing the color settings

You will now change the color settings to get a more accurate view of how the file will print.

Certification Ready 5.1

What are some factors that need to be considered when saving files for print use?

Follow these steps to edit Color Settings

Step-by-Step

1. If **ps0401_work.psd** is not open choose File > Open Recent > **ps0401_work.psd**. You can use the Open Recent command to easily locate your most recently opened files. The file opens.

2. Choose Edit > Color Settings. The Color Settings dialog box appears.

3. From the Color Settings drop-down menu, choose North America Prepress 2 as shown in Figure 4-15. This provides you with a color profile based upon typical printing environments in North America. Press OK to close the Color Settings dialog box.

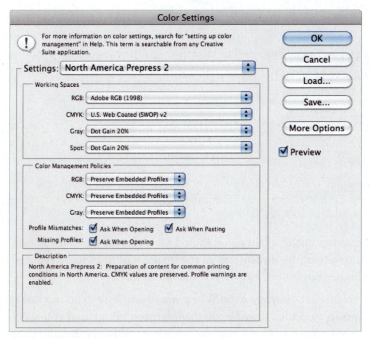

Figure 4-15: Select the North America Prepress 2 color setting.

4. Choose the Zoom tool (🔍) from the Tools panel, and then click and drag to create a zoom area around the text at the top of the image. The text is magnified to fill the entire display area.

Certification Ready 2.4

What is the difference between RGB and CMYK?

5. Choose View > Proof Colors. Notice a slight change in the color of the red stroke around the text, as the colors appear more subdued. The Proof Colors command allows you to work in the RGB format while approximating how your image will look when converted to CMYK, the color space used for printing (Figure 4-16). While you will work on images in the RGB mode, they generally must be converted to CMYK before they are printed.

Figure 4-16: The title bar reflects that you are previewing the image in CMYK.

Adjusting image size

Certification Ready 4.3

What are the differences between resampling and cropping?

Next you will adjust the image size for printing. When printing an image, you generally want a resolution of at least 150 pixels per inch. For higher-quality images, you will want a resolution of at least 300 pixels per inch. While this image was saved at 72 pixels per inch, it is larger than needed. By reducing the physical dimensions of the image, the **resolution** (number of pixels per inch) can be increased.

Step-by-Step | **Follow these steps to adjust image size**

1. Choose Image > Image Size; the Image Size dialog box appears. The image currently has a resolution of 72 pixels per inch as shown in Figure 4-17.

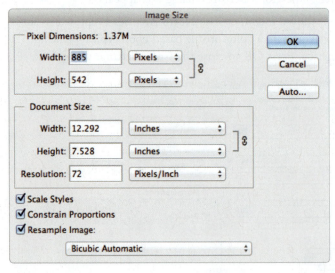

Figure 4-17: The image is at a low resolution of 72 pixels per inch.

This low resolution affects the image quality, and should be increased to print the best image possible. For this to occur, the dimensions of the image will need to be reduced so the image will be of a higher resolution, but will be smaller in size.

Resampling changes the amount of image data. When you resample up, you increase the number of pixels. New pixels are added, based upon the interpolation method you select. While resampling adds pixels, it can reduce image quality if it is not used carefully. Cropping an image will not resample an image unless a size and resolution is defined during the crop.

2. In the Image Size dialog box, uncheck Resample Image. By unchecking the Resample Image checkbox, you can increase the resolution without decreasing image quality.

   You can use this method when resizing large image files, like those from digital cameras that tend to have large dimensions but low resolution.

3. Type **300** in the Resolution field. The size is reduced in the Width and Height text boxes to accommodate the new increased resolution but the Pixel Dimensions remain the same. For quality printing at the highest resolution, this image should be printed no larger than approximately 2.9 inches by 1.8 inches (Figure 4-18). Press OK.

   In this image, you are not adding pixels, you are simply reducing the dimensions of the image to create a higher resolution.

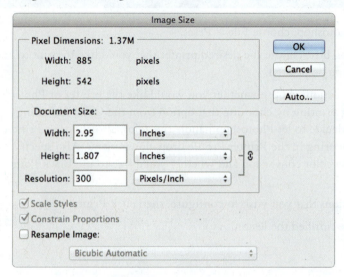

Figure 4-18: Increase resolution without decreasing quality.

4. Choose File > Save. Keep this file open for the next part of this lesson.

Saving a Photoshop PDF file

Images containing text or vector shapes may appear fine in low resolution when viewed on a computer display, even if the vector information is rasterized (converted into pixels.)When the same images are used for print projects, they should retain the resolution-independent vector elements. This keeps the text and other vector graphics looking sharp, so you do not need to worry about the jagged edges that occur when text and shapes are rasterized. To keep the vector information, you need to save the file using a format that retains both vector and bitmap data.

Follow these steps to create a Photoshop PDF	**Step-by-Step**

1. With the **ps0401_work.psd** image still open, choose File > Save As. The Save As dialog box appears.

2. In the Save As menu, navigate to the ps04lessons folder. In the Name text field, type **farm print version**. From the Format drop-down menu, choose Photoshop PDF, then press Save. Click OK to close any warning dialog box that may appear. The Save Adobe PDF dialog box appears.

3. In the Save Adobe PDF dialog box, choose Press Quality from the Adobe PDF Preset drop-down menu, and then click Save PDF. If a warning appears, indicating that older versions of Photoshop may not be able to edit the PDF file, click Yes to continue.

Certification Ready 3.5

What are some advantages and disadvantages of letting Photoshop handle color management during printing vs. letting the printer handle color management?

4. Your file has been saved in the Adobe PDF format, ready to be used in other applications such as Adobe InDesign, or shared for proofing with a reviewer who may have Adobe Acrobat or Adobe Reader.

Printing a file

Photoshop provides powerful tools for printing your image by allowing you to choose options related to color during output.

Step-by-Step | **Follow these steps to print a file**

1. With an image open in Photoshop, choose File > Print.

2. In the resulting print dialog box, choose the desired printer that you'd like to print to and specify the number copies to be printed.

3. In the color management section, choose whether you would like the printer or Photoshop to handle the color during printing by choosing that option from the Color Handling drop-down menu. If you decide to let Photoshop handle the color, also choose a Printer profile to use for color rendering in the Printer Profile drop-down menu. Also specify the rendering intent for the color conversion and whether you'd like to use Black Point Compensation or not.

4. Specify any additional options that you wish to configure, then click Print.

   Congratulations! You have finished the lesson.

Skill Summary

In this lesson you learned how to:	Objective
Demonstrate knowledge of image resolution, image size, and image file format for web, video, and print	2.1
Demonstrate knowledge of typography	2.3
Demonstrate knowledge of color correction using Photoshop CS6	2.4
Understand key terminology of digital images	2.6
Demonstrate knowledge of importing, exporting, organizing, and saving	3.3
Transform images	4.3
Demonstrate knowledge of preparing images for web, print, and video	5.1

Knowledge Assessment

True/False

Circle **T** if the statement is true or **F** if the statement is false.

T F **1.** The Image Size dialog box is divided into three main areas. Pixel Dimensions and Scale percentage.

T F **2.** Web designers should reference the top of the Image Size dialog box and print designers should reference the bottom.

T F **3.** You can drag and drop psd images into one another by using the Move tool.

T F **4.** You have to position images beside each other in order to move them from one image file to another.

T F **5.** You need to click several times on the white background of an image before it will remove the entire background of the image.

T F **6.** Clicking on an image with the Type tool will automatically create a new layer just for the type.

T F **7.** TARGA is a legacy file format used for video production.

T F **8.** By unchecking the Resample Image checkbox, you can adjust the resolution of an image without losing any image quality.

T F **9.** EPS files may contain both vector and bitmap image data.

T F **10.** PNG files are the only Web file format that does not support transparency.

Multiple Choice

Select the best response for the following statements.

1. What key needs to be held down when clicking on the file information area of the status bar to reveal more information about the active file?

    a. Shift

    b. Alt (Windows)/Option (Mac OS)

    c. Spacebar

    d. Tab

2. Which of the following is not one of the options in the Image Size dialog box?

    a. Width and Height (Pixel Dimensions)

    b. Resolution

    c. Scale Styles

    d. Stroke Weight

3. Holding down Shift while you scale an image does what while you're clicking and dragging to scale?

    a. Maintains the proportions of the image while you scale

    b. Skews the image

    c. Automatically sets the scale value to 50%

    d. Nothing

4. What is the last thing that has to be done when making changes with Edit > Transform?

    a. Finish adjusting settings in the Options panel

    b. Click Commit Transform or press Enter (Windows) or Return (Mac OS)

    c. Press ESC on your keyboard

    d. Double check your History panel

5. Which of the layers below would be fully visible in a Photoshop file?

    a. The Vector Layer

    b. Bottom-most layer in the Layer panel

    c. Mask layer

    d. Top-most layer in the Layer panel

6. Besides the Character panel, which of the following can be used to make changes to text such as font and font size?

    a. Swatches panel

    b. Options bar

    c. Layers panel

    d. Channels panel

7. Which of the following is considered a Web production format?

    a. JPEG

    b. GIF

    c. PNG

    d. All of the above

8. Which of the following is not considered a Print production format?

    a. TIFF

    b. EPS

    c. Photoshop PDF

    d. TARGA

9. When printing an image, what is the lowest recommended pixel resolution?

    a. 72

    b. 96

    c. 150

    d. 1200

10. Photoshop can save to which of the following formats?

    a. EPS

    b. PSD

    c. PSB

    d. All of the above

Competency Assessment

| Expanding the Canvas instead of the Image | Project 4-1 |

In addition to using the Crop tool to crop an image, you can also crop an image using the Canvas size dialog box.

1. Open the **ps0401.psd** image in Photoshop.

2. Choose Image > Canvas Size.

3. Change the Canvas size to 11 inches wide by 6 inches tall and set the anchor to the bottom-left corner. A dialog will appear indicating that some clipping will occur. Click proceed.

4. Choose File > Save as and save the file as **ps0401_crop.psd**.

| Understanding the effects of scaling | Project 4-2 |

One concept that's important to learn is the limitations of a raster-based image when it comes to scaling. Blowing up bitmap images beyond their original size can end up damaging an image.

1. Open the **ps0402.psd** image in Photoshop.

2. Choose Image > Image Size and with the Resample Image checkbox enabled set the width of the image to 20 inches. Essentially doubling the size of the file.

3. Choose File > Save as and save the image as **ps0402_scaled.psd**. Leave this file open and re-open the **ps0402.psd** image so that both files are open in Photoshop.

4. Choose Window > Arrange > 2-up Vertical and compare the two images.

5. Select the Note tool in Photoshop (it's found by clicking and holding on the Eyedropper tool) and click within the **ps0402_scaled.psd** image to add a note to the file. List the differences that you see in the scaled version vs. the non-scaled version and save your file.

Proficiency Assessment

| Hidden Tricks in Photoshop | Project 4-3 |

Methodology is one of the things that can always be expanded upon, no matter what your level of expertise. Understanding all the little hidden things can really help expand how efficiently you use the program.

1. Create a new document in Photoshop.

2. Select the Type tool and add some text to the document.

3. Highlight the text with the Type tool, keep it highlighted.

4. Click on the actual Font name in the Options bar and use the up and down arrows on your keyboard to cycle through your computer's fonts and see how they'd look applied to the type.

5. Duplicate the type layer and move it down in the document to create a copy. Highlight the text and repeat steps 2 through 4 to create another example. Repeat until you have 5 instances of text in your document.

6. Save the file as **ps04_text_samples.psd**.

Lesson 4

Project 4-4	Comparing File Formats

To gain a better understanding of which web formats are appropriate for different types of images, try saving a file to several web formats.

1. Open the **ps0403.psd** file in Photoshop.

2. Choose File > Save for web. In the Preset menu in the upper-right of the window, choose GIF 64 Dithered then click Save. Save the file as **ps0403.gif**.

3. Choose File > Save for web. In the Preset menu in the upper-right of the window, choose JPEG Medium then click Save. Save the file as **ps0403.jpg**.

4. Choose File > Save for web. In the Preset menu in the upper-right of the window, choose PNG 24 then click Save. Save the file as **ps0403.png**.

5. Open the files in Photoshop and compare the quality of the images to one another. In the Finder or Windows Explorer, also compare the file size of each file.

6. Create a text document or Word document and jot down some notes that you've observed regarding the quality vs. file size of each file. Save the file as **ps04_web_notes**.

Making the Best Selections

Key Terms

- Lasso tool
- Magic Wand
- Marquee tools
- Paths
- Pen tool
- Quick Mask

- Quick Selection tool
- Refine Edge
- Save Selections
- Selection

Skill	Objective
Demonstrate knowledge of color correction using Photoshop CS6	2.4
Demonstrate knowledge of layers and masks	3.2
Demonstrate knowledge of working with selections	4.1
Adjust or correct the tonal range, color, or distortions of an image	4.4
Demonstrate knowledge of drawing and painting	4.6
Demonstrate knowledge of filters	4.8

Business case

Now that you've warmed up a bit, you've decided that you want to take things up a notch. A key to really becoming proficient in Photoshop is understanding how to isolate images and manipulate them without effecting the other images nearby. There are several selection tools in Photoshop that allow you to isolate areas of images to make adjustments and affect those areas without being destructive to other elements that you would prefer go untouched.

Starting up

Before starting, make sure that your tools and panels are consistent by resetting your preferences. See "Resetting the Photoshop workspace" in the Starting up section of this book. Keep in mind that if you do not reset your Photoshop preferences you may have additonal dialog boxes appear that reference mismatched color profiles and more.

You will work with several files from the ps05lessons folder in this lesson. Make sure that you have loaded the pslessons folder onto your hard drive from *http://www.wiley.com/college/sc/adobeseries*. See "Loading lesson files" in the Starting up section of this book.

Certification Ready 4.1

Why are selections such an integral part of working with images?

Certification Ready 4.1

What are the selection commands and how do you modify the selections?

Certification Ready 4.1

What tools are used for selection?

The importance of a good selection

"You have to select it to affect it" is an old saying in the image-editing industry. To make changes to specific regions in your images, you must activate only those areas. A **selection** is an active or selected area in the file. To do this, you can use selection tools such as the Marquee, Lasso, and Quick Selection tools, or you can create a selection by painting a mask. For precise selections, you can use the Pen tool. In this lesson, you'll learn how to select pixels in an image with both pixel and pen (vector) selection techniques.

You'll start with some simple selection methods and then progress into more difficult selection techniques. Note that even if you are an experienced Photoshop user, you will want to follow the entire lesson; there are tips and tricks included that will help all levels of users achieve the best selections possible.

Using the Marquee tools

The first selection tools you'll use are the **Marquee tools**, which include Rectangular, Elliptical, Single Row, and Single Column tools. Some of the many uses for the Rectangular and Elliptical Marquee tools are to isolate an area for cropping, to create a border around an image, or simply to use that area in the image for corrective or creative image adjustment.

Step-by-Step | **Follow these steps to use the Rectangular Marquee tool**

1. In Photoshop, choose File > Browse in Bridge. Navigate to the ps05lessons folder and double-click on **ps0501_done.psd** to open the image. The completed image file appears (Figure 5-1). You can leave the file open for reference, or choose File > Close to close it.

Figure 5-1: *The completed selection file.*

2. Return to Adobe Bridge by choosing File > Browse in Bridge. Navigate to the ps05lessons folder and double-click on **ps0501.psd** to open the image. An image of a car appears.

3. Choose File > Save As. When the Save As dialog box appears, navigate to the ps05lessons folder. In the Name text field, type **ps0501_work**. Choose Photoshop from the Format drop-down menu and press Save. If the Photoshop Format Options dialog box appears, press OK.

4. Select the Rectangular Marquee tool (▭), near the top of the Tools panel.

5. Make sure that Snap is checked by choosing View > Snap. If it is checked, it is already active.

6. Position your cursor in the upper-left side of the guide in the car image, and drag a rectangular selection down toward the lower-right corner of the guide (Figure 5-2). A rectangular selection appears as you drag, and it stays active when you release the mouse.

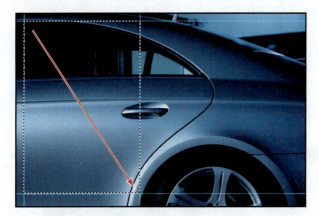

Figure 5-2: *Creating a rectangular selection in the image.*

You'll now apply an adjustment layer to lighten just the selected area of the image. You are lightening this region so that a text overlay can be placed over that part of the image.

7. If the Adjustments panel is not visible, choose Window > Adjustments and click on the Curves icon as shown in Figure 5-3; the Properties panel appears.

Figure 5-3: *Click on the Curves button to create a new Curves adjustment layer.*

8. To ensure consistent results, first click the panel menu (•≡) in the upper-right corner of the Properties panel and choose Curves Display Options. In the Show Amount of: section, select Pigment/Ink % as shown in Figure 5-4. Choosing Pigment for corrections makes the curves adjustment more representative of ink on paper. Click OK to close the Curves Display Options dialog box.

Figure 5-4: *Select Pigment/Ink % in the Curve Display options.*

Take Note...
If you do not see the entire Properties panel, including the Input and Output text fields at the bottom of the panel, click and drag the bottom of the panel to expand it.

9. Click and drag the upper-right anchor point (shadow) straight down, keeping it flush with the right side of the curve window, until the Output text field reads approximately 20, or type **20** into the Output text field (Figure 5-5). As you can see in Figure 5-6, the rectangular selection in the image is lightened to about 20% of its original value.

Take Note...
Because you used an adjustment layer, you can double-click on the Curves thumbnail in the Layers panel to re-open the Curves panel as often as you like to readjust the lightness in the rectangular selection.

Figure 5-5: *Make a curve adjustment to the selection.*

Figure 5-6: *The result.*

10. Now go back to the Layers panel, click the box to the left of the text layer named poster text; the Visibility icon (👁) appears, and the layer is now visible. The text appears over the lightened area.

11. Choose File > Save to save this file. Keep the file open for the next part of this exercise.

Creating a square selection

In this section, you'll learn how to create a square selection using the Rectangular Marquee tool.

1. Click on the Background thumbnail in the Layers panel to select it.

2. Select the Rectangular Marquee tool (▭) and position your cursor over the taillight of the car. Click and drag while holding the Shift key. Note that your selection is constrained, creating a square selection (Figure 5-7). When you have created a square (size doesn't matter), first release the mouse and then the Shift key.

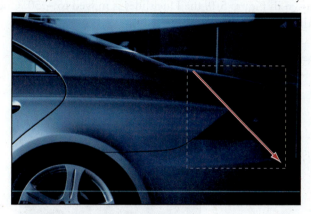

Figure 5-7: Click and drag while holding the Shift key.

3. With the square selection still active, position your cursor over the selected region of the image. Notice that an arrow with a dashed box appears (▸▫). This indicates that the selection shape can be moved without moving any of the pixel information in the image.

4. Click and drag the selection to another location. Only the selection moves. Reposition the selection over the taillight.

5. Select the Move tool (⊹) and position the cursor over the selected region. Notice that an icon with an arrow and scissors appears (▸✄). This indicates that if you move the selection, you will cut, or move, the pixels with the selection.

6. Click and drag the selection; the selected region of the image moves with the selection (Figure 5-8).

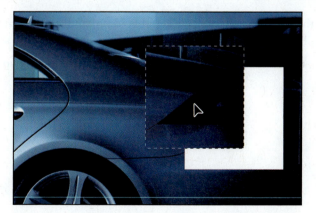

Figure 5-8: When the Move tool is selected, the pixels are moved with the selection.

7. Select Edit > Undo Move, or use the keyboard shortcut Ctrl+Z (Windows) or Command+Z (Mac OS) to undo your last step.

8. You'll now alter that section of the image. Note that in this example you edit a region of an image without creating a layer; you are affecting the pixels of the image and cannot easily undo your edits after the image has been saved, closed, and reopened. You will discover more ways to take advantage of the Adjustments panel later in this lesson.

9. Choose Image > Adjustments > Hue/Saturation.

You will now adjust the hue, or color, of this region to enhance its visibility. This technique is often used in medical and scientific research so that an area can be examined. Click and drag the Hue slider to change the color of the selected region. Select any color that you like. In this example shown in Figure 5-9, the Hue slider is moved to −150. Click OK. The new hue is applied to the taillight region (Figure 5-10).

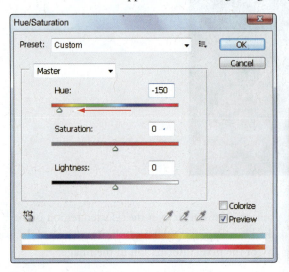

Figure 5-9: Changing the hue of the selected region.

Figure 5-10: The result.

10. Choose File > Save; keep the image open for the next part of this lesson.

Creating a selection from a center point

Step-by-Step | **Follow these steps to create a selection from a center point**

1. Select the Background layer in the Layers panel, then click and hold on the Rectangular Marquee tool (▢) and select the hidden Elliptical Marquee tool (○).

Limber up your fingers, because this selection technique requires you to hold down two modifier keys as you drag.

2. You'll now draw a circle selection from the center of the image. Place your cursor in the approximate center of the tire, and then hold down the Alt (Windows) or Option (Mac OS) key and the Shift key. Click and drag to pull a circular selection from the center origin point. Release the mouse (before the modifier keys) when you have created a selection that is surrounding the tire as seen in Figure 5-11. If necessary, you can click and drag the selection while you still have the Elliptical Marquee tool selected, or use your arrow keys to nudge the selection.

Figure 5-11: Hold down Alt/Option when dragging, to create a selection from the center.

 Take Note...
While holding down the Alt (Windows) or Option (Mac OS) key and the Shift key, you can also add the space bar to reposition the selection as you are dragging with the Marquee tool. Release the space bar to continue sizing the selection.

3. Whether you need to adjust your selection or not, choose Select > Transform Selection. A bounding box with anchor points appears around your selection. Use the bounding box's anchor points to adjust the size and proportions of the selection (Figure 5-12). Note that you can scale proportionally by holding down the Shift key when you transform the selection.

Figure 5-12: Transform your selection.

4. When you are finished with the transformation, press the check mark (✔) in the upper-right corner of the Options bar, or press the Enter (Windows) or Return (Mac OS) key to confirm your transformation change, or press the Esc key in the upper-left corner of your keyboard to cancel the selection transformation.

5. Choose File > Save. Keep this file open for the next part of this lesson.

Changing a selection into a layer

You will now move your selection up to a new layer. By moving a selection to its own independent layer, you can have more control over the selected region while leaving the original image data intact. You'll learn more about layers in Lesson 8, "Getting to Know Layers."

Follow these steps to change a selection into a layer

1. With the tire still selected, click on the Background layer to make it active. Press Ctrl+J (Windows) or Command+J (Mac OS). Think of this as the *Jump my selection to a new layer* keyboard shortcut. Alternatively, to create a new layer for your selection, you can select Layer > New > Layer Via Copy. The selection marquee disappears and the selected region is moved and copied to a new layer, named Layer 1 as you can see in Figure 5-13.

Figure 5-13: A new layer created from the selection.

2. Now you will apply a filter to this new layer. Choose Filter > Blur > Motion Blur. The Motion Blur dialog box appears. Motion Blur is just one of the many blur filters available in Photoshop CS6. You can also use blur filters such as Field blur, Iris blur, and Tilt-Shift to achieve different results such as depth of field.

3. In the Motion Blur dialog box, type **0** (zero) in the Angle text field and **45** in the Distance text field (Figure 5-14); then press OK. As you can see in Figure 5-15, a motion blur is applied to the tire.

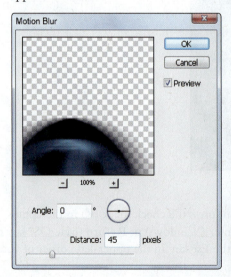

Figure 5-14: Applying the motion blur.

Figure 5-15: The result.

4. Select the Move tool (✛), move the tire slightly to the right, and press **5**. By pressing 5, you have changed the opacity of this layer to 50 percent.

5. Congratulations! You have finished the marquee selection part of this lesson. Choose File > Save, and then File > Close.

Working with the Magic Wand tool

The **Magic Wand** makes selections based on tonal similarities; it lets you select a consistently colored area, for example a blue sky, without having to trace its outline. You control the range it automatically selects by adjusting the tolerance.

Follow these steps to create a selection with the Magic Wand tool	Step-by-Step

1. Choose File > Browse in Bridge to bring Adobe Bridge forward. Then navigate to the ps05lessons folder and open the image **ps0502.psd**. An image of a kite appears.

2. Choose File > Save As; the Save As dialog box appears. Navigate to the ps05lessons folder and type **ps0502_work** into the Name text field. Make sure that Photoshop is selected from the Format drop-down menu, and press Save.

3. Select and hold on the Quick Selection tool (✓) to locate and select the hidden Magic Wand tool (✺).

4. In the Options bar, make sure the tolerance is set to **32**.

5. Position your cursor over the red portion of the kite and click once. Notice that similar tonal areas that are contiguous (touching) are selected. Place your cursor over different parts of the kite and click to see the different selections that are created. The selections pick up only similar tonal areas that are contiguous, which in this case is generally not the most effective way to make a selection.

6. Choose Select > Deselect, or use the keyboard shortcut Ctrl+D (Windows) or Command+D (Mac OS).

7. Click once in the sky at the top center of the image. The sky becomes selected as shown in Figure 5-16. Don't worry if the sky is not entirely selected, it is because those areas are outside of the tolerance range of the area that you selected with the Magic Wand tool.

Figure 5-16: *Image with the background selected.*

Take Note...
To see what is included in a selection, position any selection tool over the image. If the icon appears as a hollow arrow with a dotted box next to it, it is over an active selection. If the icon of the tool or crosshair appears, then that area is not part of the active selection.

8. Press Ctrl+0 (zero) (Windows) or Command+0 (zero) (Mac OS) to fit the picture to the screen. Then hold down the Shift key and click the area of sky that was left unselected. Those areas are added to the selection of the sky.

9. Choose Select > Inverse. Now the selection has been turned inside out, selecting the kite. Inversing a selection is a helpful technique when solid colors are part of an image, as you can make quick selections instead of focusing on the more diversely colored areas of an image.

Take Note...
If you have control over the environment when you capture your images, it can be helpful to take a picture of an object against a solid background. That way, you can create quick selections using tools like Quick Selection and the Magic Wand.

10. Don't worry if you accidentally deselect a region, as Photoshop remembers your last selection. With the selection of the kite still active, choose Select > Deselect, and the selection is deselected; then choose Select > Reselect to reselect the kite.

11. Now you will sharpen the kite without affecting the sky. Choose Filter > Sharpen > Unsharp Mask. The Unsharp Mask dialog box appears.

12. Drag the Amount slider to the right to about 150, or type **150** into the Amount text field. Leave the Radius text field at 1. Change the Threshold slider to about 10, or type **10** into the Threshold text field as you can see in Figure 5-17. There are reasons that you have entered these settings, they are just not addressed in this lesson. Read more about unsharp mask in Lesson 7, "Creating a Good Image."

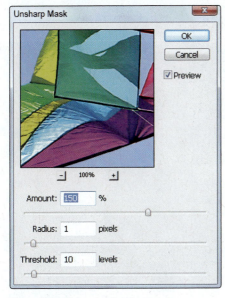

Figure 5-17: *Sharpening the selection only.*

13. Click and drag in the preview pane to bring the kite into view. Notice that in the preview pane of the Unsharp Mask dialog box, only the kite is sharpened. Position your cursor over the kite in the preview pane, and then click and hold. This temporarily turns the preview off. Release the mouse to see the Unsharp Mask filter effect applied. Press OK.

14. Choose File > Save. Then choose File > Close to close this file.

The Lasso tool

The **Lasso tool** is a free-form selection tool. It is great for creating an initial rough selection, and even better for cleaning up an existing selection. The selection that you create is as accurate as your hand on the mouse or trackpad allows it to be, which is why it lends itself to general cleaning up of selections. The best advice when using this tool is not to worry about being too precise; you can modify the selection, as you will see later in this section.

Follow these steps to use the Lasso tool	Step-by-Step

1. Choose File > Browse in Bridge to bring Adobe Bridge forward. Navigate to the ps05lessons folder and double-click on **ps0503.psd** to open the image. An image of a snowboarder appears.

2. Choose File > Save As. When the Save As dialog box appears, navigate to the ps05lessons folder. In the Name text field, type **ps0503_work**. Choose Photoshop from the Format drop-down menu and click Save.

You will now create a selection using the Lasso tool.

3. Select the Lasso tool (⌀) in the Tools panel.

4. Click slightly outside the snowboarder and drag the Lasso tool around him as shown in Figure 5-18. The lasso selection that you are making does not have to be perfect, as you will have an opportunity to edit it shortly.

Figure 5-18: *Click and drag around the snowboarder using the Lasso tool.*

Adding to and subtracting from selections

You created a selection that surrounds the snowboarder. You'll now use the Lasso tool to refine that selection.

Deleting from the selection

In this part of the exercise, you learn to subtract from your active selection.

Step-by-Step | **Follow these steps to subtract from an existing selection**

t the Lasso tool (⌀) in the Tools panel.

at your image and determine the areas of your selection that you want to delete. This include the area between the snowboarder and the selection of the sky surrounding

nd hold the Alt (Windows) or Option (Mac OS) key and notice that the cursor nto a Lasso with a minus sign. While holding the Alt/Option key, click and drag e the selected area and into the active selection. Release the mouse when you have back to your original starting point. The new Lasso selection you made is deleted e existing selection.

4. To practice this skill, press and hold the Alt/Option key, and click to start your lasso path on the edge of the snowboarder. Then, click and drag along the edge of the snowboarder for a short bit. When you want to end the lasso path, make sure to circle back around to the start point demonstrated in Figure 5-19.

Figure 5-19: Carefully drag along the edge of the snowboarder, and then circle back to your starting point, enclosing the section that you want to delete from the active selection.

You do not have to delete the sky from all the edges of the snowboarder for this exercise. However, to prepare for the next section, you will delete the section between the snowboarder's legs and the board.

5. With the Alt/Option key pressed, click anywhere on the inside edge of one of the snowboarder's legs and drag all the way around the inner edge, over the mitten, and back to the starting point (Figure 5-20). Release the mouse when you are back at the initial clicking point.

Figure 5-20: Delete the section between the snowboarder's legs from the selection.

Lesson 5

Adding to the selection

If you want to add to an active selection, press and hold the Shift key and create a closed area. Follow these steps to bring the mitten back into the active selection.

Step-by-Step	Follow these steps to add to an existing selection

1. Press and hold the Shift key and click and drag along the edge of the mitten. Make sure you drag beyond the mitten and down into the active area at the top and bottom to create a fully encompassed area to add to the selection.

2. You can continue to Shift+Drag to add areas that you missed, or Alt/Option + Drag to subtract areas that you might have selected in error.

Take Note...
Using the Shift key to add to a selection and the Alt (Windows) or Option (Mac OS) key to delete from a selection, you can edit selections created with any of the selection tools.

Saving a selection

You should always save your selection because you might accidentally delete it or you might need to reactivate it at another time.

Step-by-Step	Follow these steps to save a selection

1. Choose Select > Save Selection; the Save Selection dialog box appears.

2. Type **Snowboarder** into the Name textbox, and then press OK (Figure 5-21). Anytime that you might need to reactivate the selection, choose Select > Load Selection, and then choose the Channel named Snowboarder (Figure 5-22). Keep the other settings at the default and press OK.

Figure 5-21: Saving a selection.

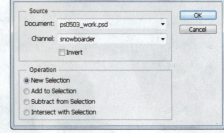

Figure 5-22: Loading a selection.

3. Choose File > Save to save this file. Keep the file open for the next part of the lesson.

Feathering the selection

In this part of the lesson, you will feather your selection (don't worry if your selection is less than perfect). Feathering is the term that Photoshop uses to describe a vignette, or fading of an image around the edges of a selection. There are many ways to feather a selection; in this section, you will learn the most visual method, which is the Refine Edge feature.

Certification Ready 4.1

When should you use feathering and anti-aliasing when making selections?

Follow these steps to feather a selection using Refine Edge

Step-by-Step

1. With the Lasso tool still selected, click Refine Edge in the Options bar. The Refine Edge dialog box appears.

2. Use the Feather slider to change the feather amount to about 5 pixels. By using the Refine Edge feature, you see a preview of the vignette immediately.

3. From the Output To drop-down menu, select Layer Mask and click OK (Figure 5-23). The image is faded as you can see in Figure 5-24, and a mask is added to the layer in the Layers panel.

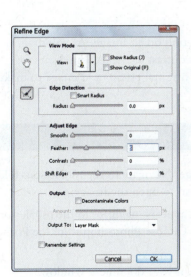

Figure 5-23: *Change the Feather to 5 pixels.*   ***Figure 5-24***: *The result.*

Layer masks essentially cover any area that was not selected at the time the mask was created. Your selection is now in a state that can be reactivated, turned off and turned on at any time. Layer Masks are discussed in more detail in Lesson 8, "Getting to Know Layers."

4. Press and hold the Shift key and click the Layer Mask in the Layers panel to turn off the mask; press and hold the Shift key and click the Layer Mask again to turn it on (Figure 5-25).

Figure 5-25: *Press and hold the Shift Key and click the layer mask to turn it off and on.*

5. Choose File > Save, and then File > Close.

Using the Quick Selection tool

The **Quick Selection tool** allows you to paint your selection on an image. As you drag, the selection expands outward and finds defined edges of contrast to use as boundaries for the selection. In this part of the lesson, you'll re-open the original ps0503.psd image to make a selection using the Quick Selection tool.

Step-by-Step	Follow these steps to use the Quick Selection tool

1. Choose File > Browse in Bridge to open Adobe Bridge. Navigate to the ps05lessons folder inside the pslessons folder. Double-click on **ps0503.psd** to open the image.

2. Choose File > Save As. When the Save As dialog box appears, navigate to the ps05lessons folder. In the Name text field, type **ps0503_workv2**. Choose Photoshop from the Format drop-down menu and click Save.

3. Choose View > Fit on Screen to see the entire image in your document window.

4. Choose the Quick Selection tool (⊘) in the Tools panel. Keep in mind that this could be hidden underneath the Magic Wand (✺) tool at this time.

5. Position your cursor over the snowboarder. You see a circle with a small crosshair in the center (⊹).

Take Note...
The circle and crosshair will not appear if you have the Caps Lock key depressed.

6. From the Options bar, click the Brush drop-down menu, and either slide the size slider to the right to a value of 10, or enter **10** into the Size text field.

7. Now, click and drag to paint over the snowboarder. You can release the mouse and continue painting the snowboarder to see that you are adding to the selection (Figure 5-26).

Adding to the Selection is the default action that you can expect, as you can see by the selected option in the Options bar (✐).

Figure 5-26: *Initial selection with the Quick Selection tool.*

If you accidently grab a part of the image that you do not want to select, press and hold the Option (Mac OS) or Alt key, and paint over the region to deselect it.

Take Note...
Adjust the Quick Selection brush size by pressing the [(left bracket) repeatedly to reduce the selection size, or the] (right bracket) to increase the selection size.

8. Save your selection by choosing Select > Save Selection, the Save Selection dialog box appears.

9. In the Name text field type **Boarder**, and then press OK, leaving the other settings at their defaults. Now you have a saved selection. Keep in mind that if you deselect your selection, or close your saved file, you can reload your selection by selecting Select > Load Selection.

10. Choose File > Save, and then File > Close to close the file.

Making difficult selections with the Refine Edge feature

Using the **Refine Edge** feature you can also improve your selection of difficult items such as fur and hair. There is still no *magic pill* for making a perfect selection, but the Refine Edge improvements certainly help by incorporating Adobe's Truer Edge Selection Technology.

Follow these steps to make a precise selection with the Refine Edge feature

1. Choose File > Browse in Bridge and open the image named **ps0504.psd**. Choose File > Save As. When the Save As dialog box appears, navigate to the ps05lessons folder. In the File name text field, type **ps0504_work**. Choose Photoshop from the Format drop-down menu and press Save. If the Photoshop Format Options dialog box appears, press OK.

2. Click and hold the Quick Selection tool, and then select the hidden Magic Wand tool (✦).

3. Click the white area off to the right of the woman; the white area becomes selected.

4. Choose Select > Inverse to invert the selection. The woman is now selected.

5. Click on the Refine Edge button in the Options bar, the Refine Edge dialog box appears. Using Refine Edge, you can modify a selection in a number of different ways including expand, contract, feather and smooth.

6. To get a better view of the hair selection, choose the Black & White option from the View drop-down menu as shown in Figure 5-27. Black & White is a viewing option that you can use to see your selection better.

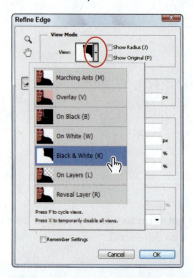

Figure 5-27: Change the View to Black & White to better see the selection edges.

7. Using the Radius slider, in the Edge Detection section, change the Radius value to **100**. This may seem like a rather drastic radius selection, but you can see that this masked the hair fairly well. If you see any color bleed from the background of the image showing up in the hair, you can try turning on the Decontaminate Colors checkbox to remove that color.

   The issue you now have is that by increasing the radius to get a better selection of hair, you also degraded the edge selection of the shoulder, beneath the hair. You will use the Erase Refinements tool to help you clean up your selection.

8. Click and hold down on the Refine Radius tool and select the Erase Refinements tool (Figure 5-28).

Figure 5-28: Clean up your selection using the Erase Refinements tool.

9. Position your cursor over an area in your image where you would like to clean up the selection (Figure 5-29). Note that you can increase or decrease your brush size by pressing the [(left bracket) or] (right bracket) keys.

10. Start painting over the areas that you do not want the refinements to take place. In this example, this is in the shoulder area, at the edge of the suit as you can see in Figure 5-30.

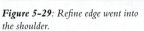

Figure 5-29*: Refine edge went into the shoulder.*

Figure 5-30*: Use the Erase Refinements tool.*

Figure 5-31*: The result, a more accurate selection of the shoulder.*

11. Select Layer Mask from the Output drop-down menu and press OK. Since you have applied a layer mask, your results are shown as a transparent selection (Figure 5-32). You can further refine this mask by using the Properties panel to adjust the mask density and possibly modifying the blending mode of the layer to blend the subject to its new background. Save and close the file.

Figure 5-32*: The completed selection.*

Using Quick Mask

Earlier in this lesson, you learned how to add to and subtract from selections. Another method for modifying selections is to use **Quick Mask**. Rather than using selection tools to modify the selection, you'll use the Paint Brush tool in the Quick Mask mode and paint to modify your selection. This is a type of art therapy for those who are selection-tool-challenged. Note that when creating a mask, by default it is the inverse of a selection; it covers the unselected part of the image and protects it from any editing or manipulations you apply.

In this lesson, you will create a mask using the Quick Mask feature, save the selection, and then copy and paste the selection into another image.

Step-by-Step	Follow these steps to create a Quick Mask

1. To see the file in its completed stage, choose File > Browse in Bridge and navigate to the ps05lessons folder. Locate the file named **ps0505_done.psd** and double-click to open it in Photoshop. A picture with a duck and penguins appears as shown in Figure 5-33. You can keep the file open for reference or choose File > Close now.

Figure 5-33: The completed exercise.

2. Choose File > Browse in Bridge to bring Adobe Bridge forward. Then navigate to the ps05lessons folder and open the image named **ps0505.psd**; an image of a duck appears.

    Choose File > Save As. When the Save As dialog box appears, navigate to the ps05lessons folder. In the File name text field, type **ps0505_work**. Choose Photoshop from the Format drop-down menu and press Save. If the Photoshop Format Options dialog box appears, press OK.

3. Select the Lasso tool (⌀) and make a quick (and rough) selection around the duck. Make sure that as you click and drag, creating a selection that encompasses the duck, the Lasso tool finishes where it started, creating a closed selection around the duck as shown in Figure 5-34. Don't worry about the accuracy of this selection, as you are going to paint the rest of the selection using Photoshop's painting tools in the Quick Mask mode.

4. Select the Quick Mask Mode button (▣) at the bottom of the Tools panel, or use the keyboard shortcut **Q**. Your image is now displayed with a red area (representing the mask) over areas of the image that are not part of the selection (Figure 5-35).

Figure 5-34: Create a rough selection using the Lasso tool.   *Figure 5-35: The selection in the Quick Mask mode.*

5. Now you will use the painting tools to refine this selection. Select the Brush tool (✏) in the Tools panel.

6. Click the Default Foreground and Background Colors button at the bottom of the Tools panel ( ), or press **D** on your keyboard, to return to the default foreground and background colors of black and white. Painting with black adds to the mask, essentially blocking that area of the image from any changes. Painting with white subtracts from the mask, essentially making that area of the image active and ready for changes.

Keep in mind that, as a default, the Quick Mask appears as red when you paint with black, and clear when you paint with white. The red indicates a masked area.

These tips will help you to make more accurate corrections on the mask:

Brush function	Brush keyboard shortcuts
Make brush size larger	] (right bracket)
Make brush size smaller	[(left bracket)
Make brush harder	Shift+] (right bracket)
Make brush softer	Shift+[(left bracket)
Return to default black and white colors	D
Switch foreground and background colors	X

7. Choose View > Actual Pixels to view the image at 100 percent. Zoom in further if necessary.

8. With black as your foreground color, start painting close to the duck as displayed in Figure 5-36, where there might be some green grass that you inadvertently included in the selection. Keep in mind that the areas where the red mask appears will not be part of the selection.

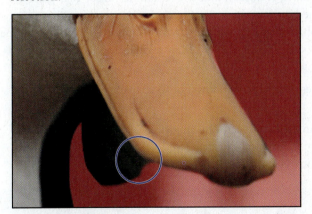

Figure 5-36: Paint the mask to make a more accurate selection.

9. If you accidentally paint into or select some of the duck, press **X** on your keyboard to swap the foreground and background colors, putting white in the foreground. Start painting with white, and you will see that this eliminates the mask, thereby making the regions that you paint with white part of the selection.

10. Continue painting until the selection is more accurate. When you are satisfied with your work, view the selection by clicking on the Quick Mask Mode button ( ), at the bottom of the Tools panel, again or pressing **Q** on your keyboard. This exits the Quick Mask mode and displays the selection that you have created as a marquee. You can press **Q** to re-enter the Quick Mask mode to fine-tune the selection even further, if necessary. Keep the selection active for the next section.

Saving selections

You spent quite some time editing the selection in the last part of this lesson. It would be a shame to lose that selection by closing your file or clicking somewhere else on your image. As mentioned earlier in this lesson, you should save your selections. In this part of the lesson you'll use the **Save Selection** feature so you can close the file, reopen it, and retrieve the duck selection whenever you need it.

Step-by-Step	Follow these steps to save a selection

1. With your duck selection active, choose Select > Save Selection.

2. Type **duck** in the Name text field (Figure 5-37) and press OK.

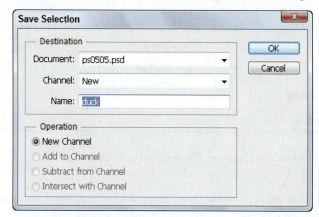

Figure 5-37: *Name your saved selection.*

Figure 5-38: *The Channels panel.*

3. If you cannot see the Channels panel, choose Window > Channels to see that you have a saved channel (or selection) named duck as shown in Figure 5-38. Selections that are saved with an image are known as alpha channels. Channels are not supported by all file formats. Only Photoshop, PDF, PICT, Pixar, TIFF, PSD, and Raw formats save alpha channels with the file.

4. Choose Select > Deselect, or press Ctrl+D (Windows) or Command+D (Mac OS), to deselect the active selection.

5. Once a selection is saved, you can easily reselect it by choosing Select > Load Selection, or by Ctrl-clicking (Windows) or Command-clicking (Mac OS) on the channel in the Channels panel. The duck selection is reactivated.

> ### Take Note...
> *You can save multiple selections in an image, but take note: your file size will increase each time you save a new selection. When multiple selections are saved, you will need to click on the Channel drop-down menu and choose which saved selection to display.*

Copying and pasting a selection

There are many different methods for moving a selection from one image to another. In this lesson, you will simply copy a selection and paste it into another image.

Certification Ready 4.1

How do you move, copy and paste a selection?

Follow these steps to copy and paste a selection

Step-by-Step

1. Choose Edit > Copy, or use the keyboard shortcut Ctrl+C (Windows) or Command+C (Mac OS).

2. Choose File > Browse in Bridge, and navigate to the ps05lessons folder. Double-click the file named **ps0506.psd** to open it in Photoshop. A photograph of penguins appears.

3. Choose File > Save As. In the Save As dialog box, navigate to the ps05lessons folder and type **ps0506_work** in the Name text field. Leave the format set to Photoshop and click Save.

4. With the image of the penguins in front, select Edit > Paste, or use the keyboard shortcut Ctrl+V (Windows) or Command+V (Mac OS). The duck selection is placed in the penguin image on its own independent layer (Figure 5-39), making it easy to reposition.

Figure 5-39: A new layer is created when the selection is pasted.   *Figure 5-40: The result.*

5. Select the Move Tool (⊹) and reposition the duck so that it is flush with the bottom of the image as shown in Figure 5-40.

6. Choose File > Save, then choose File > Close to close the file. Close any other open files without saving.

Using the Pen tool for selections

The **Pen tool** is the most accurate of all the selection tools in Photoshop. The selection that it creates is referred to as a path. A path utilizes points and segments to define a border and are also used in vector masks in Photoshop. **Paths** are not only more accurate than other selection methods, but they are also more economical, as they do not increase file size, unlike saved channel selections. This is because paths don't contain image data; they are simply outlines. In this section, you will learn how to make a basic path, and then use it to make a selection that you can use for adjusting an image's tonal values.

Learning More

Pen tool terminology

Bézier curve: Originally developed by Pierre Bézier in the 1970s for CAD/CAM operations, the Bézier curve became the underpinning of the entire Adobe PostScript drawing model. The depth and size of a Bézier curve is controlled by fixed points and direction lines.

Anchor points: Anchor points are used to control the shape of a path or object. They are automatically created by the shape tools. You can manually create anchor points by clicking from point to point with the Pen tool.

Direction lines: These are essentially the handles that you use on anchor points to adjust the depth and angle of curved paths.

Closed shape: When a path is created, it becomes a closed shape when the starting point joins the endpoint.

Simple path: A path consists of one or more straight or curved segments. Anchor points mark the endpoints of the path segments. In the next section, you will learn how to control the anchor points.

Step-by-Step

Follow these steps to make a selection based on a path

1. Choose File > Browse in Bridge to bring Adobe Bridge forward. Then navigate to the ps05lessons folder and open image **ps0507.psd**.

2. Choose File > Save As. When the Save As dialog box appears, navigate to the ps05lessons folder. In the File name text field, type **ps0507_work**. Choose Photoshop from the Format drop-down menu and press Save. If the Photoshop Format Options dialog box appears, press OK.

    This part of the exercise will guide you through the basics of using the Pen tool.

3. Select the Pen tool (✐) from the Tools panel.

4. Position the cursor over the image, and notice that an asterisk appears in the lower-right corner of the tool. This signifies that you are beginning a new path.

5. When the Pen tool is selected, the Options bar displays three path buttons: Shape layers, Paths, and Fill pixels. Click the second menu item for Paths as shown in Figure 5-41.

Figure 5-41: Select Paths in the Pen tool options.

6. Increase the zoom level by pressing the Ctrl+plus sign (Windows) or Command+plus sign (Mac OS), so that you can view the exercise file in the image window as large as possible. If you zoom too far in, zoom out by pressing Ctrl+minus sign (Windows) or Command+minus sign (Mac OS).

7. Place the pen tip at the first box in Example A, and click once to create the first anchor point of the path. Don't worry if it's not exactly on the corner, as you can adjust the path later.

8. Place the pen tip at the second box on Example A and click once. Another anchor point is created, with a line connecting the first anchor point to the second.

9. Continue clicking on each box in the exercise until you reach the last box on the path. If you're having difficulties seeing the line segments between the points on your path, you can temporarily hide the Exercise layer by clicking on the Visibility icon next to that layer.

10. Hold down the Ctrl (Windows) or Command (Mac OS) key, and click on the white background to deactivate the path that was just drawn to prepare for the next path.

   In Example A, only straight line segments were used to draw a path; now you'll use curved line segments.

11. Reposition the document in the window so that Example B is visible.

12. With the Pen tool selected, click and hold on the small square (the first anchor point in the path) and drag upward to create directional handles (Figure 5-42). Directional handles control where the following path will go. Note that when you create directional handles, you should drag until the length is the same or slightly beyond the arch that you are creating.

Figure 5-42: Click and drag with the
Pen tool to create directional handles.

13. Click and hold on the second box in Example B, and drag the directional handle downward (Figure 5-42). Keep dragging until the path closely matches the curve of Example B. Don't worry if it's not exact for this part of the lesson.

14. Click on the third box in Example B, and drag upward to create the next line segment. Continue this process to the end of the Example B diagram.

15. To edit the position of the points on the path, you'll use the Direct Selection tool (⬉). Click and hold on the Path Selection tool (⬈) and select the hidden Direct Selection tool.

16. Position the Direct Selection tool over a path segment (the area between two anchor points) and click once; the directional handles that control that line segment are displayed. Click and drag on any of the directional handles to fine-tune your line segments as shown in Figure 5-43. You can also click directly on each anchor point to reposition them if necessary.

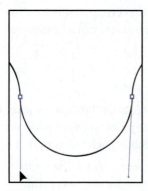

Figure 5-43: *Adjusting the directional handles using the Direct Selection tool.*

17. Choose File > Save, then choose File > Close to close the file.

Using the Pen tool to select an area of an image

Step-by-Step | **Follow these steps to use the pen tool to select an area of an image**

1. Choose File > Browse in Bridge to bring Adobe Bridge forward. Then navigate to the ps05lessons folder and open image **ps0508.psd**.

2. Choose File > Save As. When the Save As dialog box appears, navigate to the ps05lessons folder. In the Name text field, type **ps0508_work**. Choose Photoshop PSD from the Format drop-down menu and press Save. If the Photoshop Format Options dialog box appears, press OK.

3. On the keyboard, hold down the Ctrl (Windows) or Command (Mac OS) key; then press the plus sign (+) once to zoom in at 200 percent. You'll see the zoom % in the lower-left corner of your workspace. Position the apple on the left side of the image that is in focus so that you can see the entire apple in the document window.

4. Select the Pen tool (✒), and begin drawing a path around the apple using the skills you learned in the previous exercise by clicking and dragging at the top edge of the apple and dragging a handle to the right as shown in Figure 5-44.

5. Move the Pen tool further along the apple, and click and drag again, dragging out directional handles each time, creating curved line segments that match the shape of the apple (Figure 5-45).

6. When you get back to the area where you began the path, the Pen cursor has a circle next to it, indicating that when you click back on that first anchor point, it will close the path.

Figure 5-44: Creating a path around the edge of the apple.   *Figure 5-45: Continue drawing a path around the entire apple.*

7. If the Paths panel is not visible select Window > Paths. Path information is stored in the Paths panel. You see one path in the panel, named Work Path.

8. Double-click on the name Work Path in the Paths panel. The Save Path dialog box appears. Type **Apple** in the Name text field and press OK (Figure 5-46).

Figure 5-46: The Paths panel with the renamed path.

Certification Ready 2.4

How do you do a localized color correction on a portion of an image?

9. In the Paths panel click below the name of the path to deselect the path. To reselect the path, simply click on the path name.

10. Now you'll apply an adjustment to this path selection. If the Layers panel is not visible, choose Window > Layers.

11. Click and hold on the Create New fill or adjustment layer button (⬤) at the bottom of the Layers panel and select Hue/Saturation. The Adjustments panel becomes active and the Hue/Saturation adjustment is displayed.

12. Drag the Hue slider to **+116** or type **+116** into the Hue text field (Figure 5-47). You should see only the apple turn green.

13. A new adjustment layer is created, named Hue/Saturation 1 as you can see in Figure 5-48. The pen path you created is visible to the right of the Hue/Saturation adjustment layer thumbnail and acts as a mask, blocking the adjustment from occurring outside of the path. You can see the final result in Figure 5-49.

Figure 5-47: The Hue/Saturation adjustment layer.

Figure 5-48: Adjustment layer with a vector mask.

Figure 5-49: The result.

Take Note...
If you want to have multiple paths in the Paths panel, deselect any active path before you begin drawing a new path. If you don't deselect, the new path you create will be added to, and become part of, the currently active path.

14. Choose File > Save, then choose File > Close to close the file.

More Pen tool selection techniques

In the last exercise, you created a curved path. Now you'll create a path with a combination of straight lines and curves.

Step-by-Step   **Follow these steps to create a path with straight lines and curves**

1. Choose File > Browse in Bridge to bring Adobe Bridge forward. Then navigate to the ps05lessons folder and open image **ps0509.psd**.

    Choose File > Save As. When the Save As dialog box appears, navigate to the ps05lessons folder. In the Name text field, type **ps0509_work**. Choose Photoshop PSD from the Format drop-down menu and press Save. If the Photoshop Format Options dialog box appears, press OK.

2. Choose View > Fit on Screen, or use the keyboard shortcut Ctrl+0 (zero) (Windows) or Command+0 (zero) (Mac OS).

3. With the Pen tool (✐), create the first anchor point at the bottom-left side of the door by clicking once.

4. Staying on the left side of the door, click again at the location that is aligned with the top of the door frame's crossbar as shown in Figure 5-50.

Figure 5-50: The second path point.

5. Now, to set up the path for a curve segment around the arc of the door window, place the pen over the last anchor point. When you see a right slash next to the pen cursor, click and drag to pull a Bézier directional handle. As you can see in Figure 5-51, drag until the directional handle is even with the top horizontal bar inside the door window. The purpose of this handle is to set the direction of the curve segment that follows.

Figure 5-51: The Bézier handle.

6. To form the first curve segment, place the Pen tool cursor at the top of the arc of the door window, and then click, hold, and drag to the right until the curve forms around the left side of the window's arc (Figure 5-52); then release the mouse button.

Figure 5-52: The curve and its anchor point.

7. To finish off the curve, place your cursor at the right side of the door, aligned with the top of the door frame's crossbar. Click and drag straight down to form the remainder of the curve (Figure 5-53).

Figure 5-53: The completed curve.

8. Because the next segment is going to be a straight line and not a curve, you'll need to remove the last handle. Position the cursor over the last anchor point; a left slash appears next to the Pen cursor. This indicates that you are positioned over an active anchor point. Click with the Alt (Windows) or Option (Mac OS) key depressed; the handle disappears.

9. Click on the bottom-right side of the door to create a straight line segment.

10. To finish the path, continue to click straight line segments along the bottom of the door. If you need some help, look at the example below in Figure 5-54.

Figure 5-54: The completed, closed path, selected with the Direct Selection tool.

Certification Ready 4.6

How do you edit a path in Photoshop?

11. Editing paths requires a different strategy when working with curved segments. With the Direct Selection tool (↖), select the path in the image to activate it, and then select the anchor point at the top of the door. Two direction handles appear next to the selected anchor point. You also see handles at the bottom of each respective curve segment to the left and the right. These are used for adjusting the curve.

12. Select the end of one of the handles and drag it up and down to see how it affects the curve. Also drag the handle in toward and away from the anchor point. If you need to adjust any part of your path to make it more accurate, take the time to do so now.

13. Double-click on the name *Work Path in the Paths panel*, and in the Name text field, type **door**. Keep the image open for the next section.

Converting a path to a selection

Paths don't contain image data, so if you want to copy the contents of a path, you need to convert it to a selection.

| **Follow these steps to convert a path to a selection** | **Step-by-Step** |

1. Make sure that the file from the last exercise is still open.

2. Click on the path named door in the Paths panel to make the path active.

3. At the bottom of the Paths panel, there are seven path icons next to the panel trash can:

    -   **Fill path with foreground color** (◉) fills the selected path with the current foreground color.

    -   **Stroke path with brush** (○) is better used if you first Alt/Option+click on the icon and choose the tool from the drop-down menu that includes the brush you want to stroke with.

    -   **Load path as a selection** (○) makes a selection from the active path.

    -   **Make work path from selection** (◠) creates a path from an active selection.

Skill Summary

In this lesson you learned how to:	Objective
Demonstrate knowledge of color correction using Photoshop CS6	2.4
Demonstrate knowledge of layers and masks	3.2
Demonstrate knowledge of working with selections	4.1
Adjust or correct the tonal range, color, or distortions of an image	4.4
Demonstrate knowledge of drawing and painting	4.6
Demonstrate knowledge of filters	4.8

Lesson 5

Knowledge Assessment

True/False

Circle **T** if the statement is true or **F** if the statement is false.

T **F** **1.** "You have to select it to affect it" is an old saying in the image-editing industry.

T **F** **2.** You cannot change an adjustment layer's settings once you close the dialog box for the adjustment.

T **F** **3.** A selection made with the Marquee tool can be nudged into place using the arrow keys on your keyboard.

T **F** **4.** When using the Lasso tool, you can hold down Shift to add areas to the selection or hold down Alt (Windows) or Option (Mac OS) to remove areas of the selection.

T **F** **5.** Feathering is the term that Photoshop uses to describe a vignette, or fading of an image around the edges of a selection.

T **F** **6.** Items in an image such as fur and hair are impossible to select using Photoshop.

T **F** **7.** As a default, in Quick Mask mode, painting with white creates a deselected area and painting with black creates a selected area.

T **F** **8.** Selections that are saved with an image are saved as alpha channels.

T **F** **9.** Selections cannot be copied and pasted like an image.

T **F** **10.** When selecting an item with the Pen tool, the selection starts off as a Path shape.

Multiple Choice

Select the best response for the following statements.

1. To make changes to specific regions in your images, you must:

   a. Have an active selection

   b. Crop out everything else

   c. Make several copies of the image and work on different areas of each one

   d. You can't really isolate specific areas in Photoshop

2. Rectangular, Elliptical, Single Row and Single Column are all shape options for which tool?

   a. Brush

   b. Eraser

   c. Marquee

   d. Move

3. After you've made a selection with the Marquee tool, what happens if you click and drag on that area with the Move tool?

   a. You'll make a copy of that part of the image
   b. The selected region moves with the Move tool
   c. The area will scale automatically
   d. Nothing

4. Which keyboard combination draws a selection from the center point and keeps the shape constrained proportionally?

   a. Alt (Windows) or Option (Mac OS) + Tab
   b. Alt (Windows) or Option (Mac OS) + Shift
   c. Alt (Windows) or Option (Mac OS) + Control
   d. Control + Shift

5. Which tool allows you to make selections based on tonal similarities?

   a. Magic Wand
   b. Path Selection
   c. Lasso
   d. Dodge

6. When you want to make a general selection or refine an existing selection without having to worry about being too precise, what would be the best tool to use?

   a. Lasso
   b. Pen
   c. Magic Wand
   d. Magnetic Lasso

7. Which tool works like the Brush where you can paint your selection and allows you to even change the brush size when making the selection?

   a. Marquee
   b. Magnetic Lasso
   c. Lasso
   d. Quick Selection

8. What tool can be used in conjunction with the Quick Mask to refine the areas of a selection?

   a. Marquee
   b. Path Selection
   c. Brush tool
   d. Lasso

9. Out of the selection tools in Photoshop, which one is considered the most accurate?

   a. Pen
   b. Marquee
   c. Magnetic Lasso
   d. Magic Wand

10. Which of the following terminology is associated with the Pen tool?

    a. Bezier curve

    b. Anchor points

    c. Directional handles

    d. All of the above

Competency Assessment

| Project 5-1 | Commonly Known as Happy Accidents |

There are those moments when you get great unexpected results when you're going for something else entirely. It's all about trying different settings and experimenting.

1. Open the **ps0503.psd** image in Photoshop.

2. Create Curves Adjustment layer.

3. Try clicking and dragging in more extreme ways to get different color effects that you may use for a number of other moods you're trying to convey. Be creative. Even duplicate that adjustment layer once the adjustment has been applied and change the blending mode on the top layer to create even more intense visual effects!

4. Save the file as **ps0503_curve_effects.psd**.

| Project 5-2 | Adding and Subtracting Selections |

Through Load Selection you can save numerous selections and then load them, you can even get them to add and subtract from one another to modify an existing selection.

1. Open the **ps0502.psd** image in Photoshop. Make a selection.

2. Choose Select > Save Selection. Give the selection an appropriate name and click okay. Do this several times with selections overlapping each other.

3. Use Select > Load Selection and experiment with the different selections and variations in the Operations section of the Load Selection dialog box.

4. Once you have an interesting selection from performing the above steps, create a Layer Mask that masks the image using the selection.

5. Save your file as **ps0502_selections.psd**.

Proficiency Assessment

| Project 5-3 | The Magic Wand |

The Magic Wand is a bit of an old-school tool in Photoshop but is great for selecting images of similar color.

1. Open the **ps0502.psd** file in Photoshop.

2. Select the Magic Wand tool.

3. Start making selections. Experiment with the tolerance and contiguous values to better understand how the tool works. Take note that where you click on the image makes a difference in how the selection is generated.

4. Try to select each color in the kite by adjusting the tolerance values and unchecking the contiguous checkbox. When you find the best setting for a color, choose Select > Save Selection, and name your selection the color and the tolerance value used for the selection. For example, Green 75.

5. Save your file as **ps0502_wand.psd**.

| **Another Way to Load a Selection** | **Project 5-4** |

You used the Save Selection and Load Selection windows, but hey, there's a button for that second part instead.

1. Open the **ps0501_done.psd** image in Photoshop.

2. Hold down the Cmd key (Mac OS) or the Ctrl key (Windows) and click on the Layer mask of the Curves 1 layer. The selection is automatically created.

3. Choose Select > Save Selection and enter **New Rectangle** for the name. Click OK.

4. Save the file as **ps0501_selection.psd**.

Circling Back 1

Practice, practice, practice is the key to mastering the pen tool. The more you use it, the more fluid and efficient you become with it. This is true with most tools but the pen can be especially tricky and especially powerful as well with regard to making complex and professionally looking selections. Selections are something that can make or break your project and if done with rough edges or over feathering will make your project look rather amateurish.

| **Revisiting the Pen** | **Project 1** |

Some images just don't lend themselves to broad selection methods such as using the Magic Wand or Quick Selection. In those cases, you need to get in there with a tool such as the Pen tool to accurately isolate an image that is part of a more complex image or in front of a complicated background. A good example of this is the penguin photo you used earlier in this lesson.

Go ahead and launch Photoshop if you haven't already.

1. Choose File > Open and navigate to the ps05lessons folder. Open the file named **ps0506.psd**, the photograph of the penguins.

2. Save the file as **pen-exercise.psd**.

3. Zoom in on the penguin you'd like to isolate. We suggest one of the penguins on the left side of the image where you can see the whole bird from top to bottom.

4. Select the Pen tool. Make sure the Pen is set to Path in the Options bar.

5. Practice what you learned by creating a path around the penguin.

6. Edit the path as you go by pressing the Ctrl or alt (windows) or Cmd or option (Mac OS) keys to refine your path around the penguin.

7. Once you've finished with the Pen, go to the Paths panel. Double-click the work path and save it as **penguin**.

8. Convert the path to a selection.

9. With any selection tool active, click on the refine edge button in the Options bar and adjust the selection, then output to a new layer with a layer mask by choosing that option at the bottom of the Refine Edge dialog box.

Lesson 5

10. Double click the new layer name and name it **penguin**.

11. Save the file.

12. Use the Move tool and modify your new penguin layer as you wish.

Project 2   Exploring Methods

You've got a lot of selection tools in the Tools panel which is great as it allows you to try different tools for different situations. To understand which selection tool is best for each situation, we've set you up along the way with a specific image and a specific tool. You'll want to experiment though as we won't be able to be there for you in your office when you get an assignment across your desk that requires a lot of selection work.

1. Choose File > Open and navigate to the ps05lessons folder. Open the file named **ps0508.psd**; the photograph of the apples.

2. Select the Magic Wand tool. Make sure Anti-Alias and Contiguous are both checked in the Options bar.

3. Click on the main apple in the picture and notice how the selection applies.

4. Choose Select > Deselect.

5. Make adjustments to the Tolerance setting in the Options bar for the Magic Wand. Try selecting the apple again.

6. Deselect again and uncheck Contiguous for the Wand this time. Make another selection and note the difference to the area selected.

7. Continue to refine the settings of the wand and practicing making selections.

8. As you generate a selection that works, save the selection by choosing Select > Save Selection and give the selection a descriptive name.

9. Save the finished file as **Selections.psd**.

Project 3   Overlapping Selection Tricks

You've seen how you can create a selection, save it and load it back into your image. But what if you have more than one selection? There are some additional tricks to be aware of with regard to working with multiple selections.

1. Choose File > Open and navigate to the ps05lessons folder. Open the file named **ps0508.psd**, the photograph of the apples.

2. Make a selection of the big apple using any method you wish. Save the selection as **big apple**.

3. Make another selection around the apple just below the apple to the right of it. Save the selection as **small apple**.

4. Choose Select > Load Selection. Choose the big apple selection as a new selection.

5. Choose Select > Load Selection and designate the Operation as Add to Selection. This provides for a way that you can combine multiple selections into one, or even subtract one selection from another. This is very useful when working with more complex selections.

6. Save the file as **multiple_selections.psd**.

Painting and Retouching

Key Terms

- airbrush
- blending mode
- Bristle brushes
- Brush presets
- Clone Stamp tool
- CMYK
- Eyedropper tool
- gamut
- Healing Brush tool
- History panel
- opacity
- Patch tool
- retouching
- RGB

Skill	Objective
Demonstrate knowledge of color correction using Photoshop CS6	2.4
Demonstrate an understanding of and select the appropriate features and options required to implement a color management workflow	3.5
Demonstrate knowledge of retouching and blending images	4.5
Demonstrate knowledge of drawing and painting	4.6

Business case

Many photos suffer from common photographic problems that distract from the subject matter in the image. Some problems are obvious such as color cast, poor contrast, or a case of red eye. Other considerations may not be as apparent though, including things you may not see so well with the naked eye. There are several features in Photoshop (like the Histogram) that will help you to accurately analyze an image and go deeper in terms of understanding what may need to be done to correct your picture.

Starting up

Before starting, make sure that your tools and panels are consistent by resetting your preferences. See "Resetting the Photoshop workspace" in the Starting up section of this book.

You will work with several files from the ps06lessons folder in this lesson. Make sure that you have loaded the pslessons folder onto your hard drive from *http://www.wiley.com/college/sc/adobeseries*. See "Loading lesson files" in the Starting up section of this book.

Setting up your color settings

Before you begin selecting colors for painting, you should have an understanding of color modes and Photoshop's color settings. Let's start with a basic introductory overview of the two main color modes that you will use in this lesson, RGB and CMYK.

Color primer

This lesson is about painting, adding colors, and changing and retouching images. It is important to understand that what you see on the screen is not necessarily what your final viewers will see (print or web). Bright colors tend to become duller when output to a printer, and some colors can't even be reproduced on the monitor or on paper. This is due to the fact that each device—whether it's a monitor, printer, or TV screen—has a different color gamut. Color management aims to standardize color by allowing you to choose an appropriate color space for the devices in use at your organization. In addition, you can adjust settings such as the rendering intent to determine how color transformations are calculated within Photoshop.

Understanding color gamut

The **gamut** represents the number of colors that can be represented, detected, or reproduced on a specific device displayed in Figure 6-1. Although you may not realize it, you have experience with different gamuts already; your eyes can see many more colors than your monitor or a printing press can reproduce.

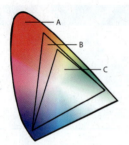

Figure 6-1

A. *Colors that your eye recognizes.*
B. *Colors that your monitor recognizes.*
C. *Colors that your printer reproduces.*

In this lesson, you will learn how you can address some of the color limitations that are inherent when working with color that is displayed or output by different devices. A quick introduction to the RGB and CMYK color models will help you to get a better grasp on what you can achieve. Understand that there are entire books on this subject, but you will at least gain enough information to be dangerous after reading this section.

If you receive a Missing or Mismatched Profile warning dialog box on any images used in this lesson, press OK to accept the default setting.

The RGB color model

The **RGB** (Red, Green, Blue) color model is an additive model in which red, green, and blue are combined in various ways to create other colors.

Follow these steps to view the RGB color model	Step-by-Step

1. Choose File > Open, and navigate to the ps06lessons folder. Open the file named **ps06rgb.psd**. An image with red, green, and blue circles appears (Figure 6-2). Try to imagine the three color circles as light beams from three flashlights with red, green, and blue colored gels.

Figure 6-2: *Red, green, blue.*

2. Select the Move tool (✛), and then check the Auto-Select checkbox in the Options bar. By checking Auto-Select Layer, you can automatically activate a layer by selecting pixel information on that layer. One at a time, click and drag the red, green, and blue circles around on the image.

Notice that white light is generated where the three colors intersect.

3. Now, turn off the visibility of the layers by selecting the Visibility icon (👁) to the left of each layer name, with the exception of the black layer. It is just like turning off a flashlight; when there is no light, there is no color.

4. Choose File > Close. Choose to not save changes.

The CMYK color model

CMYK (Cyan, Magenta, Yellow, and Black [or Key]—black was once referred to as the *Key* color) is a subtractive color model, meaning that as ink is applied to a piece of paper, these colors absorb light. This color model is based on mixing CMYK pigments to create other colors.

Ideally, by combining CMY inks together, the color black should result. In reality, the combination of those three pigments creates a dark, muddy color, and so black is added to create a panel with true blacks. CMYK works through light absorption. The colors that are seen are the portion of visible light that is reflected, not absorbed, by the objects on which the light falls.

In CMYK, magenta plus yellow creates red, magenta plus cyan creates blue, and cyan plus yellow creates green as you can see in Figure 6-3.

Figure 6-3: *Cyan, magenta, yellow, and black.*

Step-by-Step Follow these steps to view the CMYK color model

1. Choose File > Open, and navigate to the ps06lessons folder. Open the file named **ps06cmyk.psd**. An image with cyan, magenta, and yellow circles appears. Think of the colors in this file as being created with ink printed on paper.

2. With the Move tool (⊹) selected, and the Auto-Select Layer checkbox checked, individually click and drag the cyan, magenta, and yellow circles around on the image to see the color combinations that are created with ink pigments of these three colors. Notice that black appears at the intersection of all three, but, as mentioned earlier, it would never reproduce that purely on a printing press.

3. Choose File > Close to close the **ps06cmyk.psd** image. Do not save your changes.

4. Uncheck the Auto-Select Layer checkbox in the Options bar.

Working in the RGB mode

Unless you use an advanced color management system, you should do much of your creative work in the RGB mode. The CMYK mode is limited in its capabilities (fewer menu selections), and if you work in this mode, you have already made some decisions about your final image output that may not be accurate. Follow this short color primer to help you achieve the results that you expect.

In this lesson, you'll use generic profiles for your monitor and output devices. If you want to create a custom monitor profile, follow the instructions in the Photoshop Help menu, under the heading, "Calibrate and profile your monitor." You can also type **Calibrate Monitor** into the Search field on *adobe.com* to find additional helpful tips for calibrating your display.

Follow these steps to use the Proof Colors feature

1. Choose File > Browse in Bridge to bring Adobe Bridge to the front.

2. Navigate to the ps06lessons folder and open the image **ps0601.psd**. A very colorful image of a woman appears as displayed in Figure 6-4.

Figure 6-4: A colorful RGB image.

3. Press Ctrl+Y (Windows) or Command+Y (Mac OS); some of the colors become duller. By pressing Ctrl+Y/Command+Y, you have turned on the Proof Colors. This is a toggle keyboard shortcut, which means you can press Ctrl+Y/Command+Y again to turn the preview off. Note that the text in your title bar indicates whether this preview is active or not. Keep the file open for the next part of this lesson.

   The Proof Colors preview attempts to visually simulate what the colors in this image would look like if it were to be printed. This simulation is controlled by the choices you make in the color settings. This is why understanding the color settings is important, as the settings you choose not only affect your preview, but also how the image appears in its final destination; print or on-screen.

Editing color settings

For this lesson, you will adjust the color settings for Photoshop as if the final destination for this image is in print. Note that if you have Creative Suite 6 installed, you can adjust your color settings suite-wide, using Adobe Bridge. Applying color settings through Adobe Bridge saves you the time and trouble of making sure that all the colors are consistent throughout your production process. If you have the Creative Suite installed, follow the steps that are indicated for suite users; if you have Adobe Photoshop installed independently, follow the steps for adjusting Photoshop color settings only.

Certification Ready 3.5

Why is it important to define a working RGB and a working CMYK color profile?

Follow these steps to edit Color Settings

1. Choose File > Browse in Bridge to bring Adobe Bridge to the front. If you do not have the entire Creative Suite 6 installed, leave Adobe Bridge open and skip to step 3.

2. Choose Edit > Creative Suite Color Settings and select North America Prepress 2, if it is not already selected. Press the Apply button. The new color settings are applied throughout the suite applications. Note that the setting you selected is a generic setting created for a printing process that is typical in North America and automatically sets the Working spaces, Color Managment Policies, and the Conversion options. If your selections are not exactly the same, choose the setting that states it is a prepress setting.

3. Click the Return to Adobe Photoshop boomerang icon (𝄐) at the top of Bridge.

4. In Photoshop, choose Edit > Color Settings, even if you have already set them in Adobe Bridge.

5. If North America Prepress 2 is not selected in the Settings drop-down menu, choose it now. Leave the Colors Settings dialog box open.

6. While still in the Color Settings dialog box, press Ctrl+Y (Windows) or Command+Y (Mac OS) to use the toggle shortcut for the CMYK preview. You can tell if you are in the CMYK preview by looking at the title bar of the image window as is the case in Figure 6-5. Notice that CMYK appears in parentheses at the end of the title.

Figure 6-5:*The title bar indicates that this image is in the CMYK preview mode.*

It is good to get this sneak peek into what your CMYK image will look like, but there is still the issue of having many different kinds of CMYK output devices. You might have one printer that produces excellent results and another that can hardly hold a color. In the next section, you will learn about the different CMYK settings and how they can affect your image.

7. Make sure that the CMYK preview is still on. If not, press Ctrl+Y (Windows) or Command+Y (Mac OS) again. From the CMYK drop-down menu in the Working Spaces section of the Color Settings dialog box, choose U.S. Sheetfed Uncoated v2 (Figure 6-6).

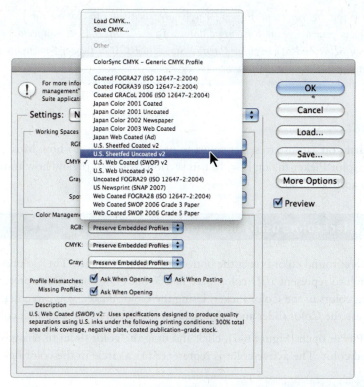

Figure 6-6:*Choose various CMYK specifications from the CMYK drop-down menu.*

Notice the color change in the image. You may need to reposition the Color Settings dialog box in order to see your image. Photoshop is now displaying the characteristics of the color space for images printed on a sheetfed press. This would be the generic setting you might choose if you were sending this image to a printing press that printed on individual sheets of paper.

8. From the CMYK drop-down menu, choose Japan Web Coated (Ad). Notice that the color preview changes again. You might use this selection if you were sending this image overseas to be printed on a large catalog or book press. A web press is a high-volume, high-speed printing press that prints on large rolls of paper rather than individual sheets.

You do not want to pick a CMYK setting simply because it looks good on your screen; you want to choose one based upon a recommendation from a printer, or you should use the generic settings that Adobe provides. The purpose of selecting an accurate setting is not only to keep your expectations realistic; it also helps you accurately adjust an image to produce the best and most accurate results.

9. From the Settings drop-down menu, choose the North America Prepress 2 setting again, and press OK. Keep the file open for the next part of this lesson.

> **Take Note...**
> *Keep in mind that if you are using your images for web only, then you can also use the preview feature to view your image on different platforms. To make this change, you would choose View > Proof Setup and choose either Internet Standard RGB or Legacy Macintosh RGB from the menu.*

Selecting colors

There are many methods that you can use to select colors to paint with in Photoshop. Most methods end up using the Color Picker dialog box. In this section, you will review how to use the Color Picker to choose accurate colors.

Step-by-Step | **Follow these steps to select colors using the Color Picker**

1. Click once on the Set foreground color box at the bottom of the Tools panel. The Color Picker appears. It is tough to represent a 3D color space in 2D, but Photoshop does a pretty good job of interpreting colors in the Color Picker. Using the Color Picker, you can enter values on the right, or use the Color slider and color field on the left to create a custom color.

2. Now, with the Color Picker open (Figure 6-7), click and drag the color slider to change the hue of your selected color. The active color is represented as a circle in the color field.

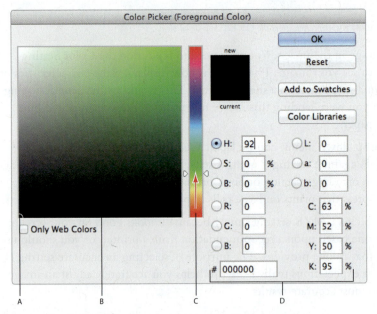

Figure 6-7: *A. Selected color.* *B. Color field.* *C. Color slider.* *D. Color values.*

3. Now, click in the color field, and then click and drag your selected color toward the upper-right corner of the color field, making it a brighter, more saturated color. To choose a lighter color, click and drag the selected color to the upper-left corner of the color field. Even though you can select virtually any color using this method, you may not achieve the best results.

4. Press Ctrl+Shift+Y (Windows) or Command+Shift+Y (Mac OS) to see how Proof Colors affects the colors in the Color Picker. Notice that colors that will not print well in CMYK show up with in gray (gamut warning). Press Ctrl+Shift+Y/Command+Shift+Y again to turn off Proof Colors.

Perhaps you are creating images for the Web and you want to work with web-safe colors only. This is very restrictive, but you can limit your color choices by checking the Only Web Colors checkbox in the Color Picker.

5. Check and uncheck the Only Web Colors checkbox to see the difference in selectable colors in the color field.

There are also warning icons in the Color Picker to help you choose the best colors for print and the Web.

6. Click in the lower-left corner of the color field and drag up toward the upper-right corner. Note that at some point, when you enter into the brighter colors, an Out of gamut for printing warning icon (⚠) appears as shown in Figure 6-8. This indicates that although you may have selected a very nice color, it is never going to print, based upon your present color settings. Click on the Out of gamut warning icon, and Photoshop redirects you to the closest color you can achieve.

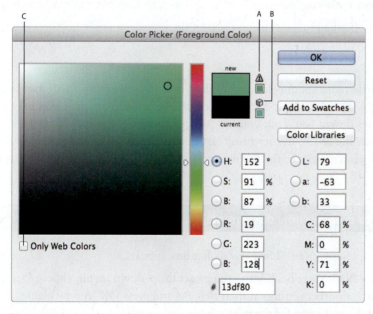

*Figure 6-8: **A.** Out of gamut for printing warning. **B.** Not a web safe color warning. **C.** Only Web Colors.*

7. Click and drag your selected color in the color field until you see the Not a web safe color alert icon (◉) appear. Click on the Not a web safe color icon to be redirected to the closest web-safe color.

8. Position the Color Picker so that you can see part of the **ps0601.psd** image, then position the cursor over any part of the image. Notice that the cursor turns into the Eyedropper tool (✎) as you can see in Figure 6-9. Click to select any color from the image.

Figure 6-9: Click outside the Color Picker to sample a color from your image.

9. Press OK in the Color Picker dialog box.

10. Choose File > Close. If asked to save changes, select No.

Starting to paint

Certification Ready 4.6

Which tools can be used for painting in Photoshop?

Now that you know a little more about color, and finding it in Photoshop, you will start to do some painting. You will work on a new blank document to begin with, but once you have the basics of the painting tools down, you'll put your knowledge to work on actual image files. The painting tools include the brush, history brush, art history brush, color replacement tool, mixer brush, pencil, and eraser tools. In the following lesson, you'll use a few of these to create the final project.

Step-by-Step | **Follow these steps to create a new document**

1. Under the File menu, choose New. The New dialog box appears.

2. Type **painting** in the Name text field. From the preset drop-down menu, choose Default Photoshop Size. Leave all other settings at their defaults and press OK. A new blank document is created; keep it open for the next part of this lesson.

Using the Color panel

Another way to select color is to use the Color panel.

| Follow these steps to access the Color panel | Step-by-Step |

1. If the Color panel is not visible, choose Window > Color. The color panel is shown below with Figure 6-10.

Place your cursor over the color ramp at the bottom of the panel, then click and drag across the displayed color spectrum. Notice that the RGB sliders adjust to indicate the color combinations creating the active color. If you have a specific color in mind, you can individually drag the sliders or key in numeric values.

Note that the last color you activated appears in the Set foreground color swatch, located in the Color panel, as well as near the bottom of the Tools panel.

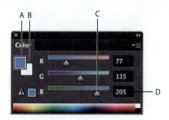

Figure 6-10

A. *Set foreground color.*
B. *Set background color.*
C. *Slider.*
D. *Color ramp.*

2. Click once on the Set Foreground Color box to open the Color Picker. Type the following values in the RGB text fields on the right side of the Color Picker dialog box: R: **74** G: **150** B: **190** (Figure 6-11). Press OK.

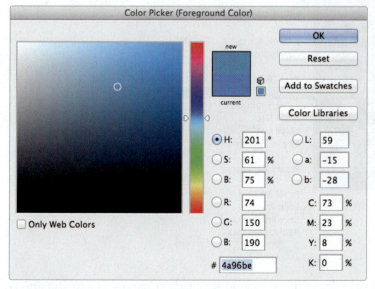

Figure 6-11: *Manually enter values in the Color Picker.*

Lesson 6

Using the Brush tool

The Brush tool paints using the foreground color. You can control the brush type, size, softness, mode, and opacity with the Brush tool Options.

Step-by-Step

Follow these steps to use the Brush tool

1. Select the Brush tool (✔) in the Tools panel.

2. Press the arrow next to the brush size in the Options bar to open the Brush Preset picker (Figure 6-12).

Figure 6-12: Press the arrow in the Brush Options bar to open the presets.

3. If you are not in the default panel view, click and hold the panel menu, which looks like a gear icon (✿), in the upper-right corner of the Brush Preset picker and choose Small Thumbnail View (Figure 6-13). **Brush presets** is a way of saving the settings defined in a brush tip so that those settings can be recalled and reused when needed.

Figure 6-13: You can use the panel menu to choose different views.

4. Position your cursor over any of the brushes to see a tooltip appear. The tooltip provides a description of the brush, such as soft, airbrush, hard, or chalk. Some will also display the brush size in pixels.

5. Locate the brush with the description Soft Round Pressure Size pixels, toward the top of the panel, and click on it.

6. Use the Size slider or enter **45** into the Size text field to change the diameter of the brush to 45 pixels as shown in Figure 6-14, and press the Enter (Windows) or Return (Mac OS) key. The brush is selected and the Brushes Preset picker is closed.

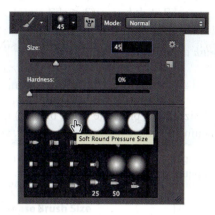

Figure 6-14: *The Brush Preset picker and the Soft Round 45 pixel brush.*

7. Position your cursor on the left side of the image window, then click and drag to paint a curved line similar to the example below in Figure 6-15. If you do not see your brush stroke, make sure that the Mode in the Options bar is set to Normal.

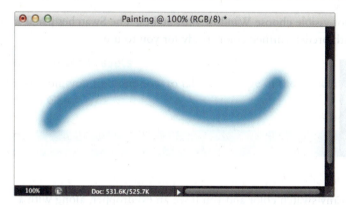

Figure 6-15: *Painted brush stroke.*

8. Using the Color panel, click on a different color from the color ramp (no specific color is necessary for this exercise). As shown in Figure 6-16, paint another brush stroke that crosses over, or intersects, with the first brush stroke.

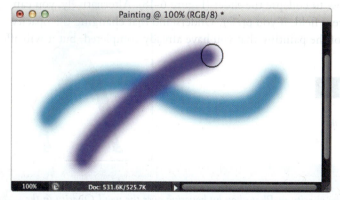

Figure 6-16: *Painting a second brush stroke.*

3. Select the Brush tool (✐) and then select the Toggle the Brush panel button (▦) in the Options bar. The Brush panel appears.

4. Select the Brush Presets tab to bring it forward and then select Small List from the panel menu. This will make it easier for you to identify the brushes by name.

5. Click on the Round Curve Low Bristle Percent preset.

6. Using the Size slider click and drag the size of the brush to approximately 205 px as shown in Figure 6-20. Note that you can preview the tip by activating the Toogle the LiveTip Brush Preview button (✎). Note that this brush preview does not work with all the brush tips.

Figure 6-20: Select the Round Curve Low Bristle brush and change the size to 205 px.

7. With the Brush tool still selected, hold down the Alt (Windows) or Option (Mac OS) key and sample a color of the woman's skin color. Choose a darker shade if possible.

8. In the Options bar, click on the Mode drop-down menu and select Multiply.

9. Using large wide brush strokes paint over the woman playing the guitar. Since you are using a blending mode with a light color, the image is still visible. If you want to erase and try again, simply press Ctrl+Z (Windows) or Command+Z (Mac OS)

Note that as you paint a preview of your brush appears (Figure 6-21), and even shows the movement of the bristles as you paint.

Figure 6-21: The image after you apply the brush stroke.

You can store your brushes for future use by taking advantage of the Brush preset feature.

10. Click on the Create new brush (⬜) button in the lower right of the Brush Presets panel. The Brush Name dialog box appears. Type the name **My Large Rounded Brush**, and press OK. As you can see in Figure 6-22, this brush now appears in the Brush Preset panel for future use.

Figure 6-22: Store your brush for future use.

Using the Airbrush feature

In this section you discover how to change the brush characteristics to act more like an airbrush. Using the **airbrush** option allows your paint to spread, much like the effect you would have using a true (non-digital) airbrush.

Follow these steps to use the Airbrush feature	Step-by-Step

1. Select Round Fan Stiff Thin Bristles from the Brush Preset panel. Make sure the size is still close to 205 px. If not, use the slider to change it to that value now.

2. Press **D** to return to the Photoshop default colors of Black and White.

3. If the Mode drop-down menu (In the Options bar) is not set to Normal, set that to Normal now.

4. Click and release with your cursor anywhere on the image to stamp a brush stroke onto the image. Do this a couple more times (Figure 6-23). You can press the [(left bracket) or] (right bracket) keys to change the size of the stamped brush.

Figure 6-23: Stamp the brush stroke to produce the effect of dabbing the brush onto the image.

5. Now, Select the Enable airbrush-style build-up effects (✍) in the Options bar. Notice that you can change the flow, or pressure, of the paint coming out of the airbrush using the Flow control to the left. In this example, this is set to 50%.

6. Using the same brush preset, click and hold on your image to notice that the paint spreads as you hold. This is illustrated in Figure 6-24.

Figure 6-24: With the Enable airbrush option the paint spreads as you hold down on the brush.

Experiment with different flows and sizes to see the effects that you have created.

7. When you are finished experimenting, return the Flow control back to 100%.

Creating a Border using the Bristle brushes

In this next section, you use a bristle brush to create an artistic border around the edge of the image. **Bristle brushes** are brush tips that simulate traditional Bristle brushes and mimic the behavior in Photoshop..

Step-by-Step	Follow these steps to use a Bristle brush

1. Select the Round Blunt Medium Stiff bristle brush from the Brush Presets panel.

2. Choose any color that you want to use for the border you are about to create. In this example we use the default black.

3. Click in the upper-left corner of the image. This is the top-left corner for your border.

Hold down the Shift key and click in the lower-left corner. By Shift+clicking you have instructed Photoshop that you want a stroke to connect from the initial click to the next.

4. Shift+click in the lower-right corner, and then continue this process until you return to your original stroke origin in the upper-left corner. The image with the completed border is shown below in Figure 6-25.

Figure 6-25: The completed border.

5. Press Ctrl+S (Windows) or Command+S (Mac OS) to save this image, then choose File > Close.

Applying color to an image

You can color anything realistically in Photoshop by using different opacity levels and blending modes. In this part of the lesson, you'll take a grayscale image and tint it with color. Understand that you can also paint color images to change the color of an object, like clothing for a catalog, or just to add interesting tints for mood and effect.

Follow these steps to apply color to a grayscale image	Step-by-Step

1. Choose File > Browse in Bridge, and then navigate to the ps06lessons folder and open image **ps0603.psd**. See Figure 6-26; a grayscale image of a small boy appears.

Figure 6-26: The original grayscale image.

2. Double-click on the Zoom tool (⊕) in the Tools panel to change the view to 100 percent. You may need to resize the image window to view more of the image.

3. Choose Image > Mode > RGB Color. This will not change the visual look of the image, but in order to colorize a grayscale image, it needs to be in a mode that supports color channels.

4. Choose File > Save As; the Save As dialog box appears. Navigate to the ps06lessons folder and type **ps0603_work** into the Name text field. Choose Photoshop from the Format drop-down menu and Press Save.

5. If you do not see the Swatches panel, choose Window > Swatches.

6. Select the Brush tool and Right-click (Windows) or Ctrl+click (Mac OS) on the canvas to open the contextual Brush Preset picker. Select the Soft Round brush (this is the first brush.) Slide the Size slider to 25 and the Hardness slider to 5 as displayed in Figure 6-27. Press Enter (Windows) or Return (Mac OS) to exit.

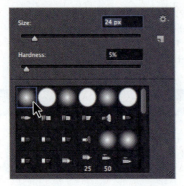

Figure 6-27: *Change the brush size to 25 pixels, and the hardness to 5%.*

7. Using the Opacity slider in the Options bar, change the opacity of the brush to 85 percent, or type **85** into the Opacity text field.

8. Position your cursor over a brown color in the Swatches panel. In this example, Dark Warm Brown is selected, but you can choose any color you want.

9. Using the Brush tool, paint the boy's hair. Notice that at 85 percent, the color is slightly transparent but still contains some of the image information underneath (Figure 6-28). You'll now paint the boy's hair more realistically.

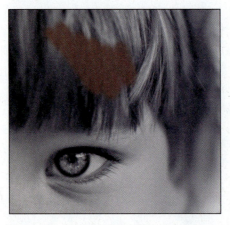

Figure 6-28: *Painting the hair at 85 percent opacity.*

10. Choose File > Revert to return the image to the last saved version. Leave the file open.

Changing blending modes

Opacity is one way to alter the appearance or strength of a brush stroke. Another method is to change the blending mode of the painting tool you are using. The **blending mode** controls how pixels in the image are affected by painting. There are many modes to select from, and each creates a different result. This is because each blending mode is unique, but also because the blending result is based upon the color you are painting with and the color of the underlying image. As you work with blending modes, you'll discover the attributes and behavior of each blending mode. For example, multiply multiplies the values of the pixels and creates a new value. With multiply, white always disappears. With the screen blending mode, colors are lightened and black disappears. In this section, you will colorize the photo by adjusting the opacity and changing the blending mode.

Certification Ready 4.5

How do blending modes change how layers interact with one another?

Certification Ready 4.5

Which blending mode would you use to remove the white background of a logo?

Follow these steps to change the blending mode of a brush

Step-by-Step

1. Make sure that **ps0603_work.psd** is still open and double-click on the Zoom tool (🔍) in the Tools panel to verify that your view is still set to 100 percent.

   Also, make sure the Swatches panel is forward and the Brush tool (✏️) is selected for this part of the lesson.

2. Make sure that you still have the brown color selected in the Swatches panel.

3. In the Options bar, change the opacity to 50 percent.

4. Select Color from the Mode drop-down list. This is where you select various blending modes for your painting tools. As shown in Figure 6-29, Color is close to the bottom of this drop-down menu, so you may have to scroll to see it.

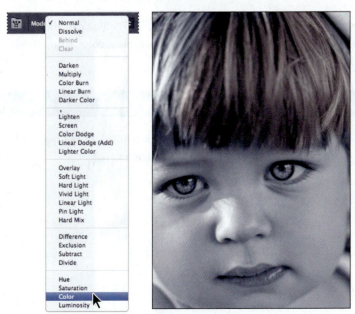

Figure 6-29: Change the blending mode to Color.

5. Using the Brush tool, paint over the boy's hair. Notice that the strength or opacity of the color varies according to the tonality of the painted area. This is because using the color blending mode you selected (Color) retains the grayscale information in the image. Where the image is lighter, the application of the brown color is lighter, and where the image is darker, the application of the brown color is darker.

6. Finish painting the hair brown, and then choose File > Save at this point so you can experiment with painting and blending modes.

Take Note...

In this example you are changing actual pixels in the image; you will find out how to make non-destructive changes in Lessons 9 and 10 of this book.

Experiment with different colors to colorize the photo. Try using different blending modes with the same color to see how differently each mode affects the colorization. Some modes may have no effect at all. Experiment all you want with painting at this point. You can choose Ctrl+Z (Windows) or Command+Z (Mac OS) to undo a brush stroke that you do not like, or use Ctrl+Alt+Z (Windows) or Command+Option+Z (Mac OS) to undo again and again.

Take Note...

Don't like what you have done in just one area of the image? Select the Eraser tool and hold down Alt (Windows) or Option (Mac OS); then click and drag to erase to the last version saved. You can also change the brush size, opacity, and hardness of the Eraser tool, using the Options bar.

7. Choose File > Revert to go back to the last saved version, and leave the file open for the next section.

The Eyedropper tool

The **Eyedropper tool** is used for sampling color from an image. This color can then be used for painting, or for use with text color. In this section, you will sample a color from another image to colorize the boy's face.

Step-by-Step | **Follow these steps to use the Eyedropper tool to sample a color**

1. Make sure that **ps0603_work.psd** is still open, choose File > Browse in Bridge, and then navigate to the ps06lessons folder and open the file named **ps0604.psd**.

2. Select Window > Arrange > 2-up Vertical to see both images.

3. Click on the title bar for the **ps0604.psd** image to bring that image forward as was done in Figure 6-30.

Figure 6-30: *Images tiled vertically.*

4. Choose the Eyedropper tool (✐) and position it over the boy's face in the color image. Click once on his left cheek. The color is selected as the foreground color in the Tools panel.

Take Note...
You can access the Eyedropper tool while you have the Brush tool selected by pressing the Alt (Windows) or option (Mac OS) Keys. When you release the Alt/Option key, you are returned to the Brush tool.

5. Select the Brush tool, then using the Options bar at the top, make sure that Color is selected from the Mode drop-down menu and that the Opacity slider is set at 15 percent.

6. Position your cursor over the image to see the brush radius size. Press the] (right bracket) key several times until the brush is approximately 150 pixels wide. You can see the size reflected in the Options bar.

7. Click on the title bar for the **ps0603_work.psd** image and with the Brush tool (✔) selected, paint the boy's face with the color you just sampled. Paint without releasing the mouse to give the face a good coverage of color.

8. Keep in mind that you have an opacity setting of 15%, which means that you can build up the skin tone color by painting over areas again. You can sculpt the image by adding more tone in the areas where you want more color as demonstrated in Figure 6-31.

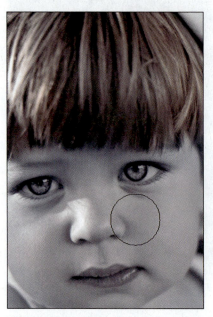

Figure 6-31: Add a light tint of skin color to the image.

9. With your Brush tool still selected, press and hold the Alt (Windows) or Option (Mac OS) key and sample the blue color from the striped shirt in the color image.

10. Press the [(left bracket) key until the brush size is about 60 pixels.

11. Press the number **5**. By pressing 5 you can indicate that you want 50% opacity. This works with all values; for instance, you can press 43 for 43%, or 2 for 20%. To change the opacity to 100% you would press 0 (zero).

12. Position the paint brush over one of the boy's eyes in the grayscale image and click to paint it blue. Repeat this with the other eye.

13. Choose File > Save, then File > Close All to close both the **ps0603_work.psd** and the **ps0604.psd** files.

Retouching images

There are many **retouching** techniques you can use to clean up an original image, from using any of the healing tools to that old standby, the Clone Stamp tool. In this lesson, you will retouch an image.

Follow these steps to open a finished file

1. To view the final image as shown in Figure 6-32, choose File > Browse in Bridge and then navigate to the ps06lessons folder and open image **ps0605_done.psd**.

Figure 6-32: The image after using the retouching tools.

2. You can choose File > Close after viewing this file, or leave it open for reference.

Using the Clone Stamp tool

One of the problems with old photographs is that they most likely contain a large number of defects. These defects can include watermarks, tears, and fold marks. There are many different ways to fix these defects; one of the most useful is the Clone Stamp tool. The **Clone Stamp tool** lets you replace pixels in one area of the image by sampling from another area. In this part of the lesson, you'll use the Clone Stamp tool, and you will also have an opportunity to explore the Clone Source panel.

Follow these steps to use the Clone Stamp tool

1. Choose File > Browse in Bridge and then navigate to the ps06lessons folder and open image **ps0605.psd**.

2. Choose File > Save As; the Save As dialog box appears. Navigate to the ps06lessons folder and type **ps0605_work** into the Name text field. Choose Photoshop from the Format drop-down menu and press Save.

    You'll first experiment with the Clone Stamp tool ( ). Don't worry about what you do to the image at this stage, as you will revert to saved when done.

3. Select the Zoom tool and click and drag a marquee around the top half of the image to zoom in closer to the face.

4. Select the Clone Stamp tool.

5. Position your cursor over the nose of the girl in the image and hold down the Alt (Windows) or Option (Mac OS) key. Your cursor turns into a precision crosshair. When you see this crosshair, click with your mouse. You have just defined the source image area for the Clone Stamp tool.

6. Now position the cursor to the right of the girl's face, then click and drag to start painting with the Clone Stamp tool. As shown in Figure 6-33, the source area that you defined is recreated where you are painting. Watch carefully, as you will see a coinciding crosshair indicating the area of the source that you are copying.

Figure 6-33: The clone source and results.

7. Press the] (right bracket) key to enlarge the Clone Stamp brush. All the keyboard commands you reviewed for the Brush tool work with other painting tools as well.

8. Type **5**. By typing a numeric value when a painting tool is active, you can dynamically change the opacity. Start painting with the Clone Stamp tool again and notice that it is now cloning at a 50 percent opacity.

9. Type **0** (zero) to return to 100 percent opacity.

10. You have completed the experimental exercise using the Clone Stamp tool.

Choose File > Revert to go back to the original image.

Repairing fold lines

You will now repair the fold lines in the upper-right corner of the image.

Step-by-Step	Follow these steps to repair fold lines with the Clone Stamp tool

1. Select the Zoom tool from the Tools panel, and if it is not already selected, check the Resize Windows To Fit checkbox in the Options bar. By checking this box, the window will automatically resize when you zoom.

2. Click approximately three times in the upper-right corner of the image. As shown in Figure 6-34, you will see fold marks that you will repair using the Clone Stamp tool.

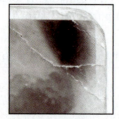

*Figure 6-34: Fold marks
that you will repair.*

3. Select the Clone Stamp tool (⬒) from the Tools panel.

4. Right-click (Windows) or Ctrl+click (Mac OS) on the image area to open the Brush Preset picker. Click on the Soft Round brush and change the Size to 13 pixels (Figure 6-35). Press Enter or the Return key.

Figure 6-35: Select the Soft Round brush.

5. Position your cursor to the left of the fold mark, approximately in the center of the fold. Hold down Alt (Windows) or Option (Mac OS), and click to define that area as the source.

6. Position the Clone Stamp tool over the middle of the fold line itself, and click and release. Depending upon what you are cloning, it is usually wise to apply a clone source in small applications, rather than painting with long brush strokes.

7. Press Shift+[(left bracket) several times to make your brush softer. This way, you can better disguise the edges of your cloning.

8. Continue painting over the fold lines in the upper-left corner. As you paint, you will see crosshairs representing the sampled area. Keep an eye on the crosshairs; you don't want to introduce unwanted areas into the image.

   It is not unusual to have to redefine the clone source over and over again. You may have to Alt/Option+click in the areas outside of the fold line repeatedly to find better-matched sources for cloning. You may even find that you Alt/Option+click and then paint, and then Alt/Option+click and paint again, until you conceal the fold mark.

   Don't forget some of the selection techniques that you learned in Lesson 5, "Making the Best Selections." You can activate the edge of the area to be retouched so that you can keep your clone stamping inside the image area and not cross into the white border (Figure 6-36).

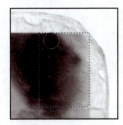

Figure 6-36: Create selections to help you control the cloning.

Take Note...

With the Clone Stamp tool, it is important to sample tonal areas that are similar to the tonal area you are covering. Otherwise, the retouching will look very obvious.

9. Choose File > Save. Keep this image open for the next part of this lesson.

The History panel

You can use the **History panel** to jump to previous states in an image. This is an important aid when retouching photos. Every action that is performed in Photoshop, is recorded as a state in the History panel. The History panel provides a way that you can selectively undo or go back to specific points in the history of a document. In this section, you will explore the History panel as it relates to the previous section, and then continue to utilize it as you work forward in Photoshop.

Step-by-Step	Follow these steps to use the History panel

1. Make sure that **ps0605_work.psd** is still open from the last section.

2. Choose Window > History. The History panel appears. As illustrated in Figure 6–37, grab the lower–right corner of the panel and pull it down to expand the panel and reveal all the previous states in History.

Figure 6–37: Resizing the History panel.

3. You see many Clone Stamp states, or a listing of any function that you performed while the image was open. As you click on each state, you reveal the image at that point in your work history. You can click back one state at a time, or you can jump to any state in the panel, including the top state, which is the state of the original image when it was first opened. You can utilize this as a strategy for redoing work that does not meet with your satisfaction.

4. If you need to redo some of the cloning that you did in the previous section, click on a state in the History panel for your starting point, and redo some of your work.

 Take Note...
All states in the History panel are deleted when the file is closed. If you want to save a state, click the Create new document button (⬚) to create a new file at the present history state.

5. Choose File > Save. Keep this file open for the next part of the lesson.

The Spot Healing Brush

The Spot Healing Brush tool paints with sampled pixels from an image and matches the texture, lighting, transparency, and shading of the pixels that are sampled to the pixels being retouched, or healed. Note that unlike the Clone Stamp tool, the Spot Healing Brush automatically samples from around the retouched area.

Certification Ready 4.5

How can you remove imperfections?

Follow these steps to use the Spot Healing Brush tool

Step-by-Step

1. With the **ps0605_work.psd** file still open, select View > Fit on Screen, or use the keyboard shortcut Ctrl+0 (zero) (Windows) or Command+0 (zero) (Mac OS).

2. Select the Zoom tool (🔍), then click and drag the lower-right section of the image to zoom into the lower-right corner as demonstrated in Figure 6-38.

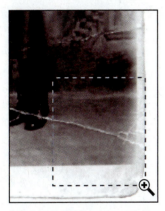

Figure 6-38: Click and drag with the Zoom tool.

Because you do not have to define a source with the Spot Healing tool, it can be easier to retouch. It is not the absolute answer to every retouching need, but it works well when retouching sections of an image that are not defined and detailed, like blemishes on skin or backgrounds.

3. Select the Spot Healing Brush tool (🖌), and then click and release repeatedly over the fold marks in the lower-right corner of the image. The tool initially creates a dark region, indicating the area that is to be retouched, but don't panic—it will blend well when you release the mouse. Now, using the Spot Healing Brush, repair the fold lines. Use the History panel to undo steps, if necessary. You can experiment with the brush size, sometimes a smaller brush size works better with this tool.

4. Choose File > Save. Keep this file open for the next part of this lesson.

The Healing Brush

The **Healing Brush tool** also lets you correct imperfections. Like the Clone Stamp tool, you use the Healing Brush tool to paint with pixels you sample from the image, but the Healing Brush tool also matches the texture, lighting, transparency, and shading of the sampled pixels. In this section, you will remove some defects in the girl's dress.

Step-by-Step	Follow these steps to use the Healing Brush tool

1. Make sure that **ps0605_work.psd** is still open from the last section, and choose View > Fit on Screen.

2. Select the Zoom tool, then click and drag over the bottom area of the girl's dress as shown in Figure 6–39.

Figure 6–39: Click and drag to zoom into the dress.

3. Click and hold on the Spot Healing Brush (✐) in the Tools panel to select the hidden tool, the Healing Brush (✐).

4. Position your cursor over an area near to, but outside, the fold line in the skirt, as you are going to define this area as your source. Hold down Alt (Windows) or Option (Mac OS), and click to define the source for your Healing Brush tool.

5. Now, paint over the fold line that is closest to the source area you defined.

6. Repeat this process; Alt/Option+click in appropriate source areas near the folds across the dress, then paint over the fold lines, using the Healing Brush tool (Figure 6–40). Don't forget to change the size using the left and right brackets, if necessary.

Figure 6–40: Define a source and then paint with the Healing Brush tool.

7. Choose File > Save, and leave this file open for the next part of this lesson.

Using the Patch tool

You may find that there are large areas of scratches or dust marks that need to be retouched. You can use the **Patch tool** to replace large amounts of an image with image data that you sample as your source. In this section, you will fix the large dusty area in the upper-left part of the image.

Follow these steps to use the Patch tool

Step-by-Step

1. With the **ps0605_work.psd** file still open, choose View Fit on Screen, or use the keyboard shortcut Ctrl+0 (zero) (Windows) or Command+0 (zero) (Mac OS).

2. Select the Zoom tool (🔍), and then click and drag to zoom into the upper-left area of the image as shown in Figure 6-41.

Figure 6-41: Click and drag to zoom into the upper-left corner.

3. Hold down on the Healing Brush tool (✐) and select the hidden Patch tool (⬤).

4. Click and drag a selection to select a small area with defects (Figure 6-42). As shown with Figure 6-43, click and drag that selection over an area of the image with fewer defects, to use that area as a source. The result is displayed in Figure 6-44.

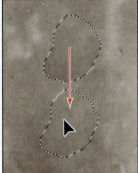

Figure 6-42: The original.   Figure 6-43: Drag with the Patch tool. Figure 6-44: The result.

5. Continue to make selections and patch with the Patch tool to clean up most of the dust marks in the upper-left corner of the image. If you find that the patch tool doesn't quite do the trick in certain instances, try the Content-Aware fill command by choosing Edit > Fill and choosing content-aware from the drop-down menu.

6. Choose File > Save. Keep the file open for the next part of this lesson.

Using the Clone Source panel

When using the Clone Source panel, you can set up to five clone sources for the Clone Stamp or Healing Brush tools to use. The sources can be from the same image you are working on or from other open images. Using the Clone Source panel, you can even preview the clone source before painting, and rotate and scale the source. In this section, you will clone the upper-left corner of the ps0605_work.psd image and rotate it to repair the upper-right corner of the image. You will also define a second clone source to add an art deco border around the edge of the image.

Step-by-Step	Follow these steps to use the Clone Source panel

1. Make sure that **ps0605_work.psd** is still open, and choose View > Fit on Screen.

2. Choose Window > Clone Source to open the Clone Source panel.

3. If it helps to zoom in to the image, press Ctrl+plus sign (Windows) or Command+plus sign (Mac OS), and then scroll to the upper-left corner.

    The Clone Source panel displays five icons, each representing a sampled source. You will start out using the first clone source, as illustrated in Figure 6-45.

Figure 6-45: *The Clone Source panel.*

4. Choose the Clone Stamp tool (⚖). Verify in the Options bar that the Mode is Normal and Opacity is 100 percent.

5. Press the] (Right bracket) until the Clone Stamp size is approximately 80 pixels. The size is indicated in the Options bar.

6. Click on the first Clone Source icon in the Clone Source panel (Figure 6-46) and position your cursor over the top-left corner of the image. As shown in Figure 6-47, hold down the Alt (Windows) or Option (Mac OS) key and click to define this corner as the first clone source.

You will now use this corner to replace the damaged corner in the upper right.

Figure 6-46*: Select the first Clone Source icon.*

Figure 6-47*: Alt/Option+click on the upper-left corner.*

7. If you zoomed into the upper-left corner, hold down the spacebar to turn your cursor into the Hand tool (🖐), then click and drag to the left. Think of the image as being a piece of paper that you are pushing to the left to see the upper-right corner of the image.

8. When you are positioned over the right corner, check the Show Overlay checkbox (if it is unchecked) in the Clone Source panel as shown in Figure 6-48. A ghosted image of your clone source is displayed as you can see in Figure 6-49. If necessary, hover over Opacity in the Clone Source panel and drag it to a lower level.

Note that you can uncheck the Clipped checkbox to see the entire clone source, but for this example, keep it checked.

Figure 6-48*: Check Show Overlay.*

Figure 6-49*: View your clone source before cloning.*

9. Now, type **90** in the Rotate text field in the Clone Source panel (Figure 6-50). The corner is rotated so that you can fit it in as a new corner in the upper-right area of the image (Figure 6-51).

Figure 6-50: Rotate your source 90 degrees.

Figure 6-51: View the results.

10. Verify that your brush size is approximately the width of the white border. You can preview the brush size by positioning your cursor over the white border. If you do not see the brush size preview, you may have your Caps Lock key selected. If necessary, make your brush smaller using the [(left bracket), or larger using the] (right bracket) keys repeatedly.

11. Make sure the corner is aligned with the outside of the underlying image (original upper-right corner) as shown in Figure 6-52 and Figure 6-53. Don't worry about aligning with the original inside border.

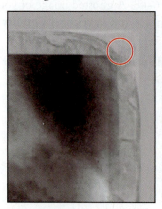 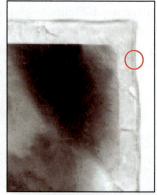

Figure 6-52: Align the corner before starting to clone.

Figure 6-53: Don't worry about aligning with the original inside border.

12. Start painting only the corner with the Clone Stamp tool. Now the corner has been added to the image. Uncheck the Show Overlay checkbox to better see your results.

13. Choose File > Save and keep this file open for the next part of this lesson.

Cloning from another source

In this section, you will open an image to clone a decoration, and then apply it to the **ps0605_work** image.

1. Choose File > Browse in Bridge and then navigate to the ps06lessons folder and double-click on the image named **ps0606.psd**. An image with a decorative border appears.

2. If the Clone Source panel is not visible, choose Window > Clone Source. Make sure that the Show Overlay checkbox is unchecked.

3. Select the Clone Stamp tool (♨) and then click on the second Clone Source icon as shown in Figure 6-54.

4. Position your cursor over the upper-left corner of the decorative border (Figure 6-55), and then hold down the Alt (Windows) or Option (Mac OS) key and click to define this area of the image as your second clone source.

Figure 6-54: Click the second Clone Source icon.

Figure 6-55: Define the correct area of the image as your second clone source.

5. Select the third Clone Source icon in the Clone Source panel.

6. Position your cursor over the upper-right corner of the decorative border, then hold down the Alt (Windows) or Option (Mac OS) key and click to define this area of the image as your third clone source.

7. Choose Window > **ps0605_work.psd** to bring that image to the front.

8. If you cannot see your entire **ps0605_work.psd** image, choose View > Fit on Screen, or use the keyboard shortcut Ctrl+0 (zero) (Windows) or Command+0 (zero) (Mac OS).

9. To make the clone of the decorative border appear *antique*, you will make some modifications to the Clone Stamp tool options. With the Clone Stamp tool selected, go to the Options bar and select Luminosity from the Mode drop-down menu. Type **50** into the Opacity text field.

10. Select the second Clone Source icon, and then check the Show Overlay check box in the Clone Source panel.

11. Position your cursor in the upper-left corner of the **ps0605_work.psd** image, and you see the preview of the decorative border. When you have the decorative corner positioned roughly in the upper-left corner, start painting. Try to follow the swirls of the design as best you can (Figure 6-56), but don't worry about being exact. The blending mode and opacity that you set in the Options bar helps to blend this into the original image. Keep in mind that when you paint with a lighter opacity, additional painting adds to the initial opacity. If it helps to see the results, turn off the Show Overlay checkbox (Figure 6-57). Check it to turn it back on for the remainder of this lesson.

Figure 6-56: Paint with the Clone tool. *Figure 6-57: The result.*

Now you will clone the third source to the upper-right corner of the image. This time, you can experiment with the position of the decoration on the image.

12. Navigate to the upper-right side of the **ps0605_work** image and select the third Clone Source icon from the Clone Source panel. You will now use the Clone Source panel to reposition the upper-right corner clone source.

13. Hold down Alt+Shift (Windows) or Option+Shift (Mac OS) and press the left, right, up, or down arrow key on your keyboard to nudge the overlay into a better position. No specific position is required for this lesson; simply find a location that you feel works well.

14. Once you have the clone source in position, start painting. Lightly paint the decoration into the upper-right corner. If you feel your brush is too hard-edged, press Shift+[(left bracket) to make it softer.

15. Choose File > Save. Keep the **ps0605_work.psd** file open for the next part of this lesson. Choose Window > **ps0606.psd** to bring that image forward. Then choose File > Close. If asked to save changes, select Don't Save.

Skill Summary

In this lesson you learned how to:	Objective
Demonstrate knowledge of color correction using Photoshop CS6	**2.4**
Demonstrate an understanding of and select the appropriate features and options required to implement a color management workflow	**3.5**
Demonstrate knowledge of retouching and blending images	**4.5**
Demonstrate knowledge of drawing and painting	**4.6**

Knowledge Assessment

True/False

Circle **T** if the statement is true or **F** if the statement is false.

T F **1.** Bright colors are always just as bright as the original color when printed.

T F **2.** Gamut represents the number of colors that can be represented, detected, or reproduced on a specific device.

T F **3.** A subtractive color model means that as ink is applied to a piece of paper, the colors absorb light.

T F **4.** Calibrating your monitor isn't really necessary when working in Photoshop.

T F **5.** Colors can shift during the printing process, ending up duller than they were originally.

T F **6.** A web press is a high-volume, high-speed printing press that prints on large rolls of paper rather than individual sheets.

T F **7.** When working in the Color Picker, the color options are only specific to print considerations.

T F **8.** Values can be typed in numerically to pick specific colors.

T F **9.** When using the Brush tool, you can hold down Alt (Windows) or Option (Mac OS) to switch to the Eyedropper tool to sample color.

T F **10.** You must work with the Brush presets that come with the program, unfortunately Photoshop does not offer a way to create custom brush presets at this time.

Multiple Choice

Select the best response for the following statements.

1. Which of the following is an additive color model?
   a. CMYK
   b. HSB
   c. RGB
   d. CMY

2. What is the advantage of working in RGB creatively versus working in CMYK?
   a. More menu selections and wider color range with RGB
   b. More color combinations are available
   c. Colors are brighter in RGB
   d. None of the above, there's no advantage

3. What is the keyboard shortcut to turn on Proof Colors?

   a. Ctrl+X (Windows) or Command+X (Mac OS)

   b. Ctrl+Y (Windows) or Command+Y (Mac OS)

   c. Shift+Y

   d. Tab+X

4. Which of the following is not a choice when picking a preset color profile in the Color Settings window?

   a. Japan Web Coated

   b. US Web Coated

   c. Australia Web Coated

   d. Uncoated

5. What color value is available when working in the Color Picker to choose a color?

   a. Lab

   b. HSB

   c. CMYK

   d. All of the above

6. Which tool can be used in conjunction to the Color Picker when you need to sample a color from an image?

   a. Lasso

   b. Eyedropper

   c. Magic Wand

   d. Marquee

7. The Brush tool uses which default base for determining the color applied to the tool?

   a. Background color

   b. Foreground color

   c. CMYK

   d. RGB

8. Soft Round, Hard Round, Round Point Stiff, and Round Angle Low Stiffness are all what?

   a. Color Presets

   b. Brush Presets

   c. Font attributes

   d. Filters

9. Which of the following is available when picking a blending mode?

   a. Multiply

   b. Screen

   c. Divide

   d. All of the above

10. What tool allows you to replace pixels in one area by sampling from another area?

    a. Clone Stamp

    b. Lasso

    c. Magic Wand

    d. Eyedropper

Competency Assessment

Creating Swatches from the Color Picker	Project 6-1

As usual, Photoshop offers a multitude of methods for completing a variety of tasks, including adding Swatches to your Swatch Library.

1. Open Photoshop.

2. Click on the Foreground color to open the Color Picker.

3. Pick a color, click Add to Swatches and give each swatch an appropriate name, repeat a few times.

4. Open the Swatches panel and take a look at the bottom colors.

5. Click on the panel menu in the Swatches panel, and choose Preset Manager. Using the shift key on your keyboard, select all of the new swatches that you created.

6. Click the Save Set button and save the file as **ps06_swatches.aco**, then click done.

7. These swatches can then be loaded onto any computer by going to the Preset Manager and choosing Load, and then navigating to the swatch file.

Trying Blending Modes on for Size	Project 6-2

You can always look up the definition of the Blending Modes in the Help section of the program, but to see them in action really paints the picture.

1. Open **ps0602.psd** in Photoshop. Create two layers, use the paint brush to paint one with a light color like yellow or white. Paint the other layer something dark like a burgundy or navy blue color. Be creative and paint some interesting designs on each layer.

2. With each of the new layers selected, try the different blending modes on each of the paint layers and notice how they interact.

3. Save the file as **ps0602_blend_modes.psd**.

Proficiency Assessment

Pushing the capabilities of the Clone Stamp tool	Project 6-3

The Clone Stamp tool is great for repairing photos as well as creating a different scene.

1. Open the **ps0605.psd** image in Photoshop.

2. Select the Clone Stamp tool.

3. Try to remove the chair in the image altogether. See how realistic you can make it look.

4. Save the file as **ps0605_clone.psd**.

Project 6-4	Adjusting History States in the Preferences

You can alter the number of History states that are available to you.

1. Open Photoshop and go to the preferences.

2. Select Performance and make adjustments to your History states. What is the maximum number of history states allowed? Create a new text file on your computer and enter the answer there. Save the file as **ps06_answer.txt**.

3. It is not recommended to set the history states to its maximum as it can because performance problems however change your history states to a number greater than the default.

Creating a Good Image

Key Terms

- Camera Raw
- Curves Adjustment
- DNG file
- highlight and shadow
- histogram

- midtones
- neutral
- red eye
- sharpening
- white and black point

Skill	Objective
Demonstrate knowledge of color correction using Photoshop CS6	2.4
Demonstrate knowledge of image-generating devices, their resulting image types, and how to access resulting images in Photoshop	2.5
Identify elements of the Photoshop CS6 user interface and demonstrate knowledge of their functions	3.1
Demonstrate knowledge of layers and masks	3.2
Demonstrate an understanding of and select the appropriate features and options required to implement a color management workflow	3.5
Adjust or correct the tonal range, color, or distortions of an image	4.4
Demonstrate knowledge of retouching and blending images	4.5
Demonstrate knowledge of filters	4.8

Business case

Many photos suffer from common photographic problems that distract from the subject matter in the image. Some problems are obvious such as color cast, poor contrast, or a case of red eye. Other considerations may not be as apparent though, including things you may not see so well with the naked eye. There are several features in Photoshop (like the Histogram) that will help you to accurately analyze an image and go deeper in terms of understanding what may need to be done to correct your picture.

Starting up

There are simple steps that you can take to create a brighter, cleaner, more accurate image. In this lesson, you'll learn how to use the Curves controls and how to sharpen your images. You'll learn what a neutral is and how to use it to color correct your images. You'll also have the opportunity to work with a Camera Raw image, using the improved Camera Raw plug-in. Although there are numerous corrections that you can make in Photoshop to improve an image, there is a lot to be said for taking the time to create a good scan, or a good digital

Certification Ready 2.5

What are some factors that determine the quality of an image when shooting using a digital camera?

capture using a digital camera. The digital camera itself can affect the quality of an image. The megapixels of the camera and the lens certainly determine quality to some extent. But more than that is how the user uses the camera. Knowing how to properly zoom, focus, and meter the subject also determines the overall quality of the iamge. The bottom line is, the more you do in the camera to get the image correct, the less you'll need to do in Photoshop and the better your image will look.

Although the following steps may at first seem time-consuming, they go quickly when not accompanied by the "whys and hows" included in this lesson. In fact, the process works almost like magic; a few steps and your image looks great!

Before starting, make sure that your tools and panels are consistent by resetting your preferences. See "Resetting Adobe Photoshop CS6 preferences" in the Starting up section of this book. You will work with several files from the ps07lessons folder in this lesson. Make sure that you have loaded the pslessons folder onto your hard drive from *http://www.wiley.com/college/sc/adobeseries*. See "Loading lesson files" in the Starting up section of this book.

Choosing your color settings

What many Photoshop users do not understand is the importance of knowing where an image is going to be published; whether for print, the Web, or even a digital device like a cell phone. You read a little about color settings in Lesson 6, "Painting and Retouching." where you discovered some of Photoshop's pre-defined settings. These help adapt the colors and values of an image for different uses. If not set properly, your images may appear very dark, especially in the shadow areas. For this lesson, you will use generic color settings that work well for a typical print image. You are also introduced to settings for other types of output, including the Web.

Step-by-Step	Follow these steps to choose your Color Settings

1. Choose Edit > Color Settings in Photoshop CS6. The Color Settings dialog box appears as displayed in Figure 7-1.

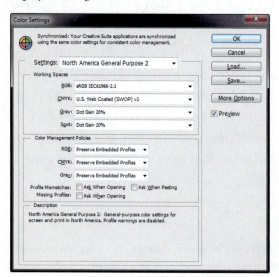

Figure 7-1: The Color Settings dialog box at its default settings.

2. As a default, North America General Purpose 2 is selected. This is a generic setting that basically indicates that Photoshop has no idea where you are using your image. Depending upon your image's final destination—print, web, or mobile, the results could vary widely. If you have another setting it is most likely due to setting your Color Settings in Adobe Bridge.

3. For this example make sure that the default settings of North America General Purpose 2 are selected. Press OK to exit the Color Settings dialog box.

Opening the file

Step-by-Step

Follow these steps to open an uncorrected image

1. Choose File > Browse in Bridge. When Adobe Bridge is forward, navigate to the ps07lessons folder that you copied onto your hard drive.

2. Locate the image named **ps0701.psd** and double-click on it to open it in Photoshop. You can also choose to right-click (Windows) or Ctrl+click (Mac OS) and select Open with Adobe Photoshop CS6. An image of a boy appears; because this is not a professional photograph, it offers many issues that need to be addressed.

Note the comparison of images: the one on the left in Figure 7-2 is uncorrected, and the one on the right in Figure 7-3 is corrected. You'll correct the image on the left in the next few steps.

Figure 7-2: The image before correction.   *Figure 7-3: The image after correction.*

3. Choose File > Save As. The Save As dialog box appears. Navigate to the ps07lessons folder on your hard drive. In the Name text field, type **ps0701_work**, choose Photoshop from the Format drop-down menu, and press Save. Leave the image open.

Why you should work in RGB

**Certification
Ready 3.5**

What is the difference
between assigning a
profile and converting
to a profile?

In this lesson, you start and stay in the RGB (Red, Green, Blue) color mode. There are two reasons for this: you find more tools are available in RGB mode, and changes to color values in RGB degrade your image less than if you are working in CMYK. If you were sending this image to a commercial printer, you would make sure your color settings were accurate, do all your retouching, and then convert your image to CMYK by choosing Image > Mode > CMYK Color.

Take Note...

If you want to see the CMYK preview while working in RGB, press Ctrl+Y (Windows) or Command+Y (Mac OS). This way, you can work in the RGB mode while you see the CMYK preview on your screen—often referred to as a soft proof. This is a toggle keyboard shortcut, meaning that if you press Ctrl+Y or Command+Y again, the preview is turned off. You may not see a difference in the image, depending upon the range of colors, but the title tab indicates that you are in CMYK preview mode by displaying /CMYK after the title of the image. For accurate rendering of color, you can use the command Edit > Assign profile which instructs Photoshop which color profile to use to render or preview the image correctly. When you want to convert an image to another color space such as RGB to CMYK, you can use the Edit > Convert to Profile command which will actually convert the image to a different color space and physically change the values in the file.

Reading a histogram

**Certification
Ready 2.4**

How do you interpret
color in an image by
using the Histogram
panel?

Understanding image histograms is probably the single most important concept to becoming familiar with Photoshop. A histogram can tell you whether your image has been properly exposed, whether the lighting is correct, and what adjustments will work best to improve your image. It will also indicate if the image has enough tonal information to produce a quality image. You will reference the Histogram panel throughout this lesson.

Step-by-Step   **Follow these steps to read a Histogram**

1. If your Histogram panel is not visible, choose Window > Histogram. The Histogram panel appears.

A **histogram** shows the tonal values that range from the lightest to the darkest in an image. Histograms can vary in appearance, but typically you want to see a full, rich, mountainous area representing tonal values. See the figures for examples of a histogram with many values, one with very few values, and the images relating to each.

Figure 7-4: A good histogram. *Figure 7-5: Image related to the good histogram..*

Figure 7-6: A poor histogram. *Figure 7-7: Image related to a poor histogram..*

Keep an eye on your Histogram panel. Simply doing normal corrections to an image can break up a histogram, giving you an image that starts to look posterized (when a region of an image with a continuous gradation of tone is replaced with several regions of fewer tones). Avoid breaking up the histogram by learning to use multi-function tools, like the Curves panel, and making changes using adjustment layers, that don't change your original image data.

2. To make sure that the values you read in Photoshop are accurate, select the Eyedropper tool (✐). Notice that the Options bar (across the top of the document window) changes to offer options specific to the Eyedropper tool. Click and hold on the Sample Size drop-down menu and choose 3 by 3 Average as demonstrated in Figure 7-8. This ensures a representative sample of an area, rather than the value of a single screen pixel.

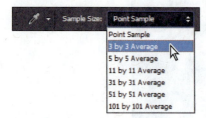

Figure 7-8: Set up the Eyedropper tool to sample more pixel information.

Making the Curve adjustment

You will now address the tonal values of this image. To do this, you will take advantage of the Curves Adjustments panel. The **Curves Adjustment** provides a way to adjust the tonal range of an image by altering the input and output values. Adjustment layers can be created by using the Adjustments panel, or in the Layers panel and include several tonal options including Clarity, Temperature, Exposure, Levels, Curves, and Shadow/Highlight. To help you see the relationship between Adjustment layers and other layers, you will create one using the Layers panel.

Follow these steps to make an adjustment in the Curves panel

1. If the Layers panel is not visible, choose Window > Layers. In this example you will use an Adjustment layer to make color corrections to this image. By using adjustments, you can make changes to an image's tonal values without destroying the original image data. See Chapter 9, "Taking Layers to the Max," for more information about how to use the Adjustments panel. Leave the Curves Adjustments panel open for the next section.

2. Click and hold on the Create New Fill or Adjustment Layer button (●) at the bottom of the Layers panel, select Curves (Figure 7-9), and release the mouse. The Properties panel appears with the Curves options visible in it as you can see below in Figure 7-10.

Figure 7-9: Select the Curves Adjustment.

Figure 7-10: The Curves dialog box appears.

If you have used previous versions of Photoshop, then keep in mind that adjustments work very differently than in previous versions and could possibly be confusing to both new and existing Photoshop users. Read the tips in Figure 7-11 before you proceed any further, and refer back to them if you have any problems following future steps.

Figure 7-11

A. *Adjustment affects all layers below (click to clip to layer).*
B. *Press to view previous state.* **C.** *Reset to adjustment defaults.*
D. *Toggle layer visibility.* **E.** *Delete this adjustment layer.*

Once you choose to create an adjustment layer, it appears in the Properties panel; an example is the Curves adjustment panel that you just revealed. If you accidently leave the Curves adjustment, you can just click on the Curves adjustment located in the Layers panel, and then locate the Window > Properties panel.

3. Click on the Properties tab and click and drag it out of the d╱   ╲ea toward the left. Undocking the panel this way allows you to reposition   ╲s panel. This is important in later steps when you need to see the image   ┐he Properties panel.

Take Note...
You can also see all adjustment layer options
links to the other adjustments that you ca

If you make an error, you can undo or
Command+Z (Mac OS). If you wan.
Reset to Adjustment Defaults button (⟲)

If you want to eliminate the adjustment layer,
button (🗑).

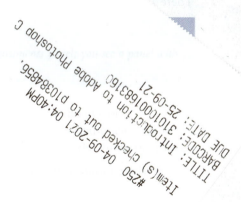

Defining the highlight and shadow

In this section, you'll set the **highlight and shadow** to predetermined values using the Set White Point and Set Black Point tools available in the Curves Adjustments panel. Before you do this, you'll determine what those values should be. This is a critical part of the process, as the default for the white point is 0, meaning that the lightest part of the image will have no value when printed, and any detail in this area will be lost.

Some images can get away with not having tonal values in very bright areas. Typically, reflections from metal, fire, and extremely sunlit areas, as well as reflections off other shiny objects like jewelry, do not have value in those reflective areas.

These are referred to as specular highlights. By leaving them without any value, it helps the rest of the image look balanced, and allows the shine to pop out of the image. See Figure 7-12 below for an example.

Figure 7-12: This image has specular highlights, which should be left with a value of zero.

Locating the White and Black Point

Back before digital imagery became so accessible, highly skilled scanner operators used large drum scanners to scan, set document dimensions, resolution, color mode, and color correct images. Back then, color experts followed many of the same steps that you will learn in this lesson. The most important step would be defining the tone curve based on what the operator thought should be defined as the lightest part of a tone curve, and the darkest.

There are many factors that can determine what appears to be a simple task. To produce the best image, you need to know where the image will be used; shiny coated paper, newsprint, or on screen only.

Before you get started, you will change a simple preference to make it easier for you to interpret the Curves Adjustment panel.

Step-by-Step | **Follow these steps to access the Curves Display Options**

1. With the Curves Adjustment panel open, click on the panel menu in the upper-right, and select Curves Display Options. The Curves Display Options dialog box appears.

2. Choose Show Amount of: Pigment/Ink % as demonstrated in Figure 7-13, then click OK.

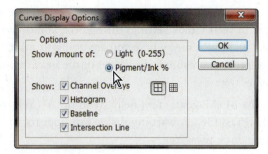

Figure 7-13: *Change the Curves panel to display curve as if it was based upon ink.*

Whether you work on print or web images it can be helpful to visually interpret the curves panel based upon ink, as this puts the lightest colors of the image in the lower left and the darkest part of the image in the upper –right.

Inputting the white and black point values

The process of defining values for the lightest and darkest points in your image is not difficult, but it helps if you know where the image is going to be used. If you have a good relationship with a printer, they can tell you what **white point** (lightest) or **black point** (darkest) values work best for their presses and material that you are printing on. Alternately, you can use the generic values suggested in this book. The values shown in this example are good for typical printing setups and for screen display.

Follow these steps to set the white and black point of an image	Step-by-Step

1. Double–click on the Set White Point button (✎) found in the Curves Adjustments panel; the Color Picker (Target Highlight Color) dialog box appears. Even though you are in RGB, you can set values in any of the color environments displayed in this window. In this example, you'll use CMYK values.

2. Type **5** in the C (Cyan) text field, **3** in the M (Magenta) text field and **3** in the Y (Yellow) text field. Leave K (Black) at 0 as show in Figure 7-14, and press OK. A warning dialog box appears; asking if you would like to save the target values, press Yes.

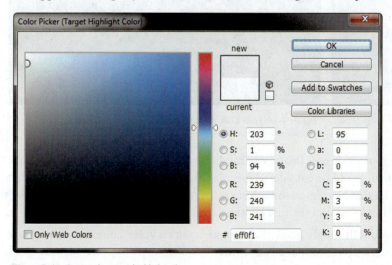

Figure 7-14: *Setting the target highlight color.*

3. Now, double-click on the Set Black Point button (🖊). The Color Picker (Target Shadow Color) dialog box appears.

If you have properly defined ink and paper in your Color Settings dialog box, you do not need to change the Black Point values. If you are not sure where you are going to print, or if you are going to use your image on screen, you can use the values in the next step of this exercise.

4. Type **65** in the C (Cyan) text field, **53** in the M (Magenta) text field, **51** in the Y (Yellow) text box and **95** in the K (Black) text field. Press OK. A warning dialog box appears, asking if you would like to save the target values; press Yes.

> **Take Note...**
> *It is important to note that your printer may be able to achieve a richer black than the one offered here. If you have a relationship with a printer, ask for their maximum black value and enter it here. Otherwise, use these standard values.*

5. Now, select the highlight slider (△), and then hold down Alt (Windows) or Option (Mac OS) and slide it to the right (Figure 7-15). Notice that the image appears posterized: this is the automatic clipping that is visible when you hold down the Alt/Option key. The clipping makes it easier to locate the darkest and lightest areas of an image—an essential task if you are trying to improve an image's tonal values.

6. In this example, the flames in the baseball hat are visible in the preview indicating that that area is recognized as one of the lightest parts of this image. If you are working on your own image and don't immediately see the lightest part of the image you can Alt/Option drag until a light part of your image is highlighted. Notice that there are other light areas in this image (Figure 7-16), but you are focusing on the primary subject, which is the boy.

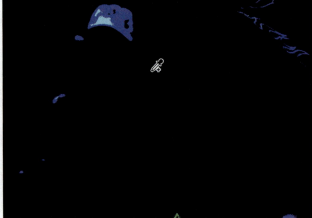

Figure 7-15: Select the highlight slider.   *Figure 7-16: Hold down the Alt/Option key while positioning the cursor over the image.*

If you are working on a different image you might notice that there are some other light areas that appear that would be considered specular highlights. It helps to remember that if a light point appears that belongs to something shiny, that you should ignore it and drag the slider to the right until you find the first legitimate (non-specular) highlight.

In the next step, you will simply mark this light area with a color sampler on the image. This way, you can refer back to it at a later time.

7. With the Set white point eyedropper (🖊) selected, hover over the image and hold down the Alt/Option key. The image now displays in the posterized view again.

Here is where it might get tricky: add the Shift key to this configuration, your cursor changes into the Color Sampler tool (🖊). As shown in Figure 7-17, click on the light area you found in the flame. A color sample appears on the image, but no change has yet been made to the image.

Figure 7-17: Add a color sample to mark the lightest point in the image.

Take Note...
If necessary, you can reposition the Color Sample by holding down the Shift key and dragging it to a new location.

8. Make sure that the Set white point eyedropper is still selected, and click on the color sampler you just placed. By clicking on the color sampler you defined this area of the image as the lightest point on the tone curve; it is adjusted to your newly defined highlight color values.

Take Note...
If this gives you unexpected results, you might have missed the color sampler. You can undo by pressing Ctrl+Z (Windows) or Command+Z (Mac OS), and then try clicking on the white area of the flame again. Keep in mind that the color sample that you dropped is only a marker; you do not have to move the sampler to change the highlight.

Now you will set the black, or darkest, part of your image.

9. If you are not seeing the entire image, press Ctrl+0 (zero) (Windows) or Command+0 (zero) (Mac OS) to make the image fit in the window.

10. Select the shadow slider (◆) on the Properties panel, and hold down the Alt/Option key and drag the slider toward the left as shown in Figure 7-18.

When dragging the slider (slowly), notice that clipping appears (Figure 7-19), indicating (with darker colors) the shadow areas of this image. Notice that there are many shadow areas in this image, but you see that the underside of the brim of the hat appears almost instantly, indicating that it is the darkest area in the image.

Figure 7-18: Select the shadow slider in the Properties panel, hold down Alt/Option key and drag slider to the left.

Figure 7-19: The clipping appears showing only the darker colors

> ### Take Note...
> *Depending upon the input device you might have, many areas display as the darkest areas of an image. This is an indication that the input device, whether a scanner or camera, does not have a large dynamic range of tonal values that it can record. You might have to take a logical guess as to what is the darkest part of the image.*

11. Make sure that the Set black point eyedropper is selected, and then hold down the Alt+Shift (Windows) or Option+Shift (Mac OS) keys and click on the darkest shadow area to leave a color sampler as displayed in Figure 7-20.

Figure 7-20: Hold down the Alt/Option key along with the Shift key and click on the darkest area.

12. With the Set black point eyedropper still selected, click on the color sampler that you dropped on the image. This has now been set as the darkest area of the image, using the values you input earlier in this example.

You should already see a difference in the image—a slight color cast has been removed and the colors look a little cleaner—but you are not done yet. The next step involves balancing the midtones (middle values) of the image.

13. Leave the Curves Properties panel visible for the next exercise.

Adjusting the midtones

In many cases, you need to lighten the **midtones** (middle values of an image) in order to make details more apparent in an image.

| **Follow these steps to adjust the midtones** | **Step-by-Step** |

1. Select the center (midtone area) of the white curve line and drag downward slightly to lighten the image in the midtones (Figure 7-21). This is the only visual correction that you will make to this image. You want to be careful that you do not adjust too much, as you can lose valuable information.

Figure 7-21

A. *Quarter tones.* **B.** *Midtones.* **C.** *Three-quarter tones.*

2. Add a little contrast to your image by clicking on the three-quarter tone area of the white curve line (the area between the middle of the curve and the top, as shown in Figure 7-22), then clicking and dragging up slightly. Again, this is a visual correction, so don't make too drastic a change. See the outcome of this change in Figure 7-23.

Figure 7-22: Click and drag the three-quarter tone up slightly.

Figure 7-23: The lightened image.

3. Keep the Curves Properties panel open for the next section of this lesson.

Take Note...

You can usually see a color cast by looking at the white and gray areas of an image, but, in some cases, you may not have any gray or white objects in your image. If these are art images, you may not want to neutralize them (for example, orange sunsets on the beach, or nice yellow candlelight images). Use the technique shown in this lesson at your discretion. It helps with a typical image, but it takes practice and experience to correct for every type of image.

Understanding neutral colors

A **neutral** is essentially anything in the image that is gray: a shade of gray, or even light to dark grays. A gray value is a perfect tool to help you measure color values, as it is composed of equal amounts of red, green, and blue. Knowing this allows you to pick up color inaccuracies by reading values in the Photoshop Info panel, rather than just guessing which colors need to be adjusted.

The first image you see below is definitely not correct. You can tell this by looking at the Info panel and seeing that the RGB values are not equal. In the second image, they are almost exactly equal. By looking at only the RGB values, you can tell that the image on the bottom is much more balanced than the image on the top.

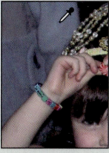

Figure 7-24: The neutrals in this image aren't balanced.

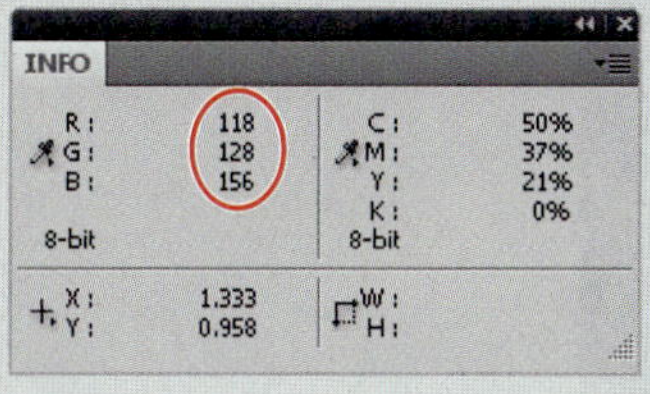

Figure 7-25: This is evident because the RGB values are not equal in value.

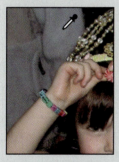

Figure 7-26: The neutrals in this image are balanced.

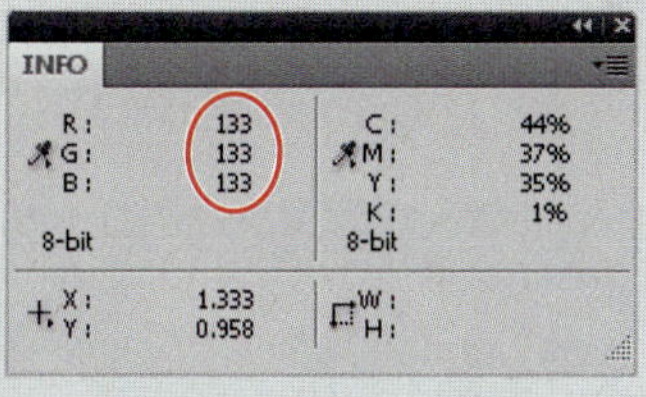

Figure 7-27: This is evident because the RGB values are equal in value.

Learning More

Take Note...

The power of the Curves panel also applies to selections. A common technique with portraits is to make a selection of the subject's face and then apply corrections.

You can quickly make a selection of a subject's face by choosing Select > Color Range and then click the Select menu and choose Skin Tones. For further refinement you could also check the "Detect Faces" checkbox.

Certification Ready 4.4

How do you make selections based on a color range?

Setting the neutral

In this section, you'll balance the neutrals in the image.

| Step-by-Step | Follow these steps to set the neutral point of an image |

1. With the Curves Properties panel still open, set another Color Sampler marker by Shift+clicking on the gray area on the baseball that is located in lower-right corner of the image (Figure 7-28). In your images, you might find a neutral in a shadow on a white shirt, a gray piece of equipment, or a counter top.

Figure 7-28: *Find a neutral gray in the image.*

Take Note...
Some photographers like to include a gray card (available at photo supply stores) in their images to help them color-balance their images.

2. If the Info panel is not open, choose Window > Info. The Info panel appears.

   In the Info panel, you see general information about RGB and CMYK values, as well as pinpoint information about the three Color Sampler markers you have created. You'll focus only on the #3 marker, as the first two were to indicate highlight and shadow.

Notice that to the right of the #3 marker in the Info panel, there are two values separated by a forward slash. You'll focus only on the set of values to the right of the slash. Depending upon where you clicked in the gray area, you could have different values. The numbers to the left of the forward slash are the values before you started making adjustments in the Curves panel. The numbers to the right of the forward slash are the new values that you are creating with your curve adjustments.

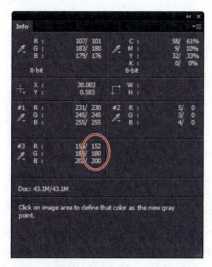

Figure 7-29: *Focus on the values to the right of the forward slash.*

3. Select the Set Gray Point button (✏).

4. Click once on the #3 marker you created as shown in Figure 7-30. The new color values may not be exactly the same, but they come closer to matching each other's values as you can see in Figure 7-31.

Figure 7-30: *Click once on the #3 marker.*

Figure 7-31: *The new color values should come close to matching each other's values..*

Take Note...
If you want more advanced correction, you can enter each of the individual color curves and adjust them separately by dragging the curve up or down, while watching the values change in the Info panel.

Certification Ready 4.4

How can you modify tonal adjustments using an adjustment layer?

5. Press Ctrl+S (Windows) or Command+S (Mac OS) to save your work file.

6. If your Layers panel is not visible, choose Window > Layers. On the Layers panel, click on the Visibility icon (👁) to the left of the Curves 1 adjustment layer to toggle off and on the curves adjustment you just made (Figure 7-32). Make sure that the Curves layer's visibility is turned back on before you move on to the next section.

Figure 7-32: *Click on the Visibility icon to turn off and on the adjustment layer.*

Certification Ready 4.4

When would you choose to adjust tone manually vs. using the auto controls?

7. Choose File > Save. Keep this file open for the next part of this lesson.

You've just made a lot of adjustments to the tonal values of this image and have seen how powerful these adjustments can be. These adjustments are necessary for images with poor tones or are badly damaged. Photoshop does contain some tools that can often do a really good job automatically. On your own, experiment with the Auto button found in many of the Adjustment panels and feel free to try the Auto Tone, Auto Contrast, and Auto Color options found under the Image menu as well.

Sharpening your image

Certification Ready 4.5

How do you sharpen an image?

Now that you have adjusted the tonal values of your image, you'll want to apply some sharpening to the image. Sharpening is just one of many filters that can be used in Photoshop to improve an image. Other useful filters for digital photographers include lens correction, adaptive wide angle, and iris blur. Each filter has specific uses for different situations.

Certification Ready 4.8

Which filter would you use to increase the detail of an image?

Sharpening is a process where an image is improved by enhancing the detail in areas of an image to improve clarity. In this section, you'll discover how to use unsharp masking. It is a confusing term, but is derived from the traditional (pre–computer) technique used to sharpen images.

Certification Ready 3.2

How do you flatten layers?

To simplify this example, you'll flatten the adjustment layer into the Background layer. Flattening layers combines them into a combined image. Once layers are flattened, they can no longer be edited but for this exercise it will simplify the sharpening process later in this lesson.

Certification Ready 3.2

What are the differences between a layered file and a flattened file?

Take Note...

If you are an advanced user, you can avoid flattening by selecting the Background layer, Shift+clicking on the Curves 1 layer, then right-clicking (Windows) or Ctrl+clicking (Mac OS) and choosing Convert to Smart Object. This embeds the selected layers into your Photoshop file, but allows you to view and work with them as one layer. If further editing is needed, you can simply double-click on the Smart Object layer, and the layers open in their own separate document.

Follow these steps to sharpen an image

1. Choose Flatten Image from the Layers panel menu, as shown in Figure 7-33 below.

Figure 7-33: Choose Flatten Image from the panel menu.

2. Choose View > Actual pixels. The image may appear very large; you can pan the image by holding down the spacebar and pushing the image around on the screen. Position the image so that you can see an area with detail, such as one of the eyes. Note that you should be in Actual Pixel view when using most filters, or you may not see accurate results on your screen.

> **Take Note...**
> *Hold down the spacebar, and click and drag on the image area to adjust the position of the image in the window.*

3. Choose Filter > Convert for Smart Filters (this step is unnecessary if you already converted your layers into a Smart Object). If an Adobe Photoshop dialog box appears informing you that the layer is being converted into a Smart Object, press OK. Smart Objects allow you to edit filters more freely. Read more about Smart Objects in Lesson 10, "Getting Smart in Photoshop." An icon (⊡) appears in the lower-right corner of the layer thumbnail, indicating that this is now a Smart Object.

4. Choose Filter > Sharpen > Unsharp Mask. The Unsharp Mask dialog box appears.

You can click and drag inside the preview pane to change the part of the image that appears there.

Lesson 7

Learning More	Unsharp masking defined

Unsharp masking is a traditional film compositing technique used to sharpen edges in an image. The Unsharp Mask filter corrects blurring in the image, and it compensates for blurring that occurs during the resampling and printing process. Applying the Unsharp Mask filter is recommended whether your final destination is in print or online.

The Unsharp Mask filter assesses the brightness levels of adjacent pixels and increases their relative contrast: it lightens the light pixels that are located next to darker pixels, as it darkens those darker pixels. You set the extent and range of lightening and darkening that occurs, using the sliders in the Unsharp Mask dialog box. When sharpening an image, it's important to understand that the effects of the Unsharp Mask filter are far more pronounced on-screen than they appear in high-resolution output, such as a printed piece.

In the Unsharp Mask dialog box, you have the following options:

Amount determines how much the contrast of pixels is increased. Typically an amount of 150 percent or more is applied, but this amount is very reliant on the subject matter. Overdoing Unsharp Mask on a person's face can be rather harsh, so that value can be set lower (150 percent) as compared to an image of a piece of equipment, where fine detail is important (300 percent+).

Radius determines the number of pixels surrounding the edge pixels that are affected by the sharpening. For high-resolution images, a radius between 1 and 2 is recommended. If you are creating oversized posters and billboards, you might try experimenting with larger values.

Threshold determines how different the brightness values between two pixels must be before they are considered edge pixels and thus are sharpened by the filter. To avoid introducing unwanted noise into your image, a minimum Threshold setting of 10 is recommended.

5. Type **150** into the Amount text box. Because this is an image of a child, you can apply a higher amount of sharpening without bringing out unflattering detail.

> ***Take Note...***
> *Click and hold on the Preview pane to turn the preview off and on as you make changes.*

6. Type **1** in the Radius text field and **10** in the Threshold text field as shown in Figure 7-34, and click OK.

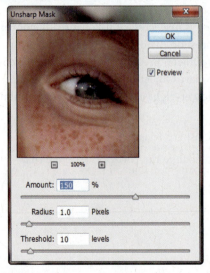

Figure 7-34: Using the Unsharp Mask dialog box.

7. Choose File > Save. Keep the file open for the next part of this lesson.

> **Take Note...**
> *Because you used the Smart Filter feature, you can turn the visibility of the filter off and on at any time by clicking on the visibility icon to the left of Smart Filters in the Layers panel. You will find out how to apply masks and use other incredible Smart Object features in Lesson 10, "Getting Smart in Photoshop."*

Comparing your image with the original

You can use the History panel in Adobe Photoshop for many functions. In this section, you'll use the History panel to compare the original image with your finished file.

Follow these steps to use the History panel   **Step-by-Step**

1. If the History panel is not visible, choose Window > History.

2. Make sure that you have the final step you performed selected. In this case, it should be the Unsharp Mask filter. If you have some extra steps because you were experimenting with the Smart Filter thumbnail, just click on the Unsharp Mask state in the History panel.

3. Click on the Create New Document from Current State button (⊞) at the bottom of the History panel. A new file is created.

4. Click back on your original image, **ps0701_work.psd**, and press Ctrl+0 (zero) (Windows) or Command+0 (zero) (Mac OS) to fit the image on your screen.

5. Click on the original snapshot located at the top of the History panel. This returns you to the original state.

6. Select Window > Arrange > 2-up Vertical to place the images side by side. Zoom into the area surrounding the small child to see that it appears almost as if a cast of color has been lifted from the image, producing a cleaner, brighter image as shown in Figures 7–35 and 7–36.

Figure 7–35*: Corrected image.*   ***Figure 7–36****: Original image..*

7. Choose File > Save, and then File > Close to close your ps0701_work files.

8. Choose File > Close for the unsharp mask file created from your History panel. When asked to save the changes, click No, or Don't Save.

Congratulations! You have finished the color-correction part of this lesson.

Taking care of red eye

Red eye typically occurs when you use a camera with a built-in flash. The light of the flash occurs too fast for the iris of the eye to close the pupil, revealing the blood-rich area alongside the iris. There are many cameras that come with features to help you avoid this phenomenon, and most professional photographers don't experience this, as they typically use a flash that is not directly positioned in front of the subject. Also, there is a solution that is built right into Photoshop.

Step-by-Step

Follow these steps to use the Red Eye tool

1. Open the image named **ps0702.psd**, click and hold down on the Spot Healing Brush tool ( ) and drag down to select the Red Eye tool ( ).

   Choose File > Save As. The Save As dialog box appears. Navigate to the ps07lessons folder on your hard drive. In the Name text field, type **ps0702_work**, choose Photoshop from the Format drop-down menu, and press Save.

2. Click and drag, creating a marquee around the eye on the left side of the image; when you release the mouse, the red eye is removed. If you missed a section, you can repeat this without damaging the areas that are not part of the red eye.

3. Now, click and drag to surround the other eye (Figure 7-37), again repeating to add any areas that are not corrected.

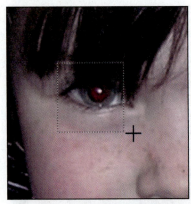

Figure 7-37: Click and drag, surrounding the iris of an eye, using the Red Eye tool to get rid of the red.

4. Choose File > Save, or use the keyboard shortcut Ctrl+S (Windows) or Command+S (Mac OS).

5. Choose File > Close to close this file.

Using the Camera Raw plug-in

In this section, you'll discover how to open and make changes to a Camera Raw file. Camera Raw really deserves more than can be covered in this lesson, but this will give you an introduction, and hopefully get you interested enough to investigate further on your own.

What is a Camera Raw file?

A **Camera Raw** image file contains the unprocessed data from the image sensor of a digital camera; essentially, it is a digital negative of your image. By working with a Raw file, you have greater control and flexibility, while still maintaining the original image file. The Camera RAW format can also be used to create 32-bit HDR (High Dynamic Range) images where multiple exposures of an image can be combined to create a wider tonal range than can typically be achieved with standard digital photography.

The Raw format is proprietary and differs from one camera manufacturer to another, and sometimes even between cameras made by the same manufacturer. This differentiation can lead to many issues, mostly that you also need the camera's proprietary software to open the Raw file, unless, of course, you are using Photoshop CS6's Camera Raw plug-in. The Camera Raw plug-in supports more than 150 camera manufacturers, and allows you to open other types of files into the Camera Raw plug-in, including TIFFs and JPEGs. If you are not sure whether your camera is supported by the Camera Raw plug-in, go to *adobe.com* and type **Support Camera Raw cameras** in the Search text field.

Follow these steps to open a Camera Raw image

1. Choose File > Browse in Bridge to launch Adobe Bridge. Navigate to the ps07lessons folder, inside the pslessons folder on your hard drive. Select the image named **ps0703.CR2**. This is a Camera Raw file from a Canon Rebel digital camera. Note that each manufacturer has its own extensions; the CR2 extension is unique to Canon cameras.

2. Double-click on the **ps0703.CR2** file to automatically launch and open the file in Photoshop's Camera Raw plug-in (Figure 7-38).

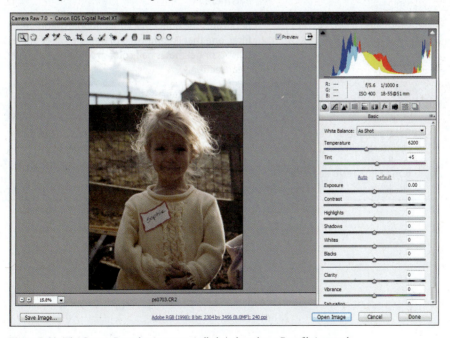

Figure 7-38: *The Camera Raw plug-in automatically launches when a Raw file is opened.*

> **Take Note...**
> *If you attempt to open a Raw file that is not recognized by the Camera Raw plug-in, you may need to update your plug-in. Go to adobe.com to download the latest version.*

Lesson 7

Certification Ready 2.5

What are some of the features of Camera Raw?

When the Camera Raw plug-in opens, you see a Control panel across the top, as well as additional tabbed panels on the right. See the table for definitions of each button in the Control panel.

Icon	Tool Name	Use
🔍	Zoom (Z)	Increases or decreases the magnification level of a Camera Raw preview.
✋	Hand (H)	Allows you to reposition a Raw image, when magnified, in the preview pane.
🖊	White Balance (I)	Balances colors in a Raw image when you click on a neutral gray area in the image.
✏	Color Sampler (S)	Reads image data and leaves markers on the Raw image.
⊙	Targeted Adjustment	Allows you to make changes in Curves, Hue, Saturation, Luminance and control grayscale conversion by clicking and dragging on the image.
⊞	Crop (C)	Crops a Raw image right in the preview pane.
⟋	Straighten (A)	Realigns an image.
⟋	Spot Removal (B)	Heals or clones a Raw image in the preview pane.
⊙	Red-Eye Removal (E)	Removes red eye from a Raw image.
✎	Adjustment Brush (K)	Paints adjustments of color, brightness, contrast, and more.
◼	Graduated Filter (G)	Replicates the effect of a conventional graduated filter, one that is composed of a single sheet of glass, plastic, or gel that is half color graduating to a half clear section.
☰	Open preferences dialog box (Ctrl+K, Command+K)	Changes preferences, such as where XMP files are saved.
↺	Rotate image 90 degrees counterclockwise (L)	Rotates an image 90 degrees counter-clockwise.
↻	Rotate image 90 degrees clockwise (R)	Rotates an image 90 degrees clockwise.

You'll have an opportunity to use several of these tools in the next lesson. Before starting, have a look at the panels on the right, and learn a bit about how they are used (Figure 7-39).

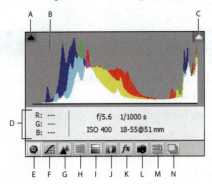

Figure 7-39

A. Shadow Clipping Warning button. B. Histogram. C. Highlight Clipping Warning button. D. Info.
E. Basic panel. F. Tone Curve panel. G. Detail. H. HSL/Grayscale. I. Split Toning. J. Lens Corrections.
K. Effects. L. Camera Calibration. M. Presets. N. Snapshots.

A. Shadow Clipping Warning button: Indicates if an image is underexposed, with large areas of shadow being clipped. Clipped shadows appear as a solid dark area if not corrected using the exposure controls.

B. Histogram: Shows you where image data resides on the tone curve.

C. Highlight Clipping Warning button: Indicates if an image is overexposed, with large areas of highlight being clipped. A clipped highlight appears as a solid white area if not corrected using the exposure controls.

D. Info: Displays the RGB readings that enable you to check your colors and balance.

E. Basic panel: Contains the main controls, such as White Balance, Exposure, and Fill Light, among others.

F. Tone Curve panel: Adjusts the tone curve. The Point tab must be brought to the front (by clicking on it) to activate point-by-point controls.

G. Detail: Adjusts Sharpening and Noise Reduction.

H. HSL/Grayscale: Allows you to create grayscale images with total control over individual colors and brightness.

I. Split Toning: Introduces additional color tones into image highlights and shadows.

J. Lens Correction: Corrects for lens problems, including fringing and vignetting.

K. Effects: Applies filters and offers the ability to create post-cropping vignetting.

L. Camera Calibration: With the Camera Calibration tab, you can shoot a Macbeth color reference chart (available from camera suppliers). Then you can set Color Samplers on the reference chart, and use the sliders to balance the RGB values shown in the Info section. Settings can be saved by selecting the Presets tab and clicking on the New Preset button in the lower-right corner, or by choosing Save Settings from the panel menu.

M. Presets: Stores settings for future use in the Presets tab.

N. Snapshots: Offers ability to save multiple versions of an image.

Using Camera Raw controls

In this section, you'll use a few of the controls you just reviewed.

Follow these steps to modify a Camera Raw image

1. Make sure that the Camera image is back to its original settings by holding down the Alt (Windows) or Option (Mac OS) key and clicking on Reset, located at the bottom-right corner. The Cancel button becomes Reset when you hold down the Alt or Option key.

2. The first thing you are going to do with this image is balance the color. You can do this with the White Balance controls. In this instance, you'll keep it simple by selecting the White Balance tool (✐) from the Control panel.

    A good neutral to balance from is the light gray section of the name tag. With the White Balance tool selected, click on the white part of the name tag as demonstrated in Figure 7-40. The image is balanced, using that section of the image as a reference.

Figure 7-40: *With the White Balance tool selected, click on the name tag.*

You'll now adjust some of the other settings available in the Basic tab, to make the image more colorful while still maintaining good color balance.

The image looks a bit underexposed; the girl's face is somewhat dark. You'll bring out more detail in the girl's face by increasing the exposure and then bringing down the highlights to recover some of the image detail.

3. Click on the Exposure slider and drag to the left until you reach the +.80 mark, or type **.80** in the Exposure text field.

4. Click on the Contrast slider in the Basic tab and drag to the right to about the +32 mark, or type **32** into the Contrast text field.

5. Recover some of the lost highlights by clicking and dragging the Highlight slider left, to the –85 mark, or by typing **–85** in the Highlight text field.

6. Increase the contrast in the image by clicking and dragging the contrast slider right, to the +60 mark, or by typing **60** into the Contrast text field.

    Increase the richness of color by using the Vibrance slider. Do not increase it too much if you plan on printing the image, as oversaturated, rich colors do not generally convert well to CMYK.

7. Drag the Vibrance slider right, over to the 25 mark as shown in Figure 7-41, or type **25** into the Vibrance text field.

Figure 7-41: Drag the Vibrance slider to the right.

8. Select the Crop tool (⌶) from the Control panel, and click and drag to select an image area that is a little closer to the girl's face as demonstrated in Figure 7-42. Double-click in the image area to accept the crop.

Figure 7-42: Cropping an image in the Camera Raw Plug-in.

Now you'll save your settings.

9. Click on the Presets tab. Press the Save Preset button (⌑) in the lower-right corner of the Presets panel. Type the name **Canon_outdoor** and press OK.

10. Keep the Camera Raw Plug-in window open for the next step.

Saving a DNG file

Next, you will save your image as a DNG file. A **DNG file** is essentially a digital negative file that maintains all the corrections you have made, in addition to the original unprocessed Raw image.

Adobe created the DNG format to provide a standard for Raw files. As mentioned previously, camera vendors have their own proprietary Raw formats and their own extensions and proprietary software to open and edit them. The DNG format was developed to provide a standard maximum-resolution format that all camera vendors would eventually support directly in their cameras. Right now, DNG provides you with the opportunity to save your original Camera Raw files in a format that you should be able to open for many years to come. Note that you can reopen the DNG over and over again, making additional changes without degrading the original image.

Step-by-Step	Follow these steps to save a DNG image

1. Press the Save Image button in the lower-left corner of the Camera Raw dialog box. The Save Options dialog box appears.

2. Leave the Destination set to Save in Same Location, then click on the arrow to the right of the second drop-down menu in the File Naming section and choose 2 Digit Serial Number as you can see in Figure 7-43. This will automatically number your files, starting with the original document name followed by 01.

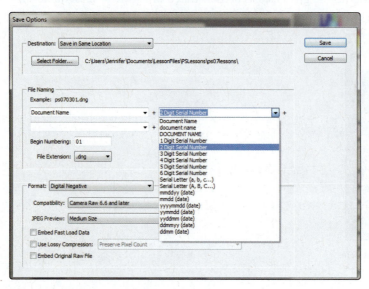

Figure 7-43: *The Camera Raw Save Options dialog box.*

3. Press Save. You are returned to the Camera Raw dialog box.

4. Click the Open Image button. The adjusted and cropped image is opened in Photoshop. You can continue working on this file. If you save the file now, you will see the standard Photoshop Save As dialog box. Note that whatever you save is a copy of the original Camera Raw file—your DNG file remains intact.

Reopening a DNG file

You'll now use Bridge to access your saved DNG file.

Follow these steps to open a DNG image	Step-by-Step

1. Access Bridge by choosing File > Browse in Bridge.

2. If you are not still in the ps07lessons folder, navigate to it now. Double-click on the file you have created, **ps070301.dng**.

   Note that the file reopens in the Camera Raw plug-in dialog box and that you can undo and redo settings, as the original has remained intact.

   Congratulations! You have completed the lesson on Camera Raw images.

Skill Summary

In this lesson you learned how to:	Objective
Demonstrate knowledge of color correction using Photoshop CS6	**2.4**
Demonstrate knowledge of image-generating devices, their resulting image types, and how to access resulting images in Photoshop	**2.5**
Identify elements of the Photoshop CS6 user interface and demonstrate knowledge of their functions	**3.1**
Demonstrate knowledge of layers and masks	**3.2**
Demonstrate an understanding of and select the appropriate features and options required to implement a color management workflow	**3.5**
Adjust or correct the tonal range, color, or distortions of an image	**4.4**
Demonstrate knowledge of retouching and blending images	**4.5**
Demonstrate knowledge of filters	**4.8**

Knowledge Assessment

True/False

Circle **T** if the statement is true or **F** if the statement is false.

T F 1. Your default working profile controls which color profiles will be used to render color on screen.

T F 2. When working in CMYK, your colors will degrade less than if you were to work in RGB.

T F 3. Tonal range values are displayed in the Histogram panel from the lightest (on the left) to darkest range of an image (on the right) of the Histogram.

T F 4. Black Point Compensation is generally used to retain detail in the shadow areas of an image when converting from one color space to another.

T F 5. You use the set white point and black point eyedropper tools to establish the opacity range of an image.

T F 6. A neutral is anything in the image that is gray, or even light to dark grays.

T F 7. You can toggle an Adjustment layer on and off by clicking on the Visibility icon for the layer.

T F 8. Adjustment layers and the layers they're affecting can never be merged, you must keep them as separate layers.

T F 9. The Unsharp Mask filter is used for correcting the blurriness of an image.

T F 10. Red eye typically occurs when the sun is out and is reflecting in people's eyes.

Multiple Choice

Select the best response for the following statements.

1. What are the default Color Settings that Photoshop first assigns unless you change it under Edit > Color Settings?
   a. North America Prepress 2
   b. North America General Purpose 2
   c. North America Newspaper
   d. North America Web / Internet

2. A histogram can convey which of the following information?
   a. If your image has proper exposure
   b. Whether the lighting was correct
   c. What adjustments will work best to improve the image
   d. All of the above

3. 3 by 3 Average, 5 by 5 Average, and 31 by 31 Average are all values behind which tool?

   a. Magic Wand
   b. Brush
   c. Eyedropper
   d. Crop

4. When using the Set white or black point eyedropper, what side tool do you get when you hold down Alt/Option + Shift?

   a. Color Sampler
   b. Color Removal
   c. Tonal Correction
   d. Hand

5. If you wanted to adjust your image to increase detail in the dark areas of an image, which tonal areas would you adjust?

   a. Highlights
   b. Midtones
   c. Shadows
   d. All of the above

6. You can usually see a color cast by looking at which color areas of an image?

   a. Gray or white
   b. White or black
   c. White or yellow
   d. Black or light blue

7. RGB, CMYK, Width, Height, X and Y coordinates are all properties displayed in which panel?

   a. Image Size
   b. Color Settings
   c. Info
   d. None of the above

8. In order to apply the Smart Filters feature, the object will first be converted to a:

   a. Flattened image
   b. JPEG
   c. Smart Object
   d. Filtered Object

9. Which panel is used when you want to backtrack and check out each stage of editing you've been working on in your image?

   a. Info
   b. Options
   c. History
   d. Adjustments

Lesson 7

10. What file format contains unprocessed data from the image sensor of a digital camera?

    a. JPEG

    b. PNG

    c. TIFF

    d. Camera Raw

Competency Assessment

Project 7-1	Levels versus Curves

Levels is a create feature to use for making quick yet accurate adjustments to the tonal range of an image in Photoshop.

1. Open the **ps0702.psd** image in Photoshop.

2. Choose Image > Adjustments > Levels or add a Levels Adjustment Layer to the image.

3. Work with the Shadow, Midtone, and Highlight slider controls in the Input Levels section to make adjustments to the tonality. Use the displayed histogram in the Input Levels section to compare the tonal value of the image to the new adjustment location.

4. Save the file as **ps0702_levels.psd**.

Project 7-2	Color Channels

So far the Curves have affected the whole RGB color range, what happens when you alter a specific color channel?

1. Open the **ps0701.psd** image in Photoshop.

2. Create a Curves Adjustment layer.

3. Instead of leaving the color channel on RGB, change it to Red and starting making adjustments. Note how the adjustments now affect the individual color channels instead of the entire image. Add a creative color cast to the image in this way.

4. Save the file as **ps0701_curves.psd**.

Proficiency Assessment

Project 7-3	Try out Smart Sharpen

Smart Sharpen is another choice to sharpen an image besides Unsharp Mask.

1. Open the **ps0701.psd** image in Photoshop.

2. Choose Filter > Convert for Smart Filters. Under the Sharpen filters, use the Smart Sharpen filter to apply this filter as a Smart Filter. Adjust the settings to your liking.

3. Save the file as **ps0701_smart_sharpen.psd**.

| Flattening Images and Merging Layers | Project 7-4 |

Flattening an image will merge all the visible layers. You can be a bit more selective about the process.

1. Open the **ps0702.psd** image in Photoshop.

2. Add several text layers to the document. Be creative, rotate the text, change the color, change the font, etc.

3. Save this file as **ps0702_live_text.psd**. Choose File > Save As, and save this file as **ps0703_flat_text.psd**.

4. Select all of the text layers in the Layers panel, and choose Merge Layers from the panel menu in the Layers panel. Save the file.

5. Discuss with your teacher or other students about the advantages and disadvantages of each method of working: Flattened vs. Live text. Is there another way that you could work with these text layers to achieve the best of both methods?

Getting to Know Layers

Key Terms

- Align and Distribute features
- clipping mask
- composition
- layer mask
- layer styles
- Visibility icon
- type layer

Skill	Objective
Demonstrate knowledge of project management tasks and responsibilities	1.3
Demonstrate knowledge of layers and masks	3.2
Demonstrate knowledge of working with selections	4.1
Demonstrate knowledge of type	4.7
Demonstrate knowledge of filters	4.8

Business case

The concept of layers is key to unlocking much of Photoshop's potential. Your projects have been pretty good so far, but now you'd like to challenge yourself as a designer and understand more about combining images together, creating layer-centric effects and understanding how to separate one image from another. Working with filters, layer styles and masks will provide you with the chance to accomplish effective layering - maximizing the edit-ability of your images.

Starting up

Before starting, make sure that your tools and panels are consistent by resetting your preferences. See "Resetting Adobe Photoshop CS6 preferences" in the Starting up section of this book.

You will work with several files from the ps08lessons folder in this lesson. Make sure that you have loaded the pslessons folder onto your hard drive from *http://www.wiley.com/college/sc/adobeseries*. See "Loading lesson files" in the Starting up section of this book.

Discovering layers

**Certification
Ready 3.2**

What are some of
the different types of
layers available?

**Certification
Ready 3.2**

How can you merge
two layers into one?

**Certification
Ready 1.3**

What are some
deliverables that may
be produced during a
project?

**Certification
Ready 3.2**

What is the difference
between hiding and
deleting a layer?

Think of layers as clear sheets of film, each containing its own image content. Layers can be stacked on top of each other, and you can see through the transparent area of each layer to view the content on the layers below. Each layer is independent of the others and can have its contents changed without affecting the others. You can reorder layers to create different stacking orders, and change the blending modes on the layers to create interesting overlays. Once you have mastered layers, you can create composites and repair image data like never before. When working on various projects, you might be asked to create comps (comparable designs), sketches, and other specifications leading up to the final design of a projects. Using layers in Photoshop CS6 can make this process significantly easier and allow you to create these deliverables efficiently which saves both time and effort on your part.

A new default image starts with only a background layer. The number of additional layers, layer effects, and layer sets that you can add to an image is limited only by your computer's memory. In this lesson, you'll find out how to take advantage of layers to create interesting composites and make non–destructive changes to your images.

Getting a handle on layers

In the first part of the lesson, you will work with the most fundamental concepts of using layers. Even if you are using layers already, it is a good idea to run through this section. Due to the fast pace of production, many users skip right into more advanced layer features without having the opportunity to learn basic layer features that can save them time and aggravation.

Creating a new blank file

In this lesson, you'll create a blank file and add layers to it one at a time.

Step-by-Step	Follow these steps to create and configure a new blank Photoshop file

1. Choose File > New. The New dialog box appears.

2. In the New dialog box, choose Default Photoshop Size from the Preset drop-down menu.

3. Choose Transparent from the Background Contents drop-down menu as shown in Figure 8-1, and press OK. By selecting Transparent, your new document starts with one layer instead of the default, opaque, Background or Regular layer.

Figure 8-1: *Create a new document with a transparent layer.*

4. You will now save the file. Choose File > Save As and navigate to the ps08lessons folder. In the Name text field, type **mylayers**. Choose Photoshop from the Format drop-down menu and press Save. If the Photoshop Format Options dialog box appears, press OK.

To help you work with layers, Photoshop provides a panel specific to layers. In addition to showing thumbnail previews of layer content, the Layers panel allows you to select specific layers, turn their visibility on and off, apply special effects, and change the order in which they are stacked.

5. If the Layers panel is not visible, choose Window > Layers. Click on the Layers tab and drag it out of the docking area for this lesson so that you can more closely follow the changes you are making.

6. If the Swatches panel is not visible, choose Window > Swatches. Click and drag on the Swatches tab to take it out of the docking area as shown in Figure 8-2.

Figure 8-2: Click on the panel tabs and drag the Swatches and Layers panels out of the docking area.

7. Select the Rectangular Marquee tool (▢) and click and drag; to constrain the marquee selection to a square, hold down the Shift key as you drag. Release the mouse when you have created a large, square marquee. Exact size is not important for this step.

8. Click on any red color in the Swatches panel. In this example, CMYK Red is used.

9. Choose Edit > Fill, or use the keyboard shortcut Shift+Backspace (Windows) or Shift+Delete (Mac OS), to open the Fill dialog box.

10. In the Use drop-down menu, select Foreground Color. Leave the other settings at their default (Figure 8-3) and press OK. The result is shown in Figure 8-4.

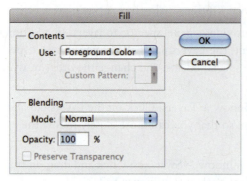

Figure 8-3*: Fill with your foreground color.*   ***Figure 8-4****: The result.*

 Take Note...
You can press Alt+Backspace (Windows) or Option+Delete (Mac OS) to automatically fill with your foreground color without opening the Fill dialog box. Keep in mind that either the Backspace or Delete key can be used for this shortcut.

11. Choose Select > Deselect to turn off the selection marquee, or use the keyboard shortcut Ctrl+D (Windows) or Command+D (Mac OS).

12. Choose File > Save.

Naming your layer

You will find that as you increase your use of layers, your Photoshop image can become quite complicated and confusing. Layers are limited only by the amount of memory you have in your computer, and so you could find yourself working with 100-layer images. To help you stay organized, and therefore more productive, be sure to name your layers appropriately.

| Step-by-Step | Follow these steps to create, name and add content to layers |

1. Double-click on the layer name, Layer 1. The text becomes highlighted and the insertion cursor appears. You can now type **red square** to provide this layer with a descriptive name.

2. You can also name a layer before you create it. Hold down the Alt (Windows) or Option (Mac OS) key and press the Create a New Layer button (⬛) at the bottom of the Layers panel. The New Layer dialog box appears as shown in Figure 8-5.

 Take Note...
As a default, new layers appear on top of the active layer. Use Ctrl+Alt (Windows) or Command+Option (Mac OS) to open the New Layer dialog box and add the new layer underneath the active layer.

3. In the Name text field, type **yellow circle**, as you are about to create a yellow circle on this layer as demonstrated in Figure 8-6.

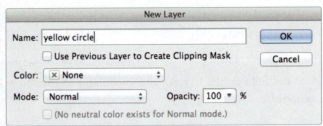

Figure 8-5: Hold down the Alt/Option key when creating a new layer so that you can name it right away.

Figure 8-6: New Layer dialog box.

> **Take Note...**
> For organizational purposes, you can change the color of the layer in the Layers panel, which can help you locate important layers more quickly.

4. For the sake of being color-coordinated, choose Yellow from the Color drop-down menu and press OK. A new layer named "yellow circle" is created. The Layer Visibility icon in the Layers panel has a yellow background. This background does not affect the actual contents of your layer.

Now you will put the yellow circle on this layer.

5. Click and hold on the Rectangular Marquee tool (▢), then choose the hidden Elliptical Marquee tool (○).

> **Take Note...**
> You can also cycle through the marquee selection tools by pressing Shift+M.

6. Click and drag while holding the Shift key down to create a circle selection in your image area as demonstrated in Figure 8-7.

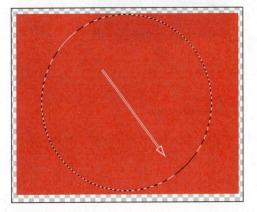

Figure 8-7: Click and drag while holding the Shift key to create a circle selection.

7. Position your cursor over the Swatches panel and click to choose any yellow color.

   In this example, CMYK Yellow is selected.

8. Use the keyboard shortcut Alt+Backspace (Windows) or Option+Delete (Mac OS) to quickly fill the selection with yellow.

9. Choose Select > Deselect, or use the keyboard shortcut Ctrl+D (Windows) or Command+D (Mac OS).

   You will now create a third layer for this file. This time, you'll use the Layers panel menu.

10. Click and hold on the Layers panel menu and choose New > Layer. The New Layer dialog box appears.

Take Note...

If you prefer keyboard shortcuts, you can type Ctrl+Shift+N (Windows) or Command+Shift+N (Mac OS) to create a new layer.

11. Type **green square** in the Name text field and choose Green from the Color drop-down menu. Press OK; a new layer is created.

12. Click and hold on the Elliptical Marquee tool to select the hidden Rectangular Marquee tool. Hold down the Shift key, then click and drag a small square selection on your document.

13. Position your cursor over the Swatches panel and click to choose any green color from the panel. In this example, CMYK Green is selected.

14. Use the keyboard shortcut Alt+Backspace (Windows) or Option+Delete (Mac OS) to quickly fill the selection with green.

15. Choose Select > Deselect, or use the keyboard shortcut Ctrl+D (Windows) or Command+D (Mac OS). The document is shown in Figure 8-8 and the Layers panel displays the three layers in Figure 8-9.

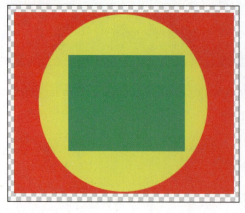

Figure 8-8: The document.

Figure 8-9: The Layers panel now shows the three layers.

16. Choose File > Save. Keep the mylayers.psd file open for the next part of this lesson.

Selecting layers

As basic as it may seem, selecting the appropriate layer can be difficult. Follow this exercise to see how important it is to be aware of layers by keeping track of which layer is active.

| Follow these steps to select and edit the content of layers | Step-by-Step |

1. You should still have the **mylayers.psd** file open from the last exercise. If not, access the file in the ps08lessons folder and select the green square layer in the Layers panel.

2. Select the Move tool (⊹) and click and drag to reposition the green square on the green square layer. Note that only the green square moves. This is because layers that are active are the only layers that are affected.

3. With the Move tool still selected, select the yellow circle layer in the Layers panel and then click and drag the yellow circle in your image file. The yellow circle moves.

4. Now, select the red square layer in the Layers panel.

5. Choose Filter > Blur > Gaussian Blur. The Gaussian Blur dialog box appears.

6. In the Gaussian Blur dialog box, type **7** in the Radius text field as shown in Figure 8-10, then press OK. Figure 8-11 shows the result of this change.

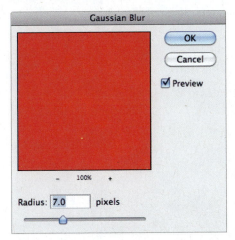

Figure 8-10: Apply a filter.

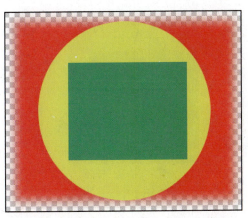

Figure 8-11: The result.

7. Choose File > Save. Keep the file open for the next part of the lesson.

Tips for selecting layers

There are several methods you can use to make sure that you are activating certain layers and changing the properties on the specific layer you want to modify.

Step-by-Step | **Follow these steps to change the properties of selected layers**

1. You should still have the **mylayers.psd** file open from the last exercise. If it is not, access the file in the ps08lessons folder and select the red square layer in the Layers panel.

2. Make sure that the Move tool (⊹) is selected, then hold down the Ctrl (Windows) or Command (Mac OS) key and select the yellow circle in the image file. Notice that the yellow circle layer is automatically selected.

3. Now, hold down the Ctrl (Windows) or Command (Mac OS) key and select the green square in the image file. The green square layer is selected. By holding down the Ctrl or Command key, you turn on an auto-select feature that automatically selects the layer that contains the pixels you have clicked on.

4. Make sure that the Move tool is still selected, and right-click (Windows) or Ctrl+click (Mac OS) on the green square. Note that when you access the contextual tools, overlapping layers appear in a list, providing you with the opportunity to select the layer in the menu that appears (Figure 8-12). Select the green square layer.

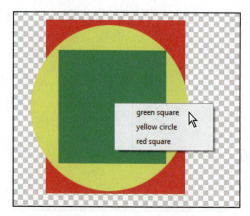

Figure 8-12: Select a layer using contextual tools.

5. Right-click (Windows) or Ctrl+click (Mac OS) on an area of the image file that contains only the red square pixels to see that only one layer name appears for you to choose from. Choose red square.

Moving layers

Layers appear in the same stacking order in which they appear in the Layers panel. For instance, in the file you have been working on in this lesson, the green square was created last and is at the top of the stacking order, essentially covering up the yellow circle and red square wherever it is positioned.

By moving the position of a layer, you can change the way an image looks, which allows you to experiment with different image compositions. A **composition** is defined as the placement or arrangement of visual elements in an image.

Follow these steps to move layers and create a composition	**Step-by-Step**

1. With the **mylayers.psd** file still open, click and drag the green square layer in the Layers panel below the red square layer, as demonstrated in Figure 8-13. Release the mouse button when you see a light bar appear underneath the red square layer. The dark line indicates the location of the layer that you are dragging. Notice that the green square may not be visible at this time because it is underneath the red square, and thus hidden.

Figure 8-13:Click and drag to reorder layers.

2. You may find it easier to use keyboard commands to move the layers' positions in the stacking order. Select the green square layer and press Ctrl+] (right bracket) (Windows) or Command+] (right bracket) (Mac OS) to move it up one level in the stacking order. Press this keyboard combination again to move the green square layer back to the top of the stacking order.

3. Select the yellow circle layer and press Ctrl+[(left bracket) (Windows) or Command+[(left bracket) (Mac OS) to put the yellow circle one level down in the stacking order, essentially placing it behind the red square. Press Ctrl+] (right bracket) (Windows) or Command+] (right bracket) (Mac OS) to move it back up one level in the layer stacking order.

    The image layers should now be back in the same order as when the image was originally created: red square on the bottom, yellow circle in the middle, and green square on the top.

4. Choose File > Save. Keep the file open for the next part of this lesson.

Changing the visibility of a layer

One of the benefits of using layers is that you can hide the layers that contain pixel data on which you are not currently working. By hiding layers, you can focus on the image editing at hand, keeping distractions to a minimum. You can hide or show layers easily by enabling or disabling the **Visibility icon** on the left side of each layer in the Layers panel.

Step-by-Step | **Follow these steps to change the visibility of selected layers**

1. With the **mylayers.psd** file still open, select the Visibility icon (👁) to the left of the red square layer (Figure 8-14). The red square disappears.

Figure 8-14: *Turn the visibility of a layer off and on by selecting the Visibility icon.*

2. Click again on the spot where the Visibility icon previously appeared. The red square layer is visible again.

3. This time, hold down the Alt (Windows) or Option (Mac OS) key, and click on the same Visibility icon. By using the Alt/Option modifier, you can hide all layers except the one you click on.

4. Alt/Option+click on the same Visibility icon to make all the layers visible again.

Using masks in a layer

There is one last feature fundamental to understand before you delve further into layers: the **layer mask** feature. Without the mask feature, making realistic composites or blending one image smoothly into another would be much more difficult.

<table><tr><td>**Follow these steps to composite layers using masks**</td><td>**Step-by-Step**</td></tr></table>

1. With the **mylayers.psd** file still open, choose the red square layer in the Layers panel.

2. Press the Add Layer Mask button (▣) at the bottom of the Layers panel as shown in Figure 8-15. A blank mask is added to the right of the red square layer.

Figure 8–15: Adding a layer mask.

3. To make sure your foreground and background colors are set to the default black and white, press **D** on your keyboard.

4. Select the Gradient tool (▬) from the Tools panel, and make sure that the Linear Gradient option is selected in the Options bar.

5. Confirm that you have the layer mask selected by clicking on it once in the Layers panel as shown in Figure 8-16.

6. Click and drag across the red square in the image from the left side of the square to the right (Figure 8-17). Note that some of the red square becomes transparent, while some remains visible. Click and drag with the Gradient tool as many times as you like. Note that in the Layers panel, wherever black appears in the mask thumbnail, the red square is transparent, as the mask is essentially hiding the red square from view.

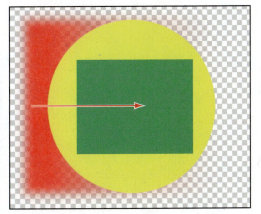

Figure 8–16: Select the layer mask.   *Figure 8–17: Click and drag using the Gradient tool across the image.*

7. Choose File > Save. Keep this file open for the next part of this lesson.

Preserve transparency

The last step in this practice file will be to apply transformations to your layers. Transformations include scaling, rotating, and distorting a layer. To help illustrate how transformations work, you will first duplicate a layer and link it to the original.

Step-by-Step	**Follow these steps to apply transformations to selected layers**

1. With the **mylayers.psd** file still open, select the green square layer.

2. Select the Move tool (⊹), and then hold down the Alt (Windows) or Option (Mac OS) key and position the cursor over the green square in the image. You will see a double-arrow cursor (▶). While still holding down the Alt/Option key, click and drag the green square to the right as displayed in Figure 8-18. A duplicate of the layer is created; release the mouse to see that a green square copy layer has been added to the Layers panel.

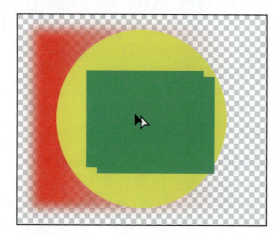

Figure 8-18: Duplicate a layer using the Alt/Option key.

3. Double-click on the green square layer name; when the text is highlighted, type the name **green square shadow**, then delete "copy" from the green square copy name.

4. Click on the green square shadow layer to select it. You'll now take advantage of a feature that allows you to fill without making a selection. Choose Edit > Fill, or use the keyboard shortcut Shift+Delete, or Shift + Backspace. The Fill dialog box appears.

5. In the Fill dialog box, choose Black from the Use drop-down menu. Leave Mode (in the Blending section) set to Normal and Opacity set to 100 percent, check Preserve Transparency as shown in Figure 8-19, and press OK. The result is displayed in Figure 8-20.

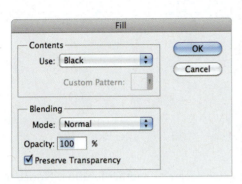

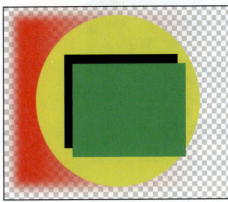

Figure 8-19: *Preserve Transparency maintains the transparent sections of a layer.*

Figure 8-20: *The result.*

Notice that because you chose to preserve the transparency, only the green pixels are changed to black and the rest of the layer (the transparent part) remains transparent. You'll use this feature later in this lesson when creating a composition from several images.

6. With the green square shadow layer still active, select Filter > Blur > Gaussian Blur. The Gaussian Blur dialog box appears.

7. In the Gaussian Blur dialog box, type **8** in the Radius text field, and press OK.

8. Using the Move tool (✛), reposition the green shadow layer so that it appears slightly off to the lower right of the green square layer, creating the look of a shadow.

9. Type **8**. When you have a layer selected, and the Move tool active, you can type a numeric value to instantly change the opacity. As shown in Figure 8-21, by typing **8**, you have changed the opacity of the green square shadow to 80 percent.

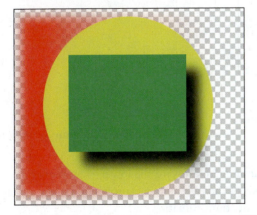

Figure 8-21: *Change the opacity of green square shadow to 80%..*

In this section, you will link the green square layer and green square shadow layer together. This allows you to move them simultaneously and also to apply transformations to both layers at the same time.

10. Select the green square layer, then Shift+click on the green square shadow layer. Both are now selected.

Preserve transparency

**Certification
Ready 3.2**

How can you link
several layers
together?

11. Select the Link Layers button (⊝⊝) at the bottom of the Layers panel as shown in
Figure 8-22. The Link icon appears to the right of the layer names, indicating that they
are linked to each other.

Figure 8-22: *Keep layers together by
linking them.*

12. Select the Move tool, and click and drag the green square to another location. Notice that
the shadow also moves. Move the squares back to the center of the image.

13. Choose Edit > Free Transform, or use the keyboard shortcut Ctrl+T (Windows) or
Command+T (Mac OS). A bounding box appears around the green square and its shadow.

14. Click on the lower-right corner handle and drag it to enlarge the squares as shown in
Figure 8-23. Release the mouse when you've resized them to your liking. No particular
size is necessary.

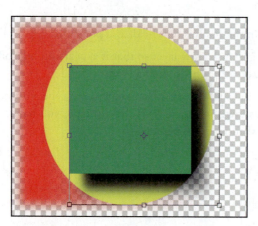

Figure 8-23: *Click and drag the bounding box to scale the
layer contents.*

15. Press the Esc key (in the upper-left corner of your keyboard) to cancel the transformation.

16. Now, choose Edit > Free Transform again, but this time hold down the Shift key while
dragging the lower-right corner of the bounding box toward the lower-right corner of
your image. Holding down the Shift key keeps the layer contents proportional as you scale.
Release the mouse when you're done with the transformation.

17. You can also enter exact scale amounts by using the Options bar. Type **150** in the W
(Width) text field and then press the Maintain Aspect Ratio button (⊝⊝). The layer contents
are scaled to exactly 150 percent. Select the checkbox in the Options bar to confirm this
transformation.

18. Choose File > Save and then File > Close to close this practice file.

Creating a composition

Now you will have the opportunity to put your practice to work by creating a composition with images and type.

Follow these steps to composite images and text using layers

1. Choose File > Browse in Bridge and navigate to the ps08lessons folder inside the pslessons folder on your computer.

2. Double-click on the file **ps0801_done.psd** to see the composition that you will create (Figure 8-24). You can keep this file open for reference, or choose File > Close.

Figure 8-24: The completed lesson file.

3. Return to Bridge and double-click on **ps0801.psd** to open it in Photoshop. An image of a blue sky with clouds appears.

4. Choose File > Save As. In the Save As dialog box, navigate to the ps08lessons folder and type **ps0801_work** into the Name text field; leave the format as Photoshop and press Save.

Moving images in from other documents

You'll start this composition by opening another file and dragging it into this file. Be aware that when moving one document into another, an image's resolution plays an important part in how that image appears proportionally in the destination file. For instance, if a 72-ppi image is moved into a 300-ppi image, it becomes relatively smaller, as the 72-ppi image takes up much less pixel space in the 300-ppi image. On the other hand, if you move a 300-ppi image into a 72-ppi image, it takes up a larger space. If you plan to create composites of multiple images, it is best to choose Image > Image Size and adjust the pixel resolutions of the images before combining them. In this section, you will learn how to check the resolution of your images before combining them into one document.

| Step-by-Step | **Follow these steps to maintain resolution while moving images** |

1. With the **ps0801_work.psd** file open, choose Image > Image Size. The Image Size dialog box appears. Notice that this image's resolution is 300 ppi as shown in Figure 8-25. Press OK.

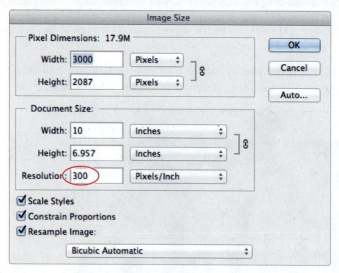

Figure 8-25: The image resolution of this file is 300 ppi.

2. Choose File > Browse in Bridge and navigate to the ps08lessons folder inside the pslessons folder on your computer.

3. Double-click on **ps0802.psd** to open it in Photoshop. An image of a boy jumping appears. For this image, you will check the resolution without opening the Image Size dialog box.

4. Click and hold on the document size box to see a pop-up window appear in the lower-left corner of the workspace (Figure 8-26). This information provides you with dimension and resolution information. Note that this image is also 300 ppi. Release the mouse button to dismiss the pop-up window.

Figure 8-26: Check the resolution in the document window.

5. Select Window > Arrange > 2-up Vertical This positions the **ps0801_work.psd** and **ps0802.psd** documents so that you can see them both at the same time.

6. Select the Move tool (⊹).

7. Hold down the Shift key, and click and drag the **ps0802.psd** image into the **ps0801_work.psd**. Holding the Shift key assures you that the layer is being placed in the exact center of the document into which it is being dragged. Release the mouse when a border appears around the **ps0801_work.psd** image.

8. Choose File > Save. Keep the file open for the next part of this lesson.

9. Click on the tab for the **ps0802.psd** file, and then click on the X in the tab or choose File > Close. You can also use the keyboard shortcut Ctrl+W (Windows) or Command+W (Mac OS) to close the file. If you are asked to save the file, choose No.

Creating a layer mask

You just created the first layer in this document. It is important to keep your layers organized as you work; the Layers panel can become cumbersome when additional layers are created without being properly named.

Follow these steps to replace a background using a layer mask

1. Double-click the word Layer 1 in the Layers panel. When the Layer 1 text becomes highlighted, type **boy**.

    Now you'll select the boy and create a layer mask to cover the background sky.

2. Select the boy layer in the Layers panel to make sure it is the active layer, then select the Quick Selection tool (☞) and start brushing over the image of the boy. A selection is created as you brush. If you accidently select the area around the jumping boy, hold down the Alt (Windows) or Option (Mac OS) key and brush over that area again to delete it from the selection (Figure 8-27).

    Because you will be turning your selection into a mask, you do not have to be perfectly precise. You can edit the selection later if necessary.

Figure 8-27: Create a selection using the Quick Selection tool.

3. With the selection still active, select the Add Layer Mask button (▣) at the bottom of the Layers panel as shown in Figure 8-28. A mask is created, revealing only your selection of the jumping boy (Figure 8-29).

Figure 8-28: Select the Add Layer Mask button.

Figure 8-29: The result.

Editing the layer mask

Your mask may not be perfect, but you can easily edit it using your painting tools. In the example shown here, the hand was not correctly selected with the Quick Selection tool and therefore created an inaccurate mask. Zoom into the image and locate a section where your selection may not be precise; it is more than likely this will be around the boy's hands (Figure 8-30).

Figure 8-30: The mask needs to be adjusted in this section.

| **Follow these steps to edit a layer mask by painting** | **Step-by-Step** |

1. Select the layer mask thumbnail that is to the right of the boy layer's thumbnail in the Layers panel as shown in Figure 8–31.

Figure 8–31: Select the layer mask thumbnail.

2. Press **D** on your keyboard to select the default foreground and background colors of black and white. Note that when working on a mask, painting with white reveals the image, while painting with black hides it.

3. Press **X** on your keyboard, and note that by pressing X you are swapping the foreground and background colors in the Tools panel. Make sure that black is the foreground color.

4. Select the Brush tool and position the cursor over an area of the image where the mask is a bit inaccurate. You see a circle representing the brush size.

> **Take Note...**
> *If you have Caps Lock selected, you will not see the brush size preview.*

If the brush size is too big or too small for the area of the mask that needs to be retouched, adjust the size before you start painting.

5. Press the] (right bracket) key to make the brush size larger, or the [(left bracket) key to make the brush size smaller.

6. Use the Opacity slider in the Options bar to change the opacity back to 100, or press **0** (zero) Pressing 0 (zero) is the keyboard shortcut for returning your brush opacity to 100%

7. Start painting the areas of the mask that were not accurate; in this case, perhaps where some of the sky on the boy layer still appears. Experiment even further by painting over the entire hand. The hand disappears.

8. Press **X** on your keyboard to bring white to the foreground, and paint over the location where the hand was, to reveal it again. You are essentially fine-tuning your mask by painting directly on it (Figure 8-32).

Figure 8-32: Painting the mask.

9. If you find that your brush should have a harder edge, press Shift+] (right bracket). For a softer edge press Shift+[(left bracket).

The benefit of working with a layer mask is that you can fine-tune and edit it as many times as you want without permanently altering the image. This gives you a lot of freedom and control, and allows you to make more accurate selections. This type of image editing is referred to as nondestructive.

10. When you are finished editing your selection, press Ctrl+0 (zero) (Windows) or Command+0 (zero) (Mac OS) to return to the Fit in Screen view. Then, to deselect the layer mask thumbnail, select the boy layer thumbnail in the Layers panel.

Cloning layers

You'll now clone (or duplicate) the boy layer two times. You'll then apply filters and adjust the opacity of the new layers.

Step-by-Step	Follow these steps to duplicate the contents of a layer

1. Select the boy layer thumbnail in the Layers panel to ensure that it is the active layer. Select the Move tool (⊕) and reposition the boy so that his feet touch the bottom of the image as shown in Figure 8-33.

Figure 8-33: Click and drag the boy layer downward.

2. With the Move tool still selected, click and hold the Alt (Windows) or Option (Mac OS) key while dragging the jumping boy image up toward the middle of the image. By holding down the Alt/Option key, you are cloning the layer (Figure 3-34). Don't worry about a precise location for the cloned layer, as you'll adjust its position later. Release the mouse before releasing the Alt/Option key.

Figure 8-34: Clone the layer of the boy jumping.

3. Click and hold down the Alt (Windows) or Option (Mac OS) key once again and drag the newly created layer upward to clone it. Position this new layer at the top of the image. There are now three layers with the boy jumping.

4. In the Layers panel, double-click on the layer named *boy copy*. When the text becomes highlighted, type **boy middle** to change the layer name.

5. Then, double-click on the layer named boy copy 2. When the text becomes highlighted, type **boy top** to change the layer name (Figure 8-35). You can see the results in Figure 8-36.

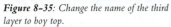

Figure 8-35: Change the name of the third layer to boy top.   *Figure 8-36: See the composition now has three images of the boy.*

6. Choose File > Save to save this file. Keep the file open for the next part of this lesson.

Creating a composition

Aligning and distributing layers

The layers may not be evenly spaced or aligned with each other. This can be adjusted easily by using the **Align and Distribute features** in Photoshop.

<table>
<tr><td>**Step-by-Step**</td><td>**Follow these steps to align and evenly space layers**</td></tr>
</table>

1. Select the boy layer and then Ctrl+click (Windows) or Command+click (Mac OS) on the boy middle and boy top layers. All three layers become selected.

    Note that when you have two or more layers selected, there are additional options in the Options bar to align and distribute your layers as displayed below in Figure 8–37.

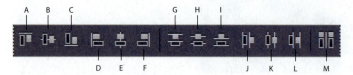

Figure 8–37

A. *Align top edges.* **B.** *Align vertical centers.* **C.** *Align bottom edges.* **D.** *Align left edges.*
E. *Align horizontal centers.* **F.** *Align right edges.* **G.** *Distribute top edges.*
H. *Distribute vertical centers.* **I.** *Distribute bottom edges.* **J.** *Distribute left edges.*
K. *Distribute horizontal centers.* **L.** *Distribute right edges.* **M.** *Auto-Align Layers.*

2. Choose the Align Horizontal Centers button (⬍) and then the Distribute Vertical Centers button (⬍). You may or may not see a dramatic adjustment here; it depends on how you positioned the layers when you created them.

3. Choose File > Save. Keep the file open for the next part of this lesson.

Take Note...

Don't confuse the Alignment options here with the more sophisticated alignment options found in the Merge to HDR and Photomerge features available in Photoshop.

Photomerge is a process that takes two or more images and automatically aligns and blends the edges of the images in order to create a seamless photo-composition. Merge to HDR is a process that takes two or more images from a set of exposures, aligns them, and then combines them to create a single high quality image.

Both these techniques generally only work with images designed for the purpose such as a panorama. Both features can be accessed by choosing File > Automate.

Applying filters to layers

Now you'll apply a filter to the boy and boy middle layers and then adjust their opacity.

| Follow these steps to add special effects to layers by applying filters | Step-by-Step |

1. Select the boy middle layer in the Layers panel.

2. Choose Filter > Blur > Motion Blur. The Motion Blur dialog box appears.

3. Type **–90** in the Angle text field, drag the distance slider to 150 (Figure 8-38), then press OK. You have created a blur that makes it look like the boy is jumping up as you can see in Figure 8-39.

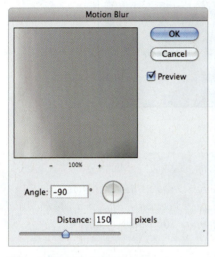

Figure 8-38: Apply the motion blur.   *Figure 8-39*: Result.

4. Choose the boy layer in the Layers panel and press Ctrl+F (Windows) or Command+F (Mac OS). This applies the last-used filter to this layer.

   You will now adjust the opacity on these layers.

5. With the boy layer still selected, click on the arrow to the right of Opacity in the Layers panel. A slider appears. Click and drag the slider to the 20 percent mark as shown in Figure 8-40.

Figure 8-40: Drag the opacity slider.

6. Make sure that the Move tool (✛) is active, and select the boy middle layer. This time, you'll change the opacity using a keyboard shortcut. Type **5**; the layer opacity is instantly changed to 50 percent. You can see the result of this adjustment in Figure 8-41.

Figure 8-41: The layers after the opacity has been adjusted.

> **Take Note...**
> *While the Move tool is active, you can type in any value to set the opacity on a selected layer. For instance, typing **23** would make the layer 23 percent opaque, and **70** would make the layer 70 percent opaque. Type **0** (zero) to return to 100 percent opacity.*

7. Choose File > Save to save this file. Keep the file open for the next part of this lesson.

Creating a type layer

You are now going to add a **type layer** to this document and apply a warp, as well as a layer style. Type layers can be used to add visual impact to an image. It can be used to create a call to attention, or something more subtle like copyright information. As Type layers are created they are added to the Layers panel and can be scaled, rotated and adjusted as needed.

Step-by-Step | **Follow these steps to create and modify a type layer**

1. In the Layers panel, select the boy top layer to make it active. The new type layer will appear directly above the active layer.

2. Select the Type tool (T) and set the following options in the Options bar (Figure 8-42):

From the font family drop-down menu, choose Myriad Pro. From the font style drop-down menu, choose Black. If you do not have Black, choose Bold.

Type **200** in the font size text field.

Figure 8-42

A. *Presets.* **B.** *Text orientation.* **C.** *Font family.* **D.** *Font style.* **E.** *Font size.* **F.** *Anti-aliasing.* **G.** *Left-align text.* **H.** *Center text.* **I.** *Right-align text.* **J.** *Text color.* **K.** *Warp text.* **L.** *Character and Paragraph panels.*

3. Now, click once on the Text color box in the Options bar. The Color Picker dialog box appears, with a Select text color pane.

4. You can either enter a color value in this window or click on a color in the color preview pane. In this example, you will click a color. Position your cursor over an area in the image that has light clouds, and click. This samples that color, and applies it to the text (Figure 8-43). Press OK to close the Color Picker.

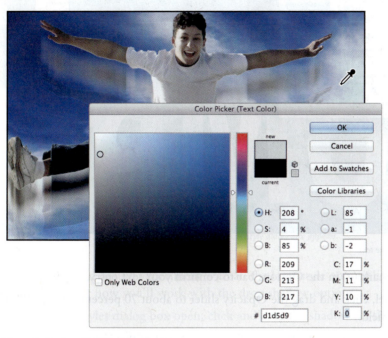

Figure 8-43: *Sample a color from your image.*

You are now ready to type.

5. Click once on the image near the boy's sneaker on the left side of the image. Exact position is not important, as it can be adjusted later.

6. Type **JUMP**, then hold down the Ctrl (Windows) or Command (Mac OS) key and drag the word Jump to approximately the bottom center of the image (Figure 8-44). By holding down the Ctrl/Command key, you do not have to exit the text entry mode to reposition the text.

Figure 8-44: *Reposition the text using the Ctrl or Command key.*

5. Click and drag from the boy's thumb on the left side of the image down to the bottom of the letter "P" in JUMP (Figure 8-48). The shape is created; don't worry about the color.

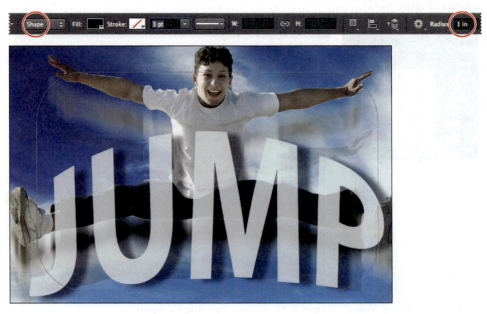

Figure 8-48: Set the shape options, then click and drag to create the shape layer.

6. In the Layers panel, click and drag the Rounded Rectangle 1 so that it is beneath the sky layer.

7. Hold down the Alt (Windows) or Option (Mac OS) key, and position your cursor over the line that separates the Rounded Rectangle 1 layer from the sky layer. When you see the Clipping Mask icon (↲□) appear, click with the mouse. The sky layer is clipped inside the shape layer as you can see in Figure 8-49. The result is displayed in Figure 8-50.

Figure 8-49: Alt/Option+click in between the layers.

Figure 8-50: The result.

8. Now, position your cursor on the line separating the sky layer from the boy layer, and Alt/Option+click on the line. The clipping now extends up into the boy layer.

9. Position the cursor on the line separating the boy layer from the boy middle layer, and Alt/Option+click again. The clipping mask is now extended to the boy middle layer.

10. Select the Move tool (⊹) and the Rounded Rectangle 1 layer. Click and drag to reposition the layer to see how the sky, boy, and boy middle layers are clipped inside the shape.

You will now trim the layers to eliminate areas you don't need.

11. Choose Image > Trim; the Trim dialog box appears. Leave the settings at the default and press OK. The image is trimmed down to the smallest possible size, without cropping out any image data.

Testing out the new Filter for the Layers panel

A new layer feature added to Photoshop CS6 is the ability to filter layers. By filtering layers, you can easily locate layers based upon attributes such as the kind of layer, the blending mode used, name, and more.

To experiment with the new filter, click on the Filter for type layers button (T) to the right of the Pick a file type drop-down menu, then click the Filter for shape layers button; only the selected type of layer appears.

Note that when you click Kind, you can choose from other attributes, such as Name, Effect, Mode, Attribute, and Color as shown in Figure 8-51.

Figure 8-51: You can filter the layers that appear in the Layers panel.

A. *Filter for pixel layers*
B. *Filter for adjustment layers*
C. *Filter for type layers*
D. *Filter for shape layers*
E. *Filter for smart objects*
F. *Turn layer filtering on/off.*

13. Choose File > Save, and then File > Close.

Congratulations! You have finished the lesson.

Skill Summary

In this lesson you learned how to:	Objective
Demonstrate knowledge of project management tasks and responsibilities	1.3
Demonstrate knowledge of layers and masks	3.2
Demonstrate knowledge of working with selections	4.1
Demonstrate knowledge of type	4.7
Demonstrate knowledge of filters	4.8

Knowledge Assessment

True/False

Circle **T** if the statement is true or **F** if the statement is false.

T F **1.** Layers are dependent on one another and cannot be changed without affecting the other layers in the image.

T F **2.** Naming layers isn't very important to the process, you can usually skip that step.

T F **3.** Holding down the spacebar when drawing will keep your shapes constrained proportionally.

T F **4.** As basic as it seems, selecting the appropriate layer can sometimes be difficult.

T F **5.** Only active layers are affected when making changes in Photoshop.

T F **6.** Layers appear on the document in the same stacking order in which they appear in the Layers panel.

T F **7.** Gradients can be used to create transparency while working with layer masks.

T F **8.** There is no way to link layers to one another without merging them.

T F **9.** Layer masks can be adjusted using the painting tools.

T F **10.** Layer styles allow you to apply effects to layers such as drop shadows and embossing.

Multiple Choice

Select the best response for the following statements.

1. Blending mode, opacity, fill and lock are all attributes of which panel?
   a. Adjustments
   b. Channels
   c. Info
   d. Layers

2. What is the keyboard shortcut for Edit > Fill?
   a. Shift+Backspace (Windows) or Shift+Delete (Mac OS)
   b. Shift+Tab
   c. Spacebar+Shift
   d. Spacebar+Tab

3. To make an image appear above all other images, the layer must be:
   a. Set to Adjust > Bring forward
   b. Moved to the bottom of the layer stack
   c. Moved to the top of the layer stack
   d. Merged with the other layers

4. What is the keyboard shortcut to set your foreground and background colors to the default black and white?

   a. X

   b. Ctrl+D

   c. D

   d. Shift+X

5. Transformations to a layer can include which of the following?

   a. Scaling

   b. Rotating

   c. Distorting

   d. All of the above

6. Which menu command will activate controls that allow you to change a number of transformation properties such as scale and rotation?

   a. Edit > Transform > Skew

   b. Edit > Transform > Rotate

   c. Edit > Free Transform

   d. Edit > Transform > Perspective

7. Which key do you need to hold down when dragging on an image to make a copy of it?

   a. Shift

   b. Alt (Windows) / Option (Mac OS)

   c. Spacebar

   d. None of the above

8. Bend, Horizontal Distortion, and Vertical Distortion are all characteristics of:

   a. Warp Text

   b. Free Transform

   c. Perspective

   d. Skew

9. In the Layer Style dialog box, which of the following is not an option?

   a. Stroke

   b. Color Overlay

   c. Warp Text

   d. Outer Glow

10. What allows you to use the content of one layer to mask the layers above it?

   a. It depends on the opacity value on each layer

   b. Blending modes

   c. Clipping Mask

   d. Chroma Keying

Competency Assessment

| Project 8-1 | **Altering the Transparency Settings** |

You know that crazy checkerboard pattern that's in the background while you're working with transparency in Photoshop? Well, you can alter that if you don't find the initial pattern to your satisfaction.

1. Create a new blank file in Photoshop; be sure to set the Background Contents to Transparent.

2. Go to the Preferences section of Photoshop.

3. In the Preferences, select the Transparency and Gamut settings and start to make adjustments in the Transparency Settings section.

4. Take a screen capture of your settings and save the file as **Custom_background** with the file extension of your choice.

| Project 8-2 | **Other Blurs** |

The Gaussian Blur is kind of a classic when it comes to Photoshop's filters. Let's try some of the other blurs as there quite a few to choose from.

1. Open the **ps0802.psd** file in Photoshop.

2. Select the Background layer and choose Filter > Convert for Smart Filters.

3. Choose Filter > Blur > Radial Blur. Try experimenting with direction to see the results.

4. Duplicate the layer and delete the smart filter. Try some of the other blur methods in the Filter > Blur menu.

5. Name each Smart Object appropriately to the filter that is applied to it.

6. Save the file as **ps0802_blur.psd**.

Proficiency Assessment

| Project 8-3 | **Creating Punch In Text** |

Did you ever see or want to create text that looks like it's cut into an image?

1. Open the **ps0802.psd** image in Photoshop.

2. Create a text layer using the settings of your choice. Big bold text will work best for this example.

3. With the text layer selected, go to the Layer Styles and experiment with the Inner Shadow settings.

4. Save the file as **ps0802_style.psd**.

| Converting Layers to Backgrounds and Vice-Versa | Project 8-4 |

You know that by double-clicking a background layer, you can save it as a regular layer. Let's look at another method and how to reverse it.

1. Open the **ps0802.psd** image in Photoshop.

2. Convert the Background layer to a regular layer by dragging the lock icon to the right of the layer to the trash can at the bottom of the panel. You just converted a background layer to a regular layer.

3. Duplicate this layer by selecting it and then right-clicking on the layer and choosing Duplicate Layer. Leave the name at the default.

4. Select the top-most layer in the layers panel and choose Layer > New > Background From Layer.

5. Save the file as **ps0802_layers.psd**.

Taking Layers to the Max

Key Terms

- adjustment layer
- contour
- emboss
- fill opacity
- gradient
- pattern fill
- tint

Skill	Objective
Demonstrate knowledge of design principles, elements, and image composition	**2.2**
Demonstrate knowledge of layers and masks	**3.2**
Adjust or correct the tonal range, color, or distortions of an image	**4.4**
Demonstrate knowledge of retouching and blending images	**4.5**
Demonstrate knowledge of filters	**4.8**

Business case

So now your boss is getting more excited with your Photoshop skills and wants to utilize those skills on a project for a new client. Her request is that you be able to present an original image from the client and then show the new version you'll be creating without destroying the original in the process. But how do you do that? You can always make a back up of the original and toggle back and forth between the original and your new version but that may not be as smooth as using Adjustment layers.

Starting up

Layers, in their simplest form, offer Photoshop users an amazing amount of flexibility to create and modify images. The more advanced features of layers offer even more options, many of which you can exploit in various ways while keeping the original image information intact.

Before starting, make sure that your tools and panels are consistent by resetting your preferences. See "Resetting Adobe Photoshop CS6 preferences" in the Starting up section of this book.

You will work with several files from the ps09lessons folder in this lesson. Make sure that you have loaded the pslessons folder onto your hard drive from *http://www.wiley.com/college/sc/adobeseries*. See "Loading lesson files" in the Starting up section of this book.

Making color changes using adjustment layers

**Certification
Ready 3.2**

What are some of the
benefits of fill and
adjustment layers
vs. making a change
directly to an image
layer?

**Certification
Ready 4.4**

How can you replace
the color in a photo
using an adjustment
layer?

Changing the color of an object in Adobe Photoshop is a pretty common practice, but how do you make it look realistic, and how can you recover the image if you make a mistake? What if you want to see three or four different variations? All these tasks can be completed easily and efficiently, using adjustment layers. An **adjustment layer** is a layer that applies any variety of tonal adjustments to an image. In this section, you'll change the color of a jacket on a model, and then, using the same adjustment layer, change it again, multiple times.

Follow these steps to change colors using adjustment layers

1. Choose File > Browse in Bridge to open Adobe Bridge.

2. Navigate to the ps09lessons folder, inside the pslessons folder you have created on your computer and double-click on **ps0901.psd** to open it in Photoshop. An image of a girl wearing a blue jacket appears.

   You will take the original jacket (Figure 9-1) and change the color of it (Figure 9-2). You will also add a pattern to the jacket, using an adjustment layer (Figure 9-3).

Figure 9-1: The original image.   *Figure 9-2: A solid color adjustment.*   *Figure 9-3: A pattern adjustment.*

3. Choose File > Save As. In the Name text field, type **ps0901_work**, and then navigate to the ps09lessons folder. Choose Photoshop from the format drop-down menu and press Save.

   The first thing that you will make is a selection with the Quick Selection tool.

4. Select the Quick Selection tool (✎), then click and drag on the jacket (Figure 9-4). If you miss some of the jacket, just paint a stroke over it to add it to the selection. If your selection goes too far, hold down the Alt (Windows) or Option (Mac OS) key and click on the part of the selection that you want to deactivate.

   You can also increase or decrease your Quick Selection tool size by pressing the [(left bracket) or] (right bracket) keys.

Figure 9-4: Paint the jacket with the Quick Selection tool to make a selection.

5. If the Layers panel is not visible, choose Window > Layers.

6. Click and hold on the Create New Fill or Adjustment Layer button (◒) at the bottom of the Layers panel.

7. Select Hue/Saturation from the pop-up menu. The Properties panel appears with the Hue/Saturation options visible.

   Hue refers to the color. By changing the hue, you can essentially change the color of an object without taking away any of the shading properties, which are normally created from the neutral gray value.

8. Check the Colorize checkbox, and click and drag the Hue slider to the right to about the 70 point, or type **70** in the Hue text field.

   In the next step, you will bring the saturation down a bit so the green you are creating is less bright.

**Certification
Ready 4.4**

How can you adjust
color using Hue/
Saturation?

9. Click and drag the Saturation slider to the left to about the 20 point, or type **20** into the
    Saturation text field as shown in Figure 9-5.

Figure 9-5: *Change the color and saturation
using the Hue/Saturation sliders.*

The jacket is now green, but your selection might not be as accurate as you would like.
In the next section, you will use your painting tools to refine the mask attached to the
adjustment layer. A benefit of adjustment layers is that you can use them to paint masks at
any point in the process to modify your selection.

10. Choose File > Save. If the Format Options dialog box appears, press OK.

Take Note...
*If you inadvertently close any images while working on a project, you can quickly reopen
them by choosing File > Open Recent, and selecting the file from the drop-down menu.*

Refining the adjustment layer mask

If you take a look at the Layers panel you just created, you see a Hue/Saturation adjustment
layer that has a mask thumbnail to the right of the layer thumbnail. You can activate this mask
separately, and then use painting tools to refine it.

Step-by-Step | **Follow these steps to fine-tune a mask by painting**

1. Alt+click (Windows) or Option+click (Mac OS) on the adjustment mask thumbnail, to
    the right of the Hue/Saturation thumbnail in the Layers panel.

The mask appears. You are not doing anything to the mask at this time, but you should take a look at what the actual mask looks like. Notice that where there is white, the hue and saturation changes take place. Where the mask is black, the changes are not occurring (Figure 9-6). Using the painting tools in Photoshop, you can edit a mask by painting black and white and even varying opacities to control the results of the adjustment layer.

Figure 9-6: *Where the mask is white, the Hue/Saturation change is occurring.*

2. To return to the normal layer view, click once on the word *Background* in the Layers panel.

   You will now make changes to the adjustment mask thumbnail.

3. Click once on the adjustment mask thumbnail (Figure 9-7) (to the right of the Hue/Saturation adjustment layer thumbnail).

Figure 9-7: *Paint on the adjustment layer's mask to refine your selection.*

4. Now, select the Brush tool (✔), and press **D** on your keyboard to set the colors to the default of black and white. Note that when in a mask, white is the foreground color and black is the background color.

5. Adjust your brush size as needed to paint the areas in the mask that might not have been selected, and thus not affected, when you created the adjustment layer (Figure 9-8).

Take Note...
Refine Edge (covered in Lesson 5, "Making the Best Selections,") is actually the best method to use to select hair, but for this exercise, you will use the Brush tool to help you understand the process of painting your selection on a mask.

Figure 9-8: Paint the areas that may have been missed with your original selection.

Take Note...
You can make your brush size larger by pressing the] (right bracket) key and smaller by pressing [(left bracket) key. Make your brush harder by pressing Shift+] and softer by pressing Shift+[.

6. Press **X** on your keyboard to swap the foreground and background colors. Black is now the foreground color.

7. Now, find a section of your image—perhaps the hand tucked in underneath the elbow—that has the Hue/Saturation change applied to it in error.

You will paint this area with the black paint brush, with the mask active, to block the change from occurring there.

Take Note...

It is very easy to deselect the mask and paint on your actual image. Avoid this by clicking once on the Layer mask thumbnail, just to be sure!

8. Adjust your paint brush to the right size and softness, and paint over the hand to reveal the actual flesh color as shown in Figure 9-9.

Figure 9-9:Eliminate the areas that may have been included, in error, in the original selection.

Take Note...

If you did such an accurate selection that you have no areas to repair, paint an area somewhere on your image anyway, just to see the effects of painting black on the mask. When you are done experimenting, press **X** *to swap back to the white foreground color and repair the mask, as necessary.*

Adjusting the Hue/Saturation layer

Now that you have created an accurate mask, the next few steps will be rather simple. Perhaps your client has suggested that you use a more vibrant violet for the blazer. In this section, you will apply more color to the blazer, and also edit the existing hue and saturation.

Step-by-Step	**Follow these steps to adjust hue and saturation settings**

1. Click once on the adjustment layer thumbnail to reopen the Hue/Saturation information in the Properties panel as displayed in Figure 9-10.

Figure 9-10: *Click on the adjustment layer thumbnail to change the settings.*

2. On the Properties panel, click and drag the Hue slider to the right to about the 260 point, or type **260** into the Hue text field.

3. Click and drag the Saturation slider to the right to about the 40 point, or type **40** into the Saturation text field (Figure 9-11).

The green is now changed to a violet.

Figure 9-11: *Readjusting the Hue and Saturation.*

You can reopen the Hue/Saturation adjustment layer as many times as you like.

4. Choose File > Save, and keep the image open for the next section.

Adding a pattern fill layer

You can add a pattern and apply it to an image using a fill layer, this effect is called a **pattern fill**. This gives you the ability to scale the pattern, as well as adjust the opacity and blending modes. In this section, you will create a simple pattern that will be scaled and applied to the image, using a new fill layer.

Defining the pattern

You can create a pattern in Photoshop out of any pixel information that you can select with the Rectangular Marquee. In this section, you will use the entire image area as the pattern, but you could also activate a smaller portion of an image and define it as a pattern.

1. Leave the **ps0901_work.psd** file open, and open an additional image. Choose File > Browse in Bridge to open Adobe Bridge.

2. If you are not already there, navigate to the ps09lessons folder, inside the pslessons folder you created on your computer and double-click on the file named **ps0902.psd**. An image of an ornate pattern appears as you can see in Figure 9-12.

Figure 9-12: Define a pattern from an entire image, or just a rectangular selection.

Because you are using the entire image to create the pattern, you do not need to select anything.

3. Choose Edit > Define Pattern. The Pattern Name dialog box appears. Type **ornate** in the Name text field (Figure 9-13), and press OK.

Figure 9-13: Defining a pattern for future use.

4. Choose File > Close to close the image without making any changes.

Applying the pattern

You will now apply the pattern to the jacket, using a new fill layer.

Step-by-Step	Follow these steps to apply, scale and modify a new pattern

1. You spent a fair amount of time perfecting your mask, and you certainly don't want to have to do that again. Hold down the Ctrl (Windows) or Command (Mac OS) key and click on the Layer mask thumbnail of your adjustment layer. The mask is activated as a selection.

Take Note...
You can Ctrl/Command+click on any layer or mask to activate its contents as a selection.

2. Now that you have an active selection of the woman's blazer, click and hold on the Create New Fill or Adjustment Layer button ( ) at the bottom of the Layers panel, and choose Pattern (Figure 9-14). The Pattern Fill dialog box appears as shown in Figure 9-15.

   Your new pattern swatch should be visible. If it is not, click on the downward arrow to the right of the visible swatch to select a different pattern.

Figure *9-14*: Select the Pattern Fill layer.

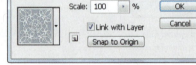

Figure *9-15*: The Pattern Fill dialog box appears.

Figure *9-16*: The result.

The result may be a little unexpected at first (Figure 9-16), as no scaling or blending mode has been applied to this fill pattern yet.

3. With the Pattern Fill dialog box still open, use the Scale slider to set the scale of the pattern to 25 percent, or type **25** into the Scale text field, and press OK.

4. With your new Fill layer still selected, click and hold on Normal in the blending mode drop-down menu on the Layers panel, and choose Multiply (Figure 9-17). You can view the result in Figure 9-18.

Figure 9-17: Select Multiply. *Figure 9-18: The result.*

You can experiment with other blending modes to see how they affect the final rendering of the pattern.

> **Take Note...**
> *If you select your Move tool, and then select a blending mode from the Set the blending mode drop-down menu, you can press Shift + (↓) Down Arrow to move down the list of different blending options. Press Shift + (↑) Up Arrow to move up the list of blending options.*

5. Choose File > Save and then File > Close to close this image.

Congratulations! You have finished the adjustment layer section of this lesson.

Using the Black & White adjustment layer

Photoshop contains some powerful adjustment layer options that can adjust color and tone in an image including channel mixer, gradient map, photo filter, invert, posterize, and lens correction. Using these adjustment layers is easy as you'll see in this exercise. Photoshop contains some powerful adjustment layer options that can adjust color and tone in an image including channel mixer, gradient map, photo filter, invert, posterize, and lens correction. Using these adjustment layers is easy as you'll see in this exercise.

Changing color images to grayscale is easy—you just switch the color mode using Image > Mode > Grayscale, right? Not if you want to achieve the best possible conversion from color to black and white. In this section, you will learn how to use the Black & White adjustment layer.

Step-by-Step	Follow these steps to convert an image using a Black & White adjustment layer

1. Choose File > Browse in Bridge to open Adobe Bridge.

2. Navigate to the ps09lessons folder, inside the pslessons folder you created on your computer and double-click on the file named **ps0903.psd**. A cityscape appears as shown in Figure 9-19.

You will convert this cityscape image to grayscale.

3. Choose File > Save As; the Save As dialog box appears. Navigate to the ps09lessons folder. In the Name text field, type **ps0903_work** and select Photoshop from the Format drop-down menu. Press Save.

4. Click on the Create New Fill or Adjustment Layer button (⬤) at the bottom of the Layers panel and select Black & White. The Black and White settings become active in the Properties panel.

   This window may appear very confusing at first. Without some assistance, it would be difficult to decipher which color adjustments are going to affect the image and where. Fortunately, Adobe has created some helpful features to make a better conversion easier for users.

5. Click on the pointing Finger icon (👆) in the Properties panel to make that option active.

6. Click and hold on the sky in the image; a pointing finger with a double arrow (👆) appears. The color that would make changes to that part of the image (the sky) is affected.

7. Continue holding down on the sky image, and drag to the right; notice that you automatically lightened the blues in the sky (Figure 9-20). Click and drag to the left to make the conversion darker. View Figure 9-21 to see the slider change in the Properties panel for the Blues.

Figure 9-20: Click and drag in the sky area to automatically adjust the color.

Figure 9-21: The Properties panel shows the change with Blues.

8. Now, click on the darker streaming car lights in the image; the Reds are highlighted. Click and drag to the right to lighten them (Figure 9-22). View Figure 9-23 to see the slider change in the Properties panel for the Red color. You can just make visual adjustments for this image, but if you were concerned about maintaining certain values, you would want to have the Window > Info panel open.

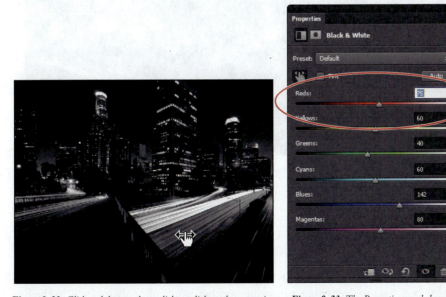

Figure 9-22: Click and drag on the car lights to lighten the conversion.

Figure 9-23: The Properties panel shows the change with Reds.

9. You can turn the visibility of this adjustment layer off and on by clicking on the Visibility icon (👁) to the left of the Black & White 1 adjustment layer.

10. Choose File > Save. Keep the file open for the next section of this lesson.

Adding a tint

In this section, you will add a tint to your image. A **tint** of color can be added to an RGB image to create a nice effect.

> **Take Note...**
>
> *The Black & White adjustment layer is disabled in CMYK mode.*

Step-by-Step	**Follow these steps to add a tint effect to an RGB image**

1. Double-click on the Black & White 1 layer thumbnail (⬤) icon (to the left of the Black & White 1 name and mask) in the Layer's panel. This activates the Black & White settings in the Properties panel.

2. Check the *Tint* checkbox as displayed in Figure 9-24. See the result in Figure 9-25.

   You can click on the color box to the right of the Tint checkbox to assign a color from the color libraries.

Figure 9-24: Apply a tint of color.   *Figure 9-25: The result.*

3. Click once on the Color box to the right of the *Tint* checkbox; the Color Picker (Tint Color) dialog box appears.

4. Press the Color Libraries button; the Color Libraries dialog box appears. From the Book drop-down menu, select Pantone+ Solid Coated, if it is not already selected.

5. Type **642** quickly, without pausing between typing the numbers. There is no text field in this dialog box, and so, by typing a Pantone number, you can easily locate it in the list of colors. Type too slowly and you could have an inaccurate color selection. You can try it again if Pantone 642 C is not selected. Press OK to close the Color Libraries dialog box. The color tint is assigned Pantone 642 C.

6. Choose File > Save. Leave the file open for the next section of this lesson.

Applying a gradient to the adjustment layer

The next step is a simple one that adds an interesting blending technique for using adjustment layers. By applying a **gradient** to the mask, you can blend the Black & White effect into a color image.

Follow these steps to enhance blending using a gradient mask	Step-by-Step

1. Press **D** on your keyboard to make sure that you are back to the default foreground and background colors of black and white.

2. Click once on the Black & White adjustment layer mask thumbnail to select it (Figure 9-27).

3. Select the Gradient tool (▪), and type **0**. By typing **0**, you are assigning 100 percent opacity to the gradient.

4. Click and drag from the left side of the image to the right as shown in Figure 9-26. A gradient is created in the same direction and angle as the line you draw.

   When you release the Gradient tool, there is a blend from the black-and-white adjustment to the original color image. If you don't like the angle or transition, you can re-drag the gradient as many times as you want. Click and drag a short line for a shorter gradient transition, or click and drag a longer line for a more gradual transition.

   If your colors are opposite to the ones in this example, your foreground and background colors could be reversed. Press **X** to reverse your colors and try again.

Figure 9-26: Click and drag with the Gradient tool to create a gradient mask. **Figure 9-27**: *The layer mask.*

Take Note...
The Gradient tool can create straight-line, radial, angle, reflected, and diamond blends. Select the type of gradient from the Options bar across the top of the Photoshop work area. If you want to drag a straight gradient line, hold down the Shift key while dragging to constrain the gradient to a 0-degree, 45-degree, or 90-degree angle.

5. Choose File > Save. Keep the file open for the next part of this lesson.

   Congratulations! You have completed the Black & White adjustment layer section of this lesson.

Layer styles

By using layer styles, such as shadows, glows, and bevels, you can change the appearance of images on layers. Layer styles are linked to the layer that is selected when the style is applied, but they can also be copied and pasted to other layers. When you combine masks with layer styles and use the Properties panel to refine those masks, the possibilities are endless. Combinations of styles can also be saved as a custom style to be applied to other layers.

Creating the text layer

In this section, you will create a text layer and apply a combination of effects to it. Then you will save the combined effects as a new style to apply to another layer. You should still have the file **ps0903_work.psd** open from the last lesson.

Step-by-Step | **Follow these steps to create and edit a text layer**

1. Select the Type tool (T) and click anywhere on the image. Type **CITY LIGHTS**.

2. Press Ctrl+A (Windows) or Command+A (Mac OS) to select all the text. Alternatively, you can choose Select > All from the menu bar.

   Get ready for a three-key command. It may seem awkward if you haven't used this combination before, but it is used in most other Creative Suite applications to resize text visually, and is a huge time-saver.

3. Hold down Ctrl+Shift+> (Greater Than) (Windows) or Command+Shift+> (Mac OS), and repeatedly press the > key. The text enlarges. You can change the combination to include the < (Lesser Than) key to reduce the size of the text. No particular size is needed; you can choose a size that you prefer.

   If you would rather not use the key command, type **85** in the font size text field in the Options bar at the top of the Photoshop workspace.

   Next, you will find a typeface that you want to use. Again, no particular typeface is required for this exercise. Pick one that you like, but make sure that it is heavy enough to show bevel (edge) effects. The font in the example is Rockwell, but you can choose any available font from your font list. The goal here is to create some visual hierarchy in the image. You don't want the text to be too big or overpowering. Changing the font, font size, line spacing and indentation of the text are just a few ways that this can be done.

4. Make sure the Type tool is still active and the text is selected, by pressing Ctrl+A (Windows) or Command+A (Mac OS), or by choosing All from the Select menu.

5. Now, highlight the font family name in the Type tool Options bar at the top of the Photoshop workspace (Figure 9-28), and press the up arrow (↑) or down arrow (↓) keys to scroll through your list of font families (Figure 9-29).

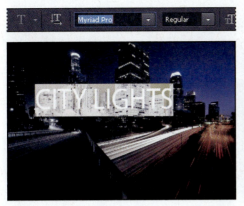 

Figure 9-28: *Select the text and then select the font name in Options bar.*

Figure 9-29: *Press the down or up arrows to change the font the selection. Your font selection may differ from this example.*

If you would rather not use the font shortcut, you can select the font you want from the Font family drop-down menu in the Options bar.

If your Swatches panel is not visible, choose Window > Swatches to bring it forward.

6. With the text still selected, choose White from the Swatches panel. Press the Commit check mark (✔) in the far right of the Options bar to commit your type changes.

> ***Take Note...***
> *Do not leave the Type tool to select the Move tool and reposition the text. If you want to reposition your text, keep the Type tool selected and simply hold down the Ctrl (Windows) or Command (Mac OS) key while dragging.*

Applying the Outer Glow layer style

Now you will apply a combination of layer effects to the text layer you just created.

Follow these steps to apply layer styles to type for effect   **Step-by-Step**

1. Click on the text layer name CITY LIGHTS, which is to the right of the Text layer indicator in the Layers panel, to make sure the layer is active.

2. Click on the Add a Layer Style button (*fx*) at the bottom of the Layers panel, and select Outer Glow from the pop-up menu (Figure 9-30). The Layer Style dialog box appears. The default settings may be too subtle, so you will make some changes.

Figure 9-30*: Select the Outer Glow style.*

There are many options available for each layer style. As a default, certain blending modes and opacities, as well as spread size and contours (edges), are already determined. In the next step, you will change the contour and the size of the outer glow.

<table>
<tr><td>What is a layer style contour?</td><td></td></tr>
</table>

When you create custom styles, you can use contours to create unique edge effects and transitions. A **contour** is a property found in layers that controls how an object is shaded. As you can see in the examples shown here, the same style can look very different. In Figure 9-31, the Cone contour is displayed. In Figure 9-32, the Cone-Inverted contour is shown and in Figure 9-33, you can see the Ring-Double contour.

Figure 9-31: The Cone contour.

 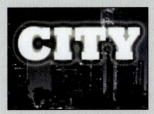

Figure 9-32: The Cone-Inverted contour.

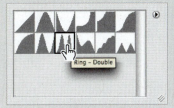 

Figure 9-33: The Ring-Double contour.

3. Select the arrow to the right of the Contour thumbnail in the Quality section of the Layer Style dialog box. The Contour Presets dialog box appears. Click on the Half Round contour as shown in Figure 9-34. Double-click on the Half Round contour to close the dialog box.

Layer styles

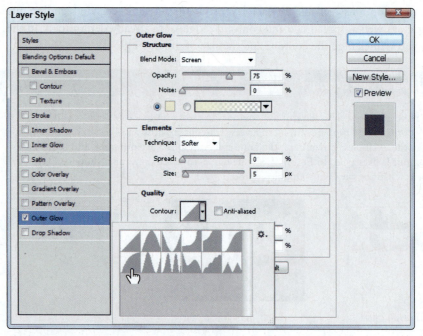

Figure 9-34: Select a preset contour for the Outer Glow style.

Take Note...
You can open the Contour Editor (Figure 9-35) and create your own custom contours by clicking on the Contour thumbnail instead of selecting the arrow to the right of the thumbnail.

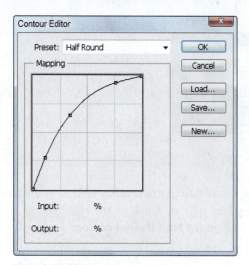

Figure 9-35: Editing a contour.

Now you will change the size of the outer glow.

4. In the Elements section of the Layer Style dialog box, drag the Size slider to the number 60 (Figure 8-36), or type **60** into the Size text field. As shown in Figure 9-37, the glow becomes more apparent.

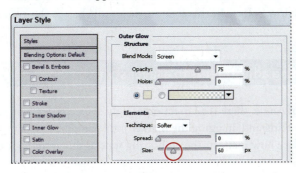

Figure 9-36: Drag the size slider to 60.   *Figure 9-37: The result.*

5. Keep the Layer Style dialog box open for the next step.

Applying the Bevel and Emboss layer style

You will now apply a second style. The Layer Style dialog box should still be open. If it is not, you can double-click on the word Effects in the Layers panel. This reopens the Layer Styles dialog box.

| Follow these steps to apply additional layer styles to your text | Step-by-Step |

1. Click on Bevel and Emboss in the Styles list on the left side of the Layer Style dialog box. The Bevel and Emboss effect is applied, and the options appear on the right.

> **Take Note...**
> *If you check a style, the options do not appear on the right. You must click on a style name for its options to appear.*

2. From the Style drop-down menu in the Structure section of the Layer Style dialog box, choose Emboss as shown in Figure 9-38. The result of this change is displayed in Figure 9-39. **Emboss** is an effect that produces the appearance of a 3D surface.

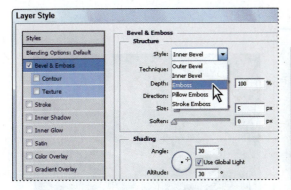

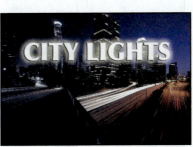

Figure 9-38: Experiment with the different Bevel and Emboss structures. *Figure 9-39: The result.*

You can experiment with many bevel and embossing styles. You can change the Technique to be Smooth, Chisel Hard, or Chisel Soft, or even direct the embossing to go down or up, using the Direction radio buttons. Experiment with these options; no particular settings are needed for this exercise.

Changing the shading

You will now change the shading. In the Shading section of the Bevel and Emboss Layer Style dialog box, there are several choices that relate to light, including the Angle, Gloss Contour (as discussed earlier), or Highlight and Shadow colors. In this section, you will change the angle of the light and the highlight color.

Step-by-Step	Follow these steps to make shading adjustments to a layer style

1. In the Shading section to the right of Angle, there is a Direction of light source slider. You can change the current light angle by clicking and dragging the marker indicating the current light angle. Click and drag the marker to see how it affects the embossing style as shown in Figure 9-40.

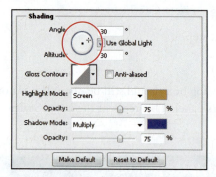

Figure 9-40: Click and drag inside the circle to change the direction of the light source.

Use Global light is checked as a default. This assures you that all other effects that rely on a light source use the same angle that you determine for this style.

2. Click and hold to select Normal from the Highlight Mode blending drop-down menu.

3. Now, click on the white box to the right of Highlight Mode. This opens the Select highlight color picker and allows you to sample a color from your image, or create your own highlight color using the Color Picker. Choose any yellow-gold color; in this example shown in Figure 9-41, an RGB value of R: 215, G: 155, B: 12 is used. Press OK.

4. Click on the Shadow color box, to the right of Shadow Mode, and change the color to blue. In the example shown in Figure 9-42, an RGB value of R: 30, G: 15, B: 176 is used. View the results in Figure 9-42.

  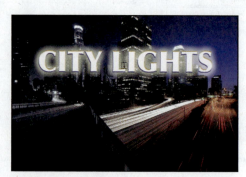

Figure 9-41: Set a highlight color.

Figure 9-42: Set a shadow color.

Figure 9-43: The resulting bevel and emboss.

5. Press OK to close the Color Picker. Keep the Layer Style dialog box open for the final step in this project.

Changing the fill opacity

In addition to setting opacity, which affects layer styles as well as the contents of the layer, you can adjust the fill opacity. The **fill opacity** affects only the contents of the layer, keeping the opacity of any layer styles that have been applied at the original opacity. This is a very easy method to use to make text look like it is embossed on paper or engraved in stone.

Follow these steps to edit fill opacity to add text effects

Step-by-Step

1. Select the Blending Options: Default. This is the top-most item underneath the Styles panel.

2. Click and drag the Fill Opacity slider to the left. In the example in Figure 9-44, it is dragged to the 20 percent point. Keep the Layer Style dialog box open for the next part of the lesson. View the result in Figure 9-45.

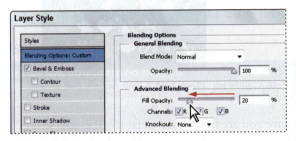

Figure 9-44: *Changing the fill opacity does not affect the layer style opacity.*

Figure 9-45: *The result as semi-transparent text.*

Saving the style

Now you will save the style you created.

Follow these steps to save a layer style for future use

Step-by-Step

1. With the Layer Styles dialog box still open, click on the New Style button, on the right side of the window. The New Style dialog box appears.

2. Type **my glow** in the Name text field as displayed in Figure 9-46, and press OK.

Figure 9-46: *Saving a style from combined styles.*

3. Press OK in the Layer Styles dialog box. The style is now added to the Styles panel.

Knowledge Assessment

True/False

Circle **T** if the statement is true or **F** if the statement is false.

T **F** **1.** When applying the Hue / Saturation adjustment layer, a layer mask is automatically added.

T **F** **2.** You can activate a mask and edit it separately from the adjustment (such as Hue and Saturation) that it's attached to.

T **F** **3.** You can make adjustments to an Adjustment layer by single clicking on it.

T **F** **4.** You can create a pattern in Photoshop out of any pixel information that you wish by selecting an area of a file or by using the entire file.

T **F** **5.** The best way to convert an image to black and white is to choose Image > Mode > Grayscale.

T **F** **6.** Pantone color libraries are not accessible through Photoshop, only print layout programs like InDesign have those libraries installed.

T **F** **7.** Layer styles (like drop shadows, glows, etc.) can be copied and pasted from one layer to another.

T **F** **8.** Contour shape is one of the attributes that can be used to adjust edge effects on an image.

T **F** **9.** Photoshop only has basic shapes available to use for drawing, such as arrows in one basic shape category.

T **F** **10.** Changing opacity affects layer styles as well as the contents of the layer.

Multiple Choice

Select the best response for the following statements.

1. Hue refers to what?

    a. Brightness

    b. Color

    c. Contrast

    d. Tonality

2. What is the keyboard shortcut to adjust brush size of the Brush tool?

    a. Left and Right Arrows

    b. Up and Down Arrows

    c. Left and Right Bracket keys

    d. Period and Comma

3. Darken, Linear Burn, Lighten, and Dissolve are all considered:

   a. Contrast settings

   b. Tonal qualities

   c. Saturation values

   d. Blending modes

4. The Black and White adjustment layer is disabled in what color mode?

   a. RGB

   b. CMYK

   c. HSB

   d. LAB

5. Straight-line, radial, angle, reflected and diamond are all types of:

   a. Patterns

   b. Symbols

   c. Gradients

   d. Blending modes

6. Which of the following is not considered an emboss style?

   a. Smooth

   b. Chisel Hard

   c. Chisel Medium

   d. Chisel Soft

7. Changing which value will affect only the content of the layer as opposed to including any layer styles that have been applied?

   a. Blend mode

   b. Opacity

   c. Fill Opacity

   d. None of the above

8. Fill Opacity, Channels, and Knockout are all properties of:

   a. General Blending

   b. Advanced Blending

   c. Transparency Settings

   d. Blend modes

9. Angle, Gloss, and Contour are all settings in which layer style?

   a. Bevel and Emboss

   b. Drop Shadow

   c. Satin

   d. None of the above

10. When choosing ways to view the various styles available in the Styles panel, which of the following view is available?

   a. Text Only

   b. Small Thumbnail

   c. Small List

   d. All of the above

2. Holding the Shift key, click and drag any corner anchor point toward the center until you see an amount close to 25 percent in the W and H text fields in the Options bar, or type **25** into the W and H text boxes. Reposition the butterfly to the upper-right corner of the image. Press Enter (Windows) or Return (Mac OS) to commit the change.

3. In the Layers panel, double-click on the layer name, ps1005, to highlight the text name. Type **Butterfly 4** and press Enter (Windows) or Return (Mac OS).

4. Now, double-click the Butterfly 4 layer thumbnail in the Layers panel (do not click on the layer name or the layer itself, but specifically on the Smart Object thumbnail). A dialog box appears, reminding you that you need to save the document after you edit the contents (Figure 10-11). Press OK. The **ps1005.psd** file is now open on your screen.

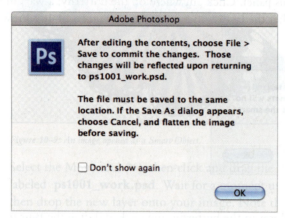

Figure 10-11: *A warning dialog box appears when you edit a Smart Object.*

By double-clicking on the Smart Object layer, you open the original file as a separate document. You'll now make some adjustments to the original image. In this case, you will be adjusting the hue and saturation.

5. In the Adjustments panel immediately above your layers, click the Hue/Saturation icon as shown in Figure 10-12 to open the Properties panel.

Figure 10-12: *Click the Hue/Saturation icon.*

The Properties panel for the Hue/Saturation settings appears. Using an adjustment layer ensures that your original pixel data remains untouched.

6. Drag the Hue slider to the left to approximately the –180 mark, or type **–180** in the Hue text box. This adjusts the color of the butterfly to blue. Click the Properties tab to close the panel.

7. Choose File > Save. This is the crucial step. As noted in the dialog box in step 4, you must save the current document without renaming it. Choose File > Close to close the image.

8. In the **ps1001_work.psd** file, notice that the blue butterfly has been updated. This is because Butterfly 4 is a Smart Object layer connected, or linked, to the original file, which is now embedded inside the **ps1001_work.psd** file.

Suppose you need to adjust the settings of the hue/saturation layer again; you can return to the adjustment layer to make any necessary changes.

9. Double-click on the Butterfly 4 layer thumbnail to reopen the source file. The warning dialog box you saw previously appears. Press OK.

> *Take Note...*
> *This dialog box can be turned off by clicking the* Don't Show Again *checkbox in the lower-left corner.*

10. In your layers panel, double-click the Layer thumbnail icon on the Hue/Saturation layer to reopen the Properties panel with the Hue/Saturation options visible as shown in Figure 10-13.

Figure 10-13: *Double-click the Layer thumbnail icon to reopen the Properties panel for Hue/Saturation.*

11. In the Properties panel, click and drag the Saturation slider to **–**60, or type **–60** in the Saturation text field. This tones down the bright blue. Click the Properties tab to close this panel.

12. Choose File > Save, and then File > Close to close the file. As before, the butterfly in your work image has been automatically updated.

Using this combination of adjustment layers and Smart Objects gives you tremendous flexibility with your layers. Adjustment layers and Smart Objects encourage you to experiment without fear of destroying the integrity of the original image. As you will see in the next exercise, this ability to edit the contents of a Smart Object has even more power when you have multiple Smart Objects.

8. Select the Brush tool (), and click and hold on the arrow to the right of the Brush Preset picker in the Options bar at the top of your screen. Select the Soft Round brush preset, and use the slider to change the Size value to approximately 45 (Figure 10-22).Click on the Options bar to make the Brush Preset picker disappear.

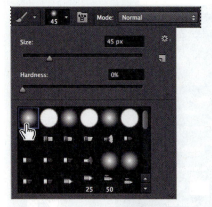

Figure 10-22: *Select the Soft Round brush and change the size to 45.*

Take Note...
For more information about working with Photoshop brushes, please review Lesson 6, "Painting and Retouching."

---

9. Press **D** on your keyboard to revert the foreground and background colors back to the default of black and white. Press **X** on your keyboard to swap the foreground and background colors. Black is now the foreground color and white is the background color.

10. Place your brush at the top of the butterfly, and begin painting from left to right and then downward. As you paint, the filter effects are concealed by the layer mask you are adding.

Take Note...
For an in-depth look at layer masks, please review Lesson 8, "Getting to Know Layers."

11. Continue painting downward until only the bottom half of the butterfly is blurred. Press the letter **X** on your keyboard to swap the foreground color to white (Figure 10-23). Now, paint over the top half again, and notice how the effect is revealed again. By toggling between white and black, and painting on the Smart Filter mask, you can reveal or conceal the filter effects (Figure 10-24).

Figure 10-23: Paint on the butterfly.   *Figure 10-24: The resulting mask.*

12. Press **X** on your keyboard to set black as the foreground color, and then paint the mask to hide virtually all the filter effect at the top part of the image. There are also areas at the bottom right that you will want to hide. You want your Butterfly 4 layer to look approximately the same as the example shown here in Figure 10-25. The effect is still not exactly what you need, but in the next section, you will fine-tune the motion blur effect.

Figure 10-25: The Butterfly 4 layer at this point.

Lesson 11

Fading your filter

Now that you have made some clouds, you'll fade the effect of the Cloud filter. The **Fade command** gives you the opportunity to change the opacity and blending mode of a filter effect immediately after you have applied it. Fade also works with the erasing, painting, and color adjustment tools.

Step-by-Step	Follow these steps to change the Cloud effect using the Fade command

1. Choose Edit > Fade Clouds. The Fade dialog box appears. Check the Preview option to preview the effect if it is not already checked.

 Take Note...
If Fade Clouds is not available, you did something else with the file after using the Clouds filter. Use the Window > History panel to select the Clouds state, then select Edit > Fade Clouds again.

2. Drag the slider to the left to adjust the opacity from 100 percent down to 50 percent as shown in Figure 11-4. Leave the Mode drop-down menu set to Normal, then press OK. View the results shown in Figure 11-5 and keep this file open for the next part of this lesson.

Figure 11–4: The Fade dialog box.

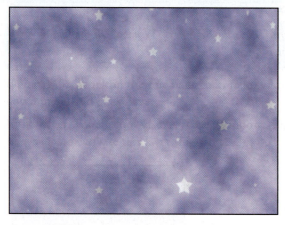

Figure 11–5: Fading the effect of the Cloud filter.

Using the Filter Gallery

The **Filter Gallery** allows you to apply more than one filter to an image at a time, and rearrange the order in which the filters are applied.

Note that not all filters are available in the Filter Gallery, and that the Filter Gallery is not available in CMYK, Lab, or Bitmap mode.

Follow these steps to select layers and access the Filter Gallery

1. With **ps1101_work.psd** open, click the Visibility icon (👁) next to the layer group named monsters. Three monsters appear.

2. Expand the layer group by clicking on the triangle immediately to the left of the monsters layer group as shown in Figure 11-6. This displays the monster1, monster2, and monster3 layers that are included in this group. Figure 11-7 shows the composition with the three monsters. Layer groups are a great way to nest layers and are easily created by clicking on the Create a new group button and dragging layers into the group.

Figure 11-6: Click on the arrow to the left of the monsters group.

Figure 11-7: The individual monster layers are revealed.

3. Select the monster1 layer.

4. Press **D** on your keyboard to return to the default foreground and background colors of black and white.

5. Choose Filter > Filter Gallery. The Filter Gallery dialog box appears.

6. Press Ctrl+– (minus sign) (Windows) or Command+– (minus sign) (Mac OS) four times to zoom to 25%.

You have just applied filters from the Filter Gallery to the monster3 layer (Figure 11-14), much the same way you applied filters to the monster1 and monster2 layers. The difference is that you converted monster3 to a smart object before applying the filters.View the results in Figure 11-13. This offers you the opportunity to make changes, or even delete the filters at a later time.

8. In the Layers panel, double-click on Filter Gallery located underneath the monster3 layer (Figure 11-15). The Filter Gallery dialog box opens again.

Figure 11-15: *Editing a Smart Filter.*

9. In the filter effects area, select Plastic Wrap from the list of applied filters.

10. Using the sliders in the Plastic Wrap effect options, change the Highlight Strength to **20**, the Detail to **1** and the Smoothness to **1**.

11. In the filter effects area of the Filter Gallery, drag Plastic Wrap below Sponge as shown in Figure 11-16. This changes the filter order, and creates a different effect. Press OK.

Figure 11-16: *Changing the order of the filters.*

12. Choose File > Save.

Smart Filter options

Next, you will explore additional filter options. You'll start by fading the filters and by editing the Smart Filter Blending Options. You will then discover how to disable a filter and how to take advantage of the Filter effects mask thumbnail.

| Follow these steps to explore additional Smart Filter options | Step-by-Step |

1. In the Layers panel, right-click (Windows) or Ctrl+click (Mac OS) on Filter Gallery, located under the monster3 layer Smart Filter. As shown in Figure 11-17, select Edit Smart Filter Blending Options from the contextual menu.

Figure 11-17: *Editing the Blending options.*

Like the Fade option used earlier in this lesson, the Smart Filter blending options allow you to control the intensity of a filter. However, this method is non-destructive. You can change the Fade settings multiple times and not impact the original image. You can also access the Blending Options at any time, unlike the Fade dialog box, which had to be accessed immediately after applying a filter to a regular (non-smart) layer.

Lesson 11

Knowledge Assessment

True/False

Circle **T** if the statement is true or **F** if the statement is false.

T **F** **1.** Filters can be applied to all types of images including bitmaps, vectors, etc.

T **F** **2.** All filters are available under the Filter menu, regardless of color mode.

T **F** **3.** You have the opportunity to change the opacity and blending mode of a filter immediately after you have applied it.

T **F** **4.** The Filter Gallery is another way to access all the filters in Photoshop.

T **F** **5.** Filters can be layered on top of one another through the Filter Gallery.

T **F** **6.** There are destructive filters and non-destructive Smart filters.

T **F** **7.** You do not need to convert your image into a Smart Object in order to apply a Smart Filter.

T **F** **8.** Once you apply a filter to a Smart Object from the Filter Gallery, it shows up as a sub-layer within the layer panel.

T **F** **9.** Smart Filters have their own blending options.

T **F** **10.** The Fade option with Smart Filters is also non-destructive.

Multiple Choice

Select the best response for the following statements.

1. The Filter Gallery allows you to apply more than one filter to an image at a time and:
   a. Apply layer masks
   b. Rearrange the order in which the filters are applied
   c. Set the tonal curves of your image
   d. All of the above

2. Which of the following is not a feature in the Filter Gallery window?
   a. The Preview pane
   b. Filter Categories
   c. Adjustment layers
   d. List of filter effects

3. Which of the following is a filter category?
   a. Brush Strokes
   b. Distort
   c. Texture
   d. All of the above

4. In order to apply a Smart Filter, the image has to be first converted into a:

    a. Flattened image

    b. RGB image

    c. CMYK image

    d. Smart object

5. Filters can be selectively modified when applied to Smart Objects because of:

    a. Layer masks

    b. The Filter Gallery

    c. Blending modes

    d. All of the above

6. Which tool is typically used in conjunction with layer masks to help isolate the areas of an image a filter will affect?

    a. Gradient

    b. Clone Stamp

    c. Healing Brush

    d. Patch

7. When using the Create Plane Tool in the Vanishing Point dialog box, what key on the keyboard is pressed to add a perpendicular plane to an existing plane?

    a. Alt (Mac) or Option (Windows)

    b. Command (Mac) or Ctrl (Windows)

    c. Shift

    d. No keyboard key is necessary

8. Which key on the keyboard allows you to toggle back and forth between foreground and background colors?

    a. D

    b. Z

    c. X

    d. S

9. Which filter simplifies the task of editing images that are in perspective?

    a. Free transform

    b. Distort

    c. Vanishing Point

    d. None of the above

10. The four corner points of a grid can be modified by what tool within Vanishing Point?

    a. Marquee

    b. Edit Plane tool

    c. Skew tool

    d. Pen

Proficiency Assessment

Using filters to create content from scratch

It's also possible to use filters to create content from scratch. In this project, you can create content from scratch.

1. Open Photoshop and create a new file that is 8" wide by 5" tall, 150 ppi RGB color mode with a white background.

2. Set the foreground color to a new blue color, and set the background color to white.

3. Choose Filter > Render > Clouds. See how Photoshop generates a cloud-like pattern that overlays a great starting point for these artwork.

4. You now have free reign. Feel free to apply additional filters as well. Maybe you can make the clouds repeat. Don't be afraid to use other colors as well. Multiple layers on top of one another? Multiple blending modes? There are many possibilities.

5. Keep working until you have something you can discuss with your classmates. Save the file as 11-4.clouds.psd.

Proficiency Assessment

1. Open Photoshop and create a new file that is 8" wide by 5" tall, 150 ppi RGB color mode with a white background.

2. Set the foreground color to a new blue color, and set the background color to white.

3. Choose Filter > Render > Clouds. See how Photoshop generates a cloud-like pattern that overlays a great starting point for these artwork.

4. You now have free reign. Feel free to apply additional filters as well. Maybe you can make the clouds repeat.

5. Keep working until you have something you can discuss.

Creating Images for Web and Video

Key Terms

- animation
- HD video
- keyframe
- optimizing image slices
- slice
- Timeline panel

Skill	Objective
Demonstrate knowledge of image resolution, image size, and image file format for web, video, and print	2.1
Demonstrate knowledge of image-generating devices, their resulting image types, and how to access resulting images in Photoshop	2.5
Demonstrate knowledge of importing, exporting, organizing, and saving	3.3
Use Photoshop guides and rulers	4.2
Transform images	4.3
Demonstrate knowledge of preparing images for web, print, and video	5.1

Business case

You've been working on print pieces so far, now it's time to shift gears in a more multimedia direction. Your latest assignment is to create a piece that will be converted into a website. To throw an additional twist they want you to add an additional animation piece. Luckily you'll be able handle that without being a web expert or animation guru. Photoshop has come a long way from being primarily a print-based application back in the early days...

Starting up

In this lesson, you'll create a group of projects for web and video production. You'll work with still and animated graphics for each medium.

Before starting, make sure that your tools and panels are consistent by resetting your preferences. See "Resetting Adobe Photoshop CS6 preferences" in the Starting up section of this book.

In this lesson, you will work with several files from the ps12lessons folder. Make sure that you have loaded the pslessons folder from *http://www.wiley.com/college/sc/adobeseries*. See "Loading lesson files" in the Starting up section of this book.

5. Reduce the spacing between the word *a* and *kite* by clicking to insert the cursor anywhere between those letters, then press and hold the Alt+Left Arrow key (Windows) or Option+Left Arrow key (Mac OS) and press repeatedly until the space is smaller; choose the amount of space you want. In our example, the Alt/Option+Left Arrow key was pressed approximately 15 times.

> **Take Note...**
> *Alternately, you could have left no space between the words a and kite, kern out the space between by repeatedly pressing the Alt/Option+Right Arrow key.*

6. While the text is still active, click the Create warped text button (⊥) in the Options bar. The Warp Text dialog box appears. You can warp text to create all sorts of effects; in this example, the text is distorted to add a little dimension.

7. In the Warp Text dialog box, select Rise from the Style drop-down menu, and make sure that the Horizontal radio button is active.

8. Click and drag the Bend slider to the left to change the value to +10, or type **+10** into the Bend text field.

9. Verify that the Horizontal Distortion is set to 0 (zero), then click and drag the Vertical Distortion slider to the right to about the value of 25, or type **25** into the Vertical Distortion text field (Figure 12-6). Click OK. The warp is applied to the text as shown in Figure 12-7.

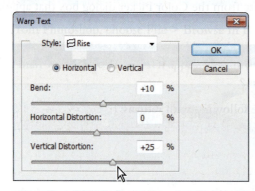

Figure 12-6: Applying the Rise warp.

Figure 12-7: Result.

10. Click the Commit check box (✔) on the right side of the Options bar to confirm your text edits. If necessary, choose the Move tool (⊹) and click and drag to reposition the text so it is visible in the upper-left corner of the image.

Adding Style to the text

Now that you have your header text created, you will add a layer style to it.

Step-by-Step	Follow these steps to apply a layer style to the text and edit it

1. With the Go Fly a Kite text layer still selected, click the Add a layer style button (*fx*) at the bottom of the Layers panel. Select Outer Glow from the layer style drop-down menu. The Layer Style dialog box appears with Outer Glow settings visible.

2. From the Blend Mode drop-down menu, choose Normal.

3. In the Structure section, click once on the Set color of glow swatch; the Color Picker appears. Click and drag the slider, on the right of the color pane, until you see blue colors in the color pane. Choose a navy blue and click OK.

4. In the Elements section, click and drag the Size slider to the right until you reach the value of 25 px, or enter **25** into the Size text field (Figure 12-8). Click OK to close the dialog box. You can see the results in Figure 12-9.

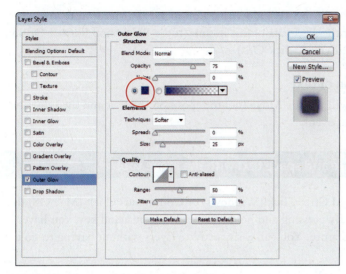

Figure 12-8: Change the options for the Outer Glow style. *Figure 12-9*: Result.

Creating the text for the links

Now that you have the header text completed, you will create the individual text layers that will serve as links.

Follow these steps to add individual text layers for the links	Step-by-Step

1. Select the Type tool (T) and click somewhere on the top right of the large kite the man is holding in the image. The blinking insert text cursor appears.

    The Type tool remembers the last settings, such as font and size. Before typing, you need to change the text size and orientation.

2. Choose 30 from the Font size drop-down menu, then click the Left align text button (≣) in the Options bar.

3. Type **Sales**, then press Ctrl+Enter (Windows) or Command+Return (Mac OS) to commit the text entry and exit the type options.

> **Take Note...**
> *Pressing Ctrl/Command+Enter or Return is the same as pressing the Commit (✔) check box in the Options bar.*

4. Position your cursor under the Sales text and click to create a new text entry. Exact position is not important, as you will reposition the text later. Type **Service**, then press Ctrl+Enter (Windows) or Command+Return (Mac OS) to commit the text entry and exit the type options.

5. Position your cursor under the word Service and click and type **About**, then press Ctrl+Enter (Windows) or Command+Return (Mac OS) to commit the text entry and exit the type options.

6. Position your cursor under the word About to make the last text entry, and click. Type the word **Contact**, then press Ctrl+Enter (Windows) or Command+Return (Mac OS) to commit the text entry and exit the type options.

7. Choose File > Save, or press Ctrl+S (Windows) or Command+S (Mac OS) to save the file. Keep this file open for the next part of this lesson. (If the Photoshop Format Options window appeared when you saved, click OK.)

Positioning and distribution of text

In this part of the lesson, you will use the Move tool to reposition the text and then distribute the vertical space between them evenly.

Step-by-Step | **Follow these steps to move and space text with the Move tool**

1. Select the Move tool (⊕) and Ctrl+Click (Windows) or Command+Click (Mac OS) the word Sales (in the image). By pressing and holding the Ctrl/Command key, you have turned on the auto-select feature. You can easily activate layers without having to go to the Layers panel.

   With the Sales layer selected, click and drag the text so it is off to the right of the curved edge of the kite.

2. Press and hold the Ctrl/Command key, click the other three text layers, and position them off to the right of the kite, following the curve of the kite image.

3. Make sure that the Layers panel is visible and select the Sales text layer. Then, Ctrl+Shift+click (Windows) or Command+Shift+Click (Mac OS) on the Service, About, and Contact text layers (in the Layers panel).

   Note that when you select three or more layers, the Align and Distribute options become visible in the Options bar. Align becomes visible with two layers selected.

4. As shown in Figure 12-10, choose Distribute vertical centers (⊜) from the Options bar. The text layers are distributed evenly as demonstrated in Figure 12-11.

Figure 12-10: Click the Distribute vertical centers button.

Figure 12-11: The selected layers now have equal amounts of vertical space between them.

Creating slices

A **slice** is a part of an image that is cut from a larger image. Think of a slice as a piece of a puzzle that, when placed alongside other related pieces, creates an entire image. An example of a sliced images is displayed in Figure 12-12. An HTML table or CSS holds the pieces together. In this example, you will use Cascading styles to create the final HTML page.

Figure 12-12: An example of a sliced image.

In the early days of the Web, slicing was used to create the appearance that a page was loading faster; a user could see the different slices loading instead of waiting for the entire image to appear. These days, slices can still be used in this way for web graphics, but it is more likely that you would use slices to precisely choose the area of an image you would like to export. You might then use the slice for a CSS background image or some other element of your web page (such as a button). In this exercise, you will create guides that will determine where the slicing of your image occurs.

Follow these steps to define guides for slicing	Step-by-Step

1. If rulers are not displayed, choose View > Rulers to show the rulers on the top and left side of the document window. Rulers are a useful visual reference to determine size and location of objects in an image. They're also a great way to change your ruler units. Simply right-click on the ruler and choose a new unit of measurement. If the rulers reveal a different unit of measurement than you desire, simply right click on a ruler and choose the desired unit of measurement from the list.

2. Choose View > Snap to turn off the snapping features for the rest of this lesson. The snapping features sometimes force the cursor to align with elements in your images, such as the edges of the text layers. Turn turn snapping back on you can choose View > Snap at any time.

   Using the rulers, you will create guides on your document that will later define where you want to slice your image.

3. Click directly on the top (horizontal) ruler, and then click and drag to pull a guide from the ruler. Continue dragging the guide; release it when the guide is just above the Sales text layer.

Certification Ready 4.2

How do you show and hide rulers?

Certification Ready 4.2

How can you change the unit of measurement on rulers?

Certification Ready 4.2

How do you add and remove guides?

Applying attributes to your slices

Now that you have defined your slices, you will apply attributes to them. The attributes that you will apply in this lesson are URL and Alt Tags. By defining a URL, a link is made from that slice to a location or file on the Web. By defining an Alt Tag, you allow viewers to read a text description of an image. This is helpful for visually impaired users and for users who have turned off the option for viewing graphics. An Alt Tag also helps search engines find more relevant content on your page.

| **Step-by-Step** | **Follow these steps to apply attributes to your slices** |

1. With the **ps1201_work.psd** file still open and the Slice Select tool (✏) still selected, select the slice containing the Sales text.

2. Click the Set options for the current slice button (▣) in the Options bar (immediately to the right of the "Hide Auto Slices" button). The Slice Options dialog box appears.

    You will be supplied with a link to a file in your lessons folder to test your links.

3. Type **sales.html** into the URL text field.

4. Type **Sales** into the Alt Tag text field as shown in Figure 12-19, and click OK.

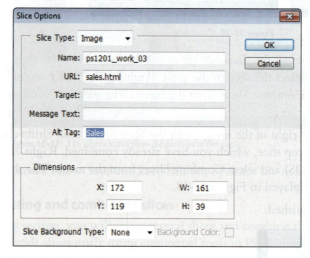

Figure 12-19: Enter the URL and Alt Tag information.

Take Note...
Your HTML file must be saved inside the ps12lessons folder in order to have a working link.

5. Now, select the slice containing the text *Service*, and choose the Set options for the current slice button in the Options bar. The Slice Options dialog box appears.

6. Type **service.html** into the URL text field and **Service** in the Alt Tag text field. Click OK.

7. Select the slice containing the text *About*, and choose the Set options for the current slice button in the Options bar. The Slice Options dialog box appears.

8. Type **about.html** into the URL text field and **About Us** in the Alt Tag text field. Click OK.

9. Select the slice containing the text *Contact*, and choose the Set options for the current slice button in the Options bar. The Slice Options dialog box appears.

10. Type **contact.html** into the URL text field and **Contact Us** in the Alt Tag text field. Click OK.

11. Choose File > Save. Keep the document open for the next part of the lesson.

> **Take Note...**
> *For this lesson, you do not put an alt tag on each slice, but we recommend that you assign a descriptive alt tag to each slice when producing images for the Web.*

Using Save For Web

The process of making an image look as good as possible at the smallest file size is called optimizing. This is important for all images that will be used on the Web, since most viewers don't want to wait long for information to appear. Optimizing images for the Web is quite different than optimizing images for print. When preparing files for print, you generally want high resolution (300 ppi) images and may want them in the CMYK color mode. File size is generally not an issue when preparing files for print. When preparing files for the Web however, you want images in the RGB color mode, you want low resolution (72 ppi) and file format is more of an issue as GIF is best for graphics that contain areas of solid color where JPEG and PNG are better for photographs.

In this part of the lesson, you'll use the Save For Web feature to optimize your navigational banner.

> **Take Note...**
> *In the previous version of Photoshop, this feature was called "Save for Web & Devices." With the removal of the Device Central feature in Photoshop CS6, the name has returned to the simpler "Save for Web."*

| **Follow these steps to explore the Save for Web feature** | **Step-by-Step** |

1. With the **ps1201_work.psd** file still open, choose File > Save For Web. The Save For Web dialog box appears.

2. Select the 2-up tab to view your original image on the top and your optimized image on the bottom as shown in Figure 12-20. Note that the window may display the original on the left side and the optimized image on the right.

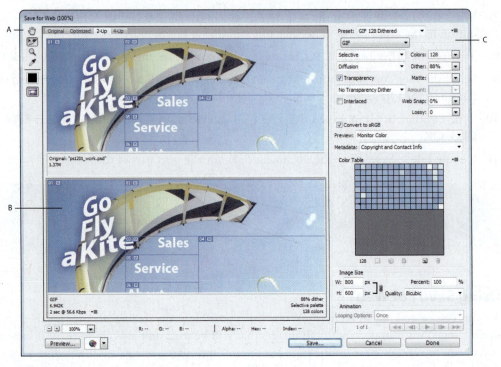

Figure 12-20

A. Toolbox. B. Preview window. C. Optimization settings.

3. Select the Hand tool (✋) and click and drag directly on the image in either window to reposition the image so you can see the four slices containing text.

The Save For Web window is broken into three main areas:

Toolbox: the Toolbox provides you with tools for panning and zooming in your image, selecting slices, and sampling color.

Preview window: in addition to having the ability to view both the original and optimized images individually, you can preview the original and optimized images side-by-side in 2-up view or with up to three variations in the 4-up view.

Optimization settings: the Optimization settings allow you to specify the format and settings of your optimized file.

How to choose web image formats

When you want to optimize an image for the Web, what format should you choose? Choose the format best suited to the type of image you are using.

Figure 12-21

GIF: an acronym for Graphic Interchange File, the GIF format is usually used on the Web to display simple colored logos, motifs, and other limited-tone imagery. The GIF format supports a maximum of 256 colors, as well as transparency. Figure 12-21 is an example of this type of image. GIF is the only one of the four formats here that supports built-in animation.

Figure 12-22

JPEG: an acronym for Joint Photographic Experts Group, the JPEG file format has found wide acceptance on the Web as the main format for displaying photographs and other continuous-tone imagery. The JPEG format supports a range of millions of colors, allowing for the accurate display of a wide range of artwork. Figure 12-22 is an example of a JPEG image.

Figure 12-23

PNG: an acronym for Portable Network Graphics. PNG was intended to blend the best of both the GIF and JPEG formats. PNG files come in two different varieties: like GIF, PNG-8 can support up to 256 colors, while PNG-24 can support millions of colors, similar to the JPEG format. Both PNG varieties support transparency and, as an improvement on GIF's all-or-nothing transparency function, a PNG file supports varying amounts of transparency so you can actually see through an image to your web page contents. Older browsers, in particular IE6, do not support PNG transparency, but this is seldom a problem, unless you specifically need to support the older browsers. Figure 12-23 is an example of a PNG.

Figure 12-24

WBMP: a standard format for optimizing images for mobile devices, WBMP files are 1-bit, meaning they contain only black and white pixel. as displayed in Figure 12-24.

4. Click the Slice Select tool (✄), then the Sales slice, then Shift+click the Service, About, and the Contact slices. Now all slices are active.

> ***Take Note...***
> *Make sure you are selecting the text slices in the Optimize preview, not the Original preview window.*

Now you will use a preset to optimize this text for the Web. Typically, artwork with lots of solid colors and text are saved as GIF or PNG-8, but images, such as photographs, fare better in size and final appearance when saved in the JPEG or PNG-24 format. In this example, you will save just the text as GIF slices, and the rest of the image slices as JPEG.

5. In the Optimize panel, on the right, choose GIF 64 No Dither from the Preset drop-down menu as displayed in Figure 12-25. The options are loaded in the optimize settings below the Preset drop-down, but can be further edited and customized, if necessary.

This is why you selected this preset:

- The GIF format was selected because the text contains a solid white color. GIF compresses images with solid colors to the smallest possible file size.

- 64 represents the number of colors that are retained when the file is saved in GIF format. GIF files use a color table model that allows up to 256 colors in an image; the fewer the number of colors, the smaller the file size. You can see the color table in the Color Table panel on the right side of the Save for Web dialog box.

- No Dither indicates that you do not want Photoshop to use dithering, or pixelation, to create colors that are not included in the 64-color panel you have specified.

Figure 12-25: *Select GIF 64 No Dither format for the slices containing text.*

Note that the file size of the optimized image (Figure 12-26), based on your current settings, is displayed at the bottom of the optimized image preview.

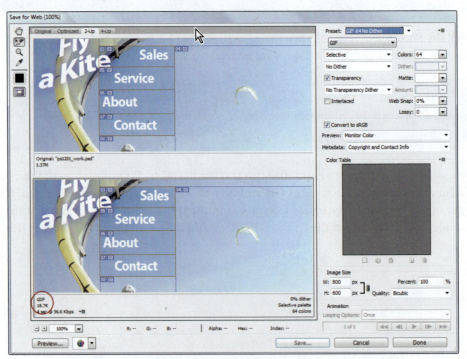

Figure 12-26: *The file size of the optimized image.*

Understanding Color Algorithms

GIFs can be reduced in size by reducing the amount of colors that create the image. This is referred to as the Color Algorithm. The Color Algorithm helps to specify the color palette that will create the final image. There are four main choices from which you can select:

Perceptual: a perceptual rendering is one where the goal is to produce a pleasing reproduction of an original. This is a good choice for illustrative graphics where color consistency or integrity is less important.

Selective: creates a color table similar to the Perceptual color table, but favoring broad areas of color and the preservation of web colors. If color integrity is important, this would be a good selection. Selective is the default option.

Adaptive: creates a custom color table by sampling colors from the predominant spectrum in the image. For example, if an image has many shades of red, the sampled colors are created from colors in the red spectrum, providing a better range of important colors.

Web: uses the standard 216-color color table common to the Windows and Mac OS 8-bit (256-color) palettes. This option ensures that no browser dither is applied to colors when the image is displayed using 8-bit color. Using the web palette can create larger files, and is becoming less of an issue as viewers increase their monitor capabilities.

Optimizing the image slices

Now that you optimized the text slices, you will optimize the remaining image slices using a different format. **Optimizing image slices** isn't always recommended, but it can work well for some images. You can optimize images even more by saving varying levels of the same format; for instance, select JPEG for all the slices, but vary the quality level, depending on the importance or location of the slice.

Follow these steps to optimize the image slices

1. Click the Optimized tab to see just this view.

2. Using the Slice Select tool (⌖), click the slice in the upper-left side of the image, then Shift+click each of the other three (non-text) slices. There should be a total of four slices selected.

3. From the Preset drop-down menu in the Optimized panel, choose JPEG Medium.

   You can test your file in a web browser directly from the Save For Web dialog box.

4. Select the Preview in default browser button at the bottom of the Save For Web dialog box as highlighted in Figure 12-27. If you have a default browser installed, your image is opened on a browser page. You can also define a browser using the Preview the optimized image drop-down menu in the lower-left corner of the Save For Web dialog box.

Notice that the slices are not apparent and the code is visible in your preview.

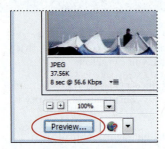

Figure 12-27: Preview the optimized image in a browser.

The slices you created for the navigation will not be working yet because this test page has not been saved into your lesson folder; it is just a temporary page.

5. Close the browser window to return to the Save For Web dialog box.

6. Choose Save; the Save Optimized As dialog box appears. Browse to the ps12lessons folder and choose HTML and Images from the Format drop-down menu. Click Save.

   An HTML page, along with the sliced images, is saved in your ps12lessons folder. You can now open the file in Dreamweaver, or any other web editing program, and continue building the page, or copy and paste the table to another page.

7. Choose File > Save to save your original image. Choose File > Close to close the file.

Saving files for video

Photoshop can be a very useful tool for preparing images for use in video programs such as Adobe Premiere, After Effects, or other video editing programs such as Final Cut Pro. Photoshop supports the creation of images using non-square pixels which helps to keep artwork correctly proportioned when used in video applications. You might use Photoshop to create a still image to be used as a title or some other element within a video. In general, most Adobe programs work extremely well with the native PSD format and require no conversion.

When importing into a non-Adobe video application, you may need to consider the support for the PSD file format and for other properties, such as transparency. Each video application has its own set of rules, and you should check with the software manufacturer for details such as file size, dimensions, file format, and title-safe areas. For this lesson, you will open a pre-built file and save it as a TIFF with an alpha channel. Most video editing applications recognize alpha channels when defining transparent areas on an image.

Follow these steps to save a file for video

1. Open the file **ps1202.psd**. The image that appears will be used as a transparent overlay in a video as shown in Figure 12-28.

Figure 12-28: An image with a largely transparent bottom half.

2. If the Layers panel is not visible, choose Window > Layers to open the Layers panel.

3. Position your cursor over the vector mask on the Shape 1 layer as shown in Figure 12-29. Press and hold the Ctrl (Windows) or Command (Mac OS) key and click the vector thumbnail for the Rectangle Shape layer. This selects everything on that layer that is not transparent.

Figure 12-29: Ctrl/Command+click the Shape 1 thumbnail in order to make a selection from a layer's contents.

4. Press and hold the Ctrl+Shift (Windows) or Command+Shift (Mac OS) keys, and click the layer thumbnail for the layer called balloon. This adds the balloon layer to the selection.

5. If the Channels panel is not visible, choose Window > Channels to open the Channels panel.

Lesson 12

5. If the Layers panel is not visible, choose Window > Layers. Select the balloon layer to make sure it is the active layer. Then, using the Move tool, click and drag the balloon so it is in the lower-left corner of the lake image as displayed in Figure 12-33.

Figure 12-33: Position the balloon to be in the lower-left corner.

6. Type **15** to change the layer to a 15% opacity.

7. Click the Duplicate selected frames button (⊒) at the bottom of the Animation panel. A second frame is added to the right of the original.

8. Verify that you still have the balloon layer selected. Then, using the Move tool, click and drag the balloon to the upper-right corner of the lake image. Type **0** (zero) to set the layer opacity at 100%.

9. Click the Add a layer style button (*fx*) at the bottom of the Layers panel, and choose Outer Glow from the list of styles. The Layer Style dialog box appears with Outer Glow selected.

10. In the Elements section of the Layer Style dialog box, click and drag the Size slider to the right until you reach approximately 70, or type **70** into the Size text field. Click OK. A glow has been applied to the balloon layer.

11. From the Animation panel menu, select Tween or click the Tween button (◌◌) at the bottom of the Animation panel.

12. On the Tween menu, confirm that tweening is set to the Previous Frame and the Frames to Add is 5 (Figure 12-34).

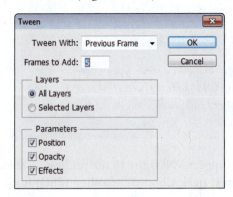

Figure 12-34: Choose to insert five frames in between the frames.

13. Click OK to add five frames to your animation. Photoshop interpolates the starting position, opacity, and layer style between the first frame and the 7th frame, thus creating an animation in which the balloon starts in the bottom-left and rises to the top-right.

 Take Note...
In addition to the number of frames to add to the animation, the Tween menu gives you the ability to choose which layers to include in your frames and which parameters to animate. As the default, all layers and parameters are included.

14. Select all the frames of your animation by clicking the first frame, pressing and holding the Shift key, and clicking the last frame. The default time for each frame is 5 seconds, which would create a very long animation; you need to reduce this time.

15. With all your frames selected, click the value for Selects frame delay at the bottom of any frame and select 0.5 as shown in Figure 12-35. Because all the frames are highlighted, the delay time of all your frames is adjusted.

Figure 12-35: Select 0.5 as the frame delay time.

Lesson 12

16. Click the Play button (▶) at the bottom of the Animation panel to preview your animation. If your animation continues to loop, press the Stop animation button (■) (same location as the Play button) to stop the animation.

> **Take Note...**
> *As a default, your animation is set to replay over and over again. If you prefer to set the number of times your animation plays, click and hold the text, Forever, that appears in the lower-left corner of the animation panel and select Once, or choose Other to input a custom value.*

17. Choose File > Save As. The Save As dialog box appears. Navigate to the ps12lessons folder and then type **animation_done** in the Name text field. Choose Photoshop (PSD) from the Format drop-down menu and click Save. Keep the file open for the next part of this lesson.

Saving an animated GIF

Now you will save the animation in a format that will recognize the frames and can be posted to the Web.

Step-by-Step	**Follow these steps to save the animation as a GIF**

1. Choose File > Save For Web.

2. In the Save For Web dialog box, choose 2-up from the display tabs at the top of the dialog box. This allows you to see the original image next to a preview of the optimized image.

3. Choose GIF 128 Dithered from the Preset drop-down menu. This is a good preset to use for an animation with multiple colors. It creates a good balance between file size and image quality.

4. Click the Preview button in the lower left to see a preview of the animated GIF. In your own projects, this would be a good way to test your animation and then return to the Save for Web interface and make adjustments. For now, just close the browser.

5. Click the Save button to save your file as a GIF animation. Navigate to the ps12lesson folder and type animation_done.gif in the File name text field.

6. In the Format drop-down menu, choose Images Only and press Save.

7. Choose File > Save to save your file, then choose File > Close to close your Photoshop document.

8. If you would like to test your file, open any browser application and choose File > Open File, and then browse to locate your GIF and open it directly into your browser window.

Creating animation for HD video

For this part of the lesson, you will create a type of on-screen graphic called a lower third. Usually seen on television and in documentary-style films, a lower third is the text and graphics that usually appear on screen to introduce a speaker. The name comes from the fact that the text and graphic take up the lower third of the frame. To create the lower third, you'll bring a graphic into a blank document and animate its opacity parameter so it fades in. Then you'll render the video file so it can be imported into a high-definition video project **HD video** contains a higher resolution picture than traditional SD (Standard Definition) video.

Working in Timeline mode

The Timeline mode of the Animation panel functions differently from the Frame mode. In the Timeline mode, each layer has parameters for position, opacity, and effects that can have key frames assigned to them individually.

Follow these steps to explore Timeline mode in the Animation panel	Step-by-Step

1. Choose File > New and choose Film & Video from the Preset drop-down menu. Click the size menu and choose the HDTV 1080p/29.97 option. This setting refers to the pixel resolution of most high-definition projects (1920 × 1080). Choose Transparent from the Background Contents drop-down menu. Click OK.

   A warning dialog box may appear, telling you that the pixel aspect ratio is for previewing purposes only. Click OK.

2. Choose View > New Guide. While the presets include guidelines to define the Action and Title safe areas of the video frame, there is nothing to indicate where your lower third should end.

3. In the New Guide dialog box, select the Horizontal radio button, type **66%** in the Position text field as shown in Figure 12-36, and click OK. This creates a new guideline 66% from the top of your document and marks the lower third of the video frame.

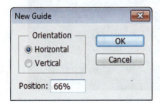

Figure 12-36: Create a guide indicating the lower third.

4. Choose File > Open and open **ps1205.psd** from the ps12lessons folder.

5. Select the Move tool (✛) and then click and drag the image (**ps1205.psd**) to the tab for your untitled document. Keep holding the mouse until the empty page toggles into view; make sure your cursor is over the image, and then release the mouse to add the lower third layer to this document.

6. You can close the **ps1205.psd** file after you drag over the contents.

7. Position the graphic so it is below the lower third guide as shown in Figure 12-37.

Figure 12-37: Position the graphic so it is below the lower third.

8. If the Layers panel is not open, choose Window > Layers. Layer 1 was created automatically when you created your document and you don't need it, so delete it by highlighting it in the Layers panel and dragging it to the Delete layer button (🗑) at the bottom of the panel.

9. If the Timeline panel is not open, choose Window > Timeline. Click the button labeled Create Video Timeline located in the middle of the Timeline panel; the video timeline appears. The video timeline in Photoshop CS6 supports basic editing, transitions, and the ability to add a music track. The various tools and icons are labeled in Figure 12-38.

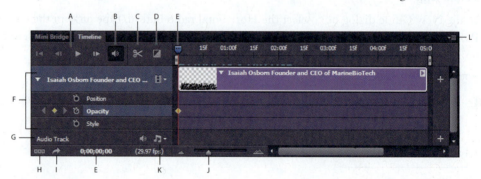

Figure 12-38

A. *Player Controls.* **B.** *Mute Audio Playback.* **C.** *Split at Playhead.* **D.** *Select a transition.* **E.** *Current Time Indicator.*
F. *Video Track Layers.* **G.** *Audio Track.* **H.** *Convert to Frame Animation.* **I.** *Render Video.* **J.** *Zoom Slider.*
K. *Add Media to Track.* **L.** *Panel Menu.*

10. In the Animation panel, click the triangle to the left of the layer name to reveal the properties.

Learning More

What are properties?

When using the video timeline, every layer has a set of default properties for Position, Opacity, and Style. In Adobe Photoshop, animation information is stored in keyframes, which represent a change in at least one property over time. A **keyframe** defines a specific point in the timeline of an animation that indicates a change. For example, if you want to have a circle move from left to right, the first keyframe would have a position property for the circle on the left and the second keyframe would have a position property for the circle on the right. Over a certain period of time, Photoshop moves the circle from one position to the other.

11. Click the stopwatch icon (⏱) next to the Opacity parameter to enable animation, this is circled in Figure 12-39. A keyframe is created at the beginning of the Timeline.

Figure 12-39: Select the stopwatch to the left of Opacity to define an opacity keyframe.

> ***Take Note...***
> *The stopwatch enables animation when it is clicked on. If clicked off, it disables animation.*
>
> *A by-product of disabling the animation of a property is that all the keyframes for that property are deleted.*

12. In the Layers panel, type **0** in the Opacity text field (Figure 12-40) and press the Enter or Return key.

Figure 12-40: Adjust the opacity so the layer is not visible.

13. Double-click the Scrub to set time field (bottom left of Timeline panel). The Set Current Time dialog box appears. Type **3:00** and click OK. This moves your Current Time Indicator to the three-second mark on the Timeline. The Current Time Indicator (the blue wedge at the top of the Timeline) indicates your animation's current time. You can also drag the Current Time Indicator, but setting the time manually is more precise.

14. In the Layers panel, type **100** in the Opacity text field, and press Enter/Return. This creates a new keyframe where your Current Time Indicator is located.

> **Take Note...**
> *This is the nature of timeline-based animation in Photoshop. If animation is enabled for a parameter, any change made to that parameter will create a new keyframe at the location of the Current Time Indicator.*

15. Return the Current Time Indicator back to the starting point by clicking on 0.0 at the beginning of the Timeline.

16. Press the Play button (▶) at the bottom of the Animation panel to preview the animation. The text fades in over three seconds. You can press the Stop button (■) when you are finished viewing the animation.

17. Choose File > Save As. The Save As dialog box appears. Navigate to the ps12lessons folder and type **ps1205_animation.psd** into the File name text field. Select Photoshop from the Format drop-down menu and click Save. Keep the file open for the next part of this lesson.

Rendering a video file

Follow these steps to render a video file in Timeline mode	Step-by-Step

1. In the lower-left corner of the Timeline panel, click the arrow icon. This is the Render Video button and it will open the Render Video window (Figure 12–41). (You can also choose File > Export > Render Video.)

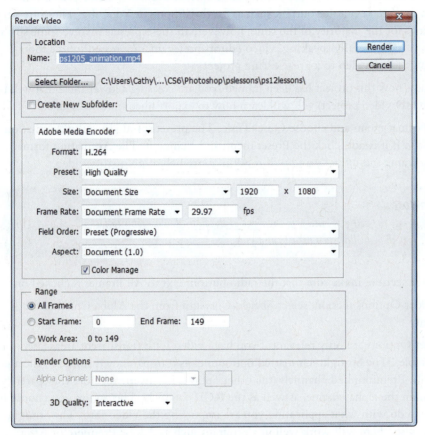

Figure 12-41: The Render Video window provides options for video export.

Note that the Render Video Window is divided into four areas: Location, File Options, Range, and Render Options.

Location: allows you to specify a name for the file that you are going to export and a location to save that file.

File Options: controls the type of file you want to create from your animation. Adobe Media Encoder is the default option here and gives you numerous options for choosing the format, size, and other parameters of the video file that you will export. The other option in this section is a Photoshop Image Sequence, which is a relatively specialized format that exports each frame of your video as an individual image file.

Range: controls the amount of the animation to export. By default, it will export the entire animation timeline, but you can limit the export range to lesser parts of the Timeline.

Render Options: controls whether an alpha channel is included in the output file along with the file's frame rate. Some exportable formats will not allow you to include an alpha channel.

2. In the Location name section, type **ps1205** into the Name text field; the default extension .mp4 should be kept. Click the Select Folder button, and navigate to the ps12lessons folder, then click OK or Choose.

3. In the File Options section, note that the Format is set to H.264. This format is the type of compression used, but there are a number of different Presets that determine the size and frame rate as well.

4. Click the Preset menu and note the multitude of options available. These presets allow you to choose a specific format for output, such as for the iPhone or YouTube. These are very useful settings for the majority of the time; however, all these presets involve some sort of compression, and generally speaking, video editors prefer uncompressed source footage if they plan on adding video to a pre-existing project.

   Because this is how this project has been framed (you are creating a lower third that will be added to an HD video project) you will learn how to export uncompressed video.

5. Click the Format menu and choose QuickTime. The preset should be set to Animation High Quality. If it is not, click the Preset menu and change it. The Animation format treats every frame individually and will result in extremely high quality video.

Take Note...
You can use the settings button to the right of the drop-down menu to format a QuickTime movie for other media, such as TV and video.

6. In the Range section, make sure that the radio button next to All Frames is clicked on.

7. In the Render Options section, select *Straight-Unmatted* from the Alpha Channel drop-down menu.

   The Render Options are only relevant if you have video with transparent areas (as you do in this example). The Straight-Unmatted option means transparency is stored in the alpha channel only. Premultiplied channels (the other options in this menu) store transparency information in the alpha channel as well as the RGB channels. The option you choose has everything to do with what application you are importing the video into. The Straight-Unmatted option here will work well in a program such as Adobe Premiere or After Effects, among others.

8. Click the Render button to create your video file. The rendering time will vary, depending on your computer hardware.

9. Choose File > Close. You can return to the native Photoshop file to make edits at a later point, if necessary. You can test your file by navigating to the ps12lessons folder and selecting your **ps1205** file. It should open the QuickTime Player, and you can view your work in action.

   Congratulations! You have finished this lesson.

Skill Summary

In this lesson you learned how to:	Objective
Demonstrate knowledge of image resolution, image size, and image file format for web, video, and print	2.1
Demonstrate knowledge of image-generating devices, their resulting image types, and how to access resulting images in Photoshop	2.5
Demonstrate knowledge of importing, exporting, organizing, and saving	3.3
Use Photoshop guides and rulers	4.2
Transform images	4.3
Demonstrate knowledge of preparing images for web, print, and video	5.1

Knowledge Assessment

True/False

Circle **T** if the statement is true or **F** if the statement is false.

T F 1. In order to work with video in Photoshop, you must have the Extended version and the QuickTime player plug-in installed on your computer.

T F 2. The auto-select feature allows you to easily activate layers without having to go to the Layers panel.

T F 3. You have to have at least 2 objects selected in order for the Align and Distribute options to become visible in the Options bar.

T F 4. From the rulers, you can drag out horizontal, vertical, diagonal and free-pivot guides.

T F 5. Slices can only be controlled separately and cannot be merged, you have to delete them if you want to make spacing adjustments.

T F 6. By defining a URL for a slice, a link is made from that slice to a location or file on the Web.

T F 7. Alt Tags allow viewers to read a text description of an image which is helpful for visually impaired users using screen readers.

T F 8. It would be best to save a photograph as a PNG-8 or GIF.

T F 9. When optimizing slices, you can only use one file format and must export all slices using that same format.

T F 10. A saved selection shows up as an alpha channel at the bottom of the Channels panel.

Adobe now requires that your computer's video support OpenGL to use the 3D capabilities, and computers running Windows XP are not able to use the 3D capabilities. Adobe recommends that you have at least 512 MB of VRAM—video memory—to use the 3D features, or you may encounter unexpected results. The complete technical requirements for Photoshop CS6 are listed at *http://www.adobe.com/products/photoshopextended/tech-specs.html*. You can find a list of video cards tested by Adobe by visiting *adobe.com* and searching for "Photoshop tested video cards."

This lesson includes the use of 3D Secondary View. Depending upon the video hardware in your computer, you may not be able to see a live preview of your work. Before starting this lesson, make sure that you have your preferences set-up to use the 3D features in Photoshop using the following instructions. The 3D features covered in this lesson are available in the Extended version of Photoshop CS6. If you are using the Standard version of Photoshop CS6, you can download a free trial of Photoshop CS6 Extended from the *adobe.com* site to follow along with this lesson.

Locating the GPU/OpenGL preferences in Photoshop CS6

Step-by-Step	Follow these steps to set the Preferences required to complete this lesson

1. In Photoshop CS6 choose Edit > Preferences > Performance (Windows) or Photoshop > Preferences > Performance (Mac OS).

2. In the Performance panel, make sure Use Graphics Processor is selected in the Graphics Processor Settings section. If the settings are grayed out, you will not be able to complete this lesson with your current computer capabilities, and will need a computer with a video card that meets the minimum video requirements provided by Adobe. You can find these at *http://www.adobe.com/products/photoshopextended/tech-specs.html*.

3. If the Graphics Processor Settings are not grayed out, click on Advanced Settings and select Advanced from the Drawing Mode drop-down menu, and then press OK.

4. Press OK again to exit the Preferences dialog box.

Getting an image ready for 3D

You will now start the 3D project by opening a file that contains many layers, layer masks, and text layers. In order to create a 3D object, these need to be converted into one layer. To keep this composition in editable form, you will select the layers and convert them to a Smart Object.

Step-by-Step	Follow these steps to convert individual layers into a Smart Object

1. Choose File > Browse in Bridge, and then navigate to the ps13lessons folder. Due to the size of some of these files, it may take longer for the file contents to appear than normal.

2. Double-click to open the file named **ps1301.psd**. A comp for the label of a soda can is visible.

3. If the Layers panel is not visible, choose Window > Layers.

4. Choose the Move tool (⊹), and then click the texture layer in the Layers panel to select it. Press and hold the Ctrl (Windows) or Command (Mac OS) key and click each layer until you reach the top text layer (called FizzyPop!) All the layers are activated.

> **Take Note...**
> *You can also click the texture layer and then Shift+click the FizzyPop! text layer to select all layers in between.*

5. Click the Layers panel menu and choose Convert to Smart Object from the panel drop-down menu. The layers appear to flatten into one layer. You can double-click this layer (Figure 13-2) at any time to reopen the composition in its original, non-flattened, form (Figure 13-1).

Figure 13-1: *Convert the multiple layers into a single Smart Object layer.*

Figure 13-2: *FizzyPop! is now a Smart Object layer.*

6. Choose File > Save As. In the Save As dialog box, navigate to the ps13lessons folder, and then type **ps1301_work.psd** into the Name text field. Choose Photoshop from the Format drop-down menu and press Save. If the Photoshop Format Options window appears, click OK.

Wrapping the image around a soda can

Now that you have consolidated the composition to one layer, you can easily map this image to a 3D mesh. **3D mesh** is the 3D shape and structure of an object. Photoshop provides you with default meshes that you can select from the 3D panel. Once this image has been wrapped around the mesh, it is considered a texture for the object.

In this exercise, you will convert your image to a 3D mesh using the 3D panel.

Step-by-Step	Follow these steps to convert the image to a 3D mesh

1. Choose Window > 3D to open the 3D panel. Click the radio button labeled Mesh from Preset, click on the drop-down menu, and then choose Soda (Figure 13-3).

Figure 13-3: *Create 3D objects from a choice of mesh presets.*

2. Click the Create button. You may be prompted to switch to the 3D workspace; click Yes if necessary. After a few moments, your flat artwork is applied to the soda mesh and you have the opportunity to see the default 3D workspace. A labeled diagram is displayed below with Figure 13-4.

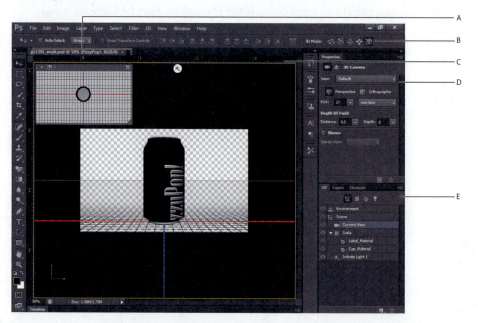

Figure 13-4

A. *3D Secondary View.* **B.** *3D Mode.* **C.** *Live Preview.* **D.** *Properties panel.* **E.** *3D panel.*

The 3D workspace is different in many ways from the traditional Photoshop workspace. Your main document window has two views by default, the main view, and the Secondary View.

3. If you do not see the Secondary View, select your Move tool, and then choose View > Show > 3D Secondary View.

Note that the 3D panel also opened to show you the elements in the 3D scene and a Properties panel, allowing you to control various properties of the scene elements.

Getting 3D images in and out of Photoshop CS6

Photoshop provides you with many preconfigured 3D shapes from which you can choose, and it also enables you to import existing files from 3D applications. Formats that you can import include:

- **.dae** (Collada)—the recommended format for interchange
- **.3ds**—3D Studio
- **.obj**—Wavefront
- **.u3d**—Universal 3D
- **.kmz**—Google Earth's format. This is the same as a zipped Collada file

---

4. Look at the 3D panel on the right side of your screen and notice that it consists of several elements, including Environment, Scene, Current View, Soda Mesh, Label_Material, Cap_Material, and Infinite Light 1.

The Current View element is highlighted, indicating that it is active. The Properties for the Current View are visible in the panel above and include properties such as the Field of View (FOV) and Depth of Field.

You will now adjust the texture that is mapped to the soda can mesh.

5. Click on the Label_Material object in the 3D panel. Depending upon your video configuration you may notice that your soda can turned white. If you cannot preview texture changes in the main view, you can use the Secondary View to see changes.

6. Click on the Select View/Camera menu located at the top of your Secondary View window and choose Front from the list of options as shown in Figure 13-5. You now see the textured version of your soda can.

If necessary, you can enlarge the size of the Secondary View by clicking and dragging the bottom-right corner of the window.

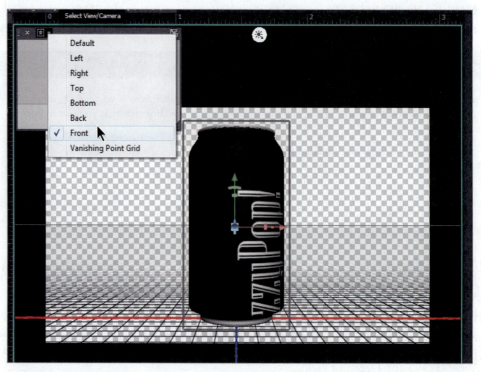

Figure 13-5: The Secondary View allows you to see changes to your 3D object in real time.

You'll notice that your texture is not wrapped correctly. The FizzyPop! text as well as the image of the man need to be wrapped horizontally across the can. In order to get this appearance, you'll edit the texture.

7. Make sure that Label_Material is still selected in the 3D panel. Click on the Texture icon to the right of the Diffuse property, in the Properties panel and then select Edit Texture (Figure 13-6). The file that opens is a .psb file which is the format Photoshop uses for textures.

Figure 13-6: Edit the texture.

8. Choose Image > Image Rotation > 90° CW. This turns the image clockwise 90 degrees.

9. Choose File > Save and then click on your **ps1301_work** image to return to it. The texture has been updated and you are looking at the top half of the man's head. In order to fit the texture you will scale it.

10. Select Label_Material in the 3D panel, and then click on the Texture icon to the right of the Diffuse property again. This time choose Edit UV Properties. This panel allows you to adjust the scaling and offset of your texture.

11. In the U Scale field type **200** (Figure 13-7) and then press the Tab key. You see the image of the man updated.

Figure 13-7: *Change the U Scale to 200 in order to adjust the scale of your texture.*

12. Click OK to confirm the change. You have adjusted the texture and in the next exercise you will adjust the position and rotation of the can.

Positioning the soda can in 3D space

Now that you have added and edited the texture of your soda can mesh, you will learn how to work with the object in Photoshop's **3D space**. You have various controls at your disposal including the ability to move, rotate and scale the mesh as well as reposition the Camera View.

Follow these steps to explore the 3D space in Photoshop	Step-by-Step

1. Click once on the soda can mesh in the 3D panel; the image changes to a silhouette with a set of 3D controls as shown in Figure 13-8. Don't try to move anything yet; when working in 3D, you first need to understand the different views and how to navigate between them.

Figure 13-8: *Click on the soda can to see 3D controls.*

2. Hover over the tip of each of the three handles of the 3D axis in the middle of the soda can silhouette:

- The red handle allows you to move the mesh on the X axis (horizontally).

- The green handle allows you to move on the Y axis (vertically).

- The blue handle allows you to move on the Z axis. The Z axis in 3D represents depth; in other words, you can move this soda can closer to you or further away.

Each handle has two other components: rotate (which is the bent line after the tip of the handle), and scale (the rectangle element after rotate). You will return to these controls a bit later; the important thing for now is to realize that any of these controls will move the soda mesh object.

As in the previous exercise, you might need to use the Secondary View in order to preview your image.

3. In the middle of the soda can silhouette, place your cursor on the bent line of the green axis; the tooltip appears indicating you can rotate around the Z Axis. Click and drag to the left until the value reaches approximately –45 degrees as displayed in Figure 13-9.

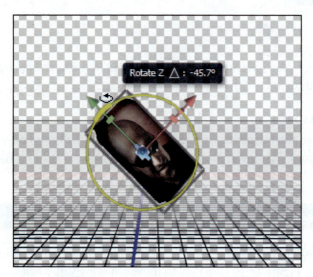

Figure 13-9: Rotating the soda can along the Z Axis.

4. Click anywhere outside of the silhouette to activate the current view again. You'll now rotate the can so the Fizzy Pop label is showing.

5. Click on the soda can and now place your cursor over the red 3D controls. Hover over the second control, making sure that you see the tooltip labeled "Rotate around Y Axis." Click and drag to the upper-right (Figure 13-10) until the you see the text on the can appear (Figure 13-11).

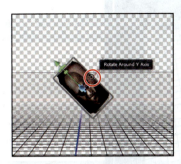

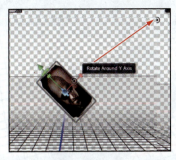

Figure 13-10: *Click and drag to the upper right.*

Figure 13-11: *Rotate the can until the text on the label appears.*

Adjusting materials and lighting

There are other important components to this 3D scene, including the label material and the lights. You will now learn how to modify the image texture on the can and then reposition the light source.

Follow these steps to adjust the label texture and lighting   Step-by-Step

1. Click the Label_Material element in the 3D panel. Notice that the Properties panel, located right above the 3D panel, lists a number of options: Diffuse, Specular, Shine, Reflection, and many more. As you saw in the first exercise, you can adjust the scale of your texture on the mesh using the Diffuse options, but keep in mind that this texture is an image, rather than a texture designed to act as a material (such as rock or steel).

   You'll now take a look at some of the other properties in this panel.

5. Move the light source so the shadow is to the bottom left of the can (the Infinite Light icon appears on the top right) as shown in Figure 13-14.

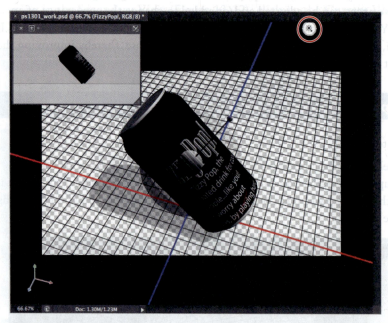

Figure 13-14: The Infinite Light icon indicates the source of the light.

6. In the Properties panel, click and drag the Intensity slider slightly to the right to a increase the value of 90% to 110%. The light source for the can is now brighter.

7. Press Ctrl+S (Windows) or Command+S (Mac OS) to save the file. Keep the **ps1301_work** file open for the next part of the lesson.

Animating the soda can

You touched on some animation techniques in Lesson 12, "Creating Images for Web and Video," now you will have the opportunity to animate the can. You can animate many of the properties of a 3D scene, including the position of the camera, lights, and the 3D object itself. After animating any of these properties, you can export the animation as video.

Step-by-Step	Follow these steps to use animation techniques on the soda can

1. Choose Window > Timeline. If the Timeline window appears in the Frame mode, click and hold the Timeline's panel menu in the top-right corner and choose Convert to Video Timeline from the drop-down menu.

2. Click the arrow to the left of FizzyPop! to expand it and view all the properties that you can animate. In this example, you will be rotating the can while maintaining a stationary camera position.

3. If necessary, use the scroll bar located on the far right-side of the Timeline panel to scroll down, and then click on the arrow to the left of 3D Meshes to expand it; the Soda mesh is visible, with the label "Soda."

4. Click the stopwatch immediately to the left of the Soda mesh as displayed in Figure 13-15; a keyframe is added, as indicated by a yellow diamond. This keyframe represents the current mesh orientation and time as the starting point for the animation.

Figure 13-15: Start the animation by clicking the stopwatch for the 3D Mesh.

5. Now click and drag the Current Time Marker (CTM) over to 3:00 in the Timeline (Figure 13-16).

Figure 13-16: Click and drag the Current Time Marker over to the 3:00 mark.

6. Click once on the soda can in your Main View to select it. Place your cursor over the second control on the red axis; make sure you see the tooltip, Rotate Around Y Axis, appear as well as the ring around the axis.

7. Click and drag straight down until the value reads approximately 145 degrees.

8. From the 3D Mode section of the tool options bar and select the 3D Roll option (Figure 13-17); Place your cursor to the right of the soda can and click and drag to the right. No exact measurements are needed here.

Figure 13-17: Choose the 3D tool and drag to the right.

9. Drag the Current Time Indicator to 0 seconds, and then press the Play button (▶) to see the animation.

At this point you could refine your animation by editing the soda can position at either of the two keyframes (0 seconds and 3 seconds) or add additional movement by creating new keyframes. You could also create much more complex animations by keyframing other properties such as the lights or the camera position.

Exporting your animation

You will now export your animation as an Mpeg4 video file. Mpeg4 is the file format frequently used for web video (although it is used elsewhere as well); it is particularly well supported for use in HTML5 video and Apple's iOS operating system on the iPod and iPad.

Step-by-Step	Follow these steps to export the animation as a video file

1. Choose File > Export > Render Video. You might see an Initialize Video progress bar appear: this is Photoshop preparing the video for export. **Render Video** is the process of generating a video file from raw video and animation data. Since this lesson is a basic introduction to the possibilities of using 3D and video, you will leave the settings in the Render Video at their default values. If you are a video professional, you will find that many of the features that you need to output a quality video are in this dialog box.

   Note that based upon the speed of your computer, this render make take a few minutes; you might want to return to this step at the end of the lesson.

2. The name **ps1301_work.mp4** should be listed in the Name text field; if not, type it now. Confirm that the folder you are saving the file to is your ps13lessons folder.

3. Leave the settings at Adobe Media Encoder, which is a dedicated application in Adobe's Creative Suite for exporting and compressing video.

   There are a number of options here you could choose to modify, including the document size, the frame rate, and more. Many of these are familiar to you if you have previously worked in digital video. Although it falls outside the scope of this lesson to discuss each of these options in depth, the last setting, 3D Quality, is worth discussing.

4. Click on the 3D Quality drop-down menu, at the bottom of the window, to see three options: Interactive, Ray Tracing Draft and Ray Tracing Final. If the quality is set to Interactive, this will result in a quick export, but not one of the highest quality (Figure 13-18). The two other options for Ray Tracing (Draft and Final) will create higher quality results,

but will take much longer to export. We discuss Ray Tracing in further detail in the next exercise.

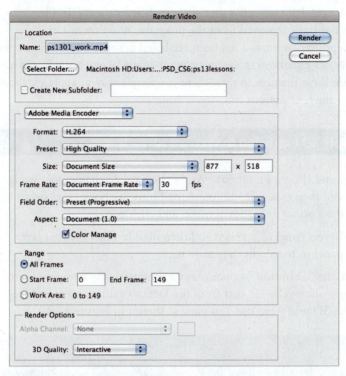

Figure 13-18: *The Render Video window provides many options for outputting digital video including the level of quality for the render.*

5. Press Render if you want to render now. Keep in mind that rendering will tie up your machine and you cannot do anything in Photoshop until it is completed (although you can cancel the render process).

   On our systems, the Interactive export was finished in 40 seconds, the Ray Traced Draft was finished in a little under five minutes, but the Ray Traced Final may take up to two hours.

6. If you have rendered, you can test the movie by opening your system's media player (QuickTime Player or Windows Media Player) and choose File > Open File to view the movie. We have also provided two versions of the rendered file in your lesson folder named **ps13_01_interactive.mp4** and **ps13_01_draft.mp4** if you would like to view these instead of rendering on your own.

7. When you are finished viewing the video, return to Photoshop and Choose File > Save to Save your file, then choose File > Close.

Creating 3D Text

In earlier versions of Photoshop, a feature called Repoussé was added that allowed you to convert 2D objects into 3D objects that you could then style in different ways. In Photoshop CS6, the Repoussé command has been removed from the program; however, all its functionality remains. The Repoussé command has been relabeled as the 3D Extrusion option in the 3D panel. You can apply 3D extrusion to vector or pixel-based layers, but you can also apply it to text. When applying these features to text, there is a simple way to apply extrusion by using the 3D text button in the text options bar.

Step-by-Step	**Follow these steps to apply 3D extrusion to text**

1. Open the file **ps1302.psd** and choose File > Save As. In the Save As dialog box, navigate to the ps13lessons folder, and then type **ps1302_work.psd** into the Name text field. Choose Photoshop from the Format drop-down menu and click Save.

2. If necessary, click on the Layers panel to access it and then double-click the text layer thumbnail in your layers panel to highlight the entire text.

3. In your Options bar, click the 3D button (3D); your text is automatically converted into a 3D scene. The Main View shows the 3D text from the Default camera view and the Secondary View shows the 3D text from the Top view as shown in Figure 13-19.

Take Note...
You can also convert a text layer by accessing the 3D panel, choosing 3D Extrusion, and then clicking Create.

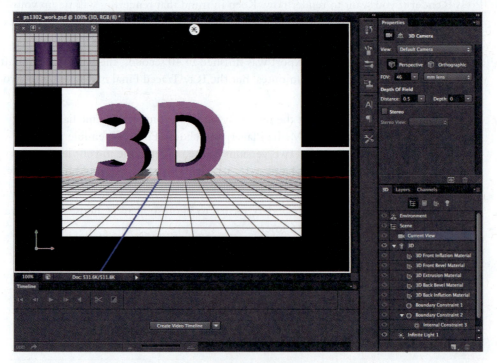

***Figure 13-19**: A text layer that has been placed into a 3D scene using extrusion.*

To understand some of the capabilities of the effect, you will modify some text properties.

4. In the Secondary View, click on the Select View/Camera menu and choose Default in order to see the 3D text at the same angle as your Main View.

5. Click the 3D text to activate it. As in all 3D objects (and as seen in the last exercise) you can modify the appearance of this object using the X, Y, and Z axes directly.

6. Click the Rotate Around Y Axis control found on the red axis (Figure 13-20) and drag to the right in order to rotate the text to the left. Drag until the value is approximately 15 degrees (Figure 13-21).

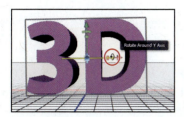

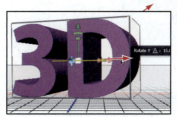

Figure 13-20: *Click on the Y Axis.*   **Figure 13-21**: *Click and drag to the right.*

At the very top of the Properties panel there are four small icons: Mesh, Deform, Cap, and Coordinates. By default you are currently in the Mesh properties.

7. Click the Deform (⬚) button at the top of the Properties panel as shown in Figure 13-22.

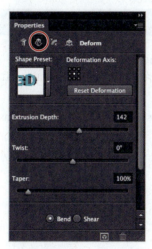

Figure 13-22: *Click on the Deform property at the top of the Properties panel.*

The Deform property allows you change the depth of the 3D object as well as twist, taper, bend, or shear the text.

8. Drag the Extrusion Depth slider to an approximate value of 300. Extrusion essentially extends the 3D object along the Z Axis; in this case, the positive value means the depth extends away from you.

9. Click the Cap button (⬚) at the top of the Properties panel. The Cap allows you to adjust the ends (called cap) of an object. You can adjust the Cap values in the Properties panel.

10. Place your cursor over the Inflation Strength icon located on the letter D in the image area. Click and drag upward to increase the Inflation Strength. You will see your 3D text inflate slightly. Change the value to approximately 11.00 as shown in Figure 13-23.

Figure 13-23: *Inflating your text directly in the Work view.*

You can also change the Inflation Angle and the Bevel Width and Bevel Angle; for now, you will leave both at their default settings.

Applying materials to the 3D mesh

Another feature of extrusion is the ability to apply materials to the 3D mesh. You can choose to apply the same material to all sides, or apply different materials to different sides.

Step-by-Step	Follow these steps to apply materials to the 3D mesh

1. In the 3D Panel, locate the 3D Front Inflation Material element. If you were to apply a texture right now, it would only be for the front of the object. To apply a material to all sides, you must select all the Material elements.

Shift+click the 3D Back Inflation Material element; this selects all five sides of the object as displayed in Figure 13-24.

Figure 13-24: *Select all materials*

2. Click the Material picker thumbnail at the top of the Properties panel. A menu appears with various Material presets. Scroll down until you find the OrangePeel material (Figure 13-25), and then click it to apply the texture to your sides.

Figure 13-25: *The OrangePeel material is applied to all sides of your 3D text.*

The texture may take a few moments to load but it will eventually update the default purple texture and will be immediately visible in the Secondary View.

3. Choose File > Save. Keep this file open for the next exercise.

Rendering and Rasterizing your 3D images

Photoshop CS6 uses a technique called ray tracing to create high-quality renders of 3D images. During ray tracing, 3D model information such as materials and lights are generated, often slowly. A high-quality final render can take a long time based on your system and the size and complexity of the 3D object; however, the results are often worth it.

| Follow these steps to render the 3D image | Step-by-Step |

1. In the 3D panel, click the panel menu at the top right and choose Render as shown in Figure 13-26. Photoshop's feedback tiling feature starts running on your screen.

Figure 13-26: *Rendering your 3D object.*

This feature is a real-time preview of the different sections of your image as they are being rendered. When the tiles stop appearing, your rendering is complete.

Based on your system's video card and other factors, even small files could take a while to render. You can pause the process at any time by clicking anywhere within your image or pressing the Esc key.

Take Note...

If an image has been paused from rendering, the Render command will now be listed as Resume Render in the 3D panel menu.

2. Choose File > Save As. In the Save As dialog box, navigate to the ps13lessons folder, and then type **ps1302_rasterized.psd** into the Name text field. Choose Photoshop from the Format drop-down menu and press Save.

When you save a file in either the PSD, PDF, or TIFF formats you preserve the 3D model information such as the lighting and 3D layers. Generally, you want to maintain this information; however, occasionally you might want to flatten your image or export your image for other uses. You can do this by rasterizing your image, just be aware that once a 3D image is rasterized, you cannot undo it, so you should always keep a master 3D backup.

3. Choose Layer > Rasterize > 3D. Your image is now converted to a standard bitmapped image that you can edit or manipulate as any other image; for example, you can make selections, apply filters, and so on.

For now, you will undo this command and return to your 3D model.

4. Choose Edit > Undo or press Command+Z (Mac OS) or Ctrl+Z (Windows).

Using your 3D layers as an element in a composite is very simple, although they can also become very involved. Here you will create a very simple composite using the gradient tool.

5. Click the background layer in the Layers panel, and then click the Gradient tool in the Tools panel. Make sure Black is the foreground color and White is the background color.

6. Place your cursor around the top of the letters, and then drag downward. Release around the bottom of the image. You may need to try this a few times, but it should be easy to create an effect that combines well with both the 3D object and its shadow (Figure 13-27).

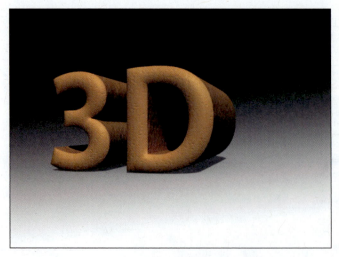

Figure 13-27: *Create a gradient effect behind the 3D rendered text.*

Exporting your 3D image

You can choose to export a 3D layer from Photoshop to a format that can be imported into 3D applications. Select a 3D layer, and then choose 3D > Export 3D Layer, and when the Save As dialog box appears, choose from one of these formats:

- Collada (DAE)
- Flash 3D
- Google Earth 4 (KMZ)
- U3D (U3D), which you can import into Acrobat 8 and 9 files.
- Wavefront|Obj (OBJ)

Save your file.

Congratulations! You have completed Lesson 13, "Introducing 3D."

Exporting your animation

Knowledge Assessment

True/False

Circle **T** if the statement is true or **F** if the statement is false.

T **F** **1.** All computers that can run Photoshop are capable of effectively running 3D features.

T **F** **2.** To access the GPU/OpenGL preferences in Photoshop, you go to Edit > Preferences > Performance (Windows) or Photoshop > Preferences > Performance (Mac OS).

T **F** **3.** Photoshop provides you with default meshes that you can select from the 3D panel.

T **F** **4.** The Secondary View allows you to see changes to your 3D object in real time.

T **F** **5.** Default, Left, Right, Top, and Front are all possible view options for a 3D object in Photoshop.

T **F** **6.** Each 3D axis handle affects one positional property (X, Y, or Z) only; scale and rotate have separate controls.

T **F** **7.** There are a preset number of lights you can work with in Photoshop; you cannot add any more than 3 to a 3D object.

T **F** **8.** Not only can you create 3D objects in Photoshop, but you can animate them as well.

T **F** **9.** Mpeg4 is a video format frequently used for web video.

T **F** **10.** Extrusion essentially extends the 3D object along the X axis.

Multiple Choice

Select the best response for the following statements.

1. Which operating system is unable to run Photoshop's 3D features?

   a. MAC OS X
   b. Windows XP
   c. Windows Vista
   d. Windows 7

2. What feature of a video's support system does Adobe now require to run the 3D capabilities?

   a. Pixel Interpolation
   b. HD
   c. OpenGL
   d. Matrix

3. Which of the following is not part of the 3D workspace options?

   a. Properties panel

   b. Live Preview

   c. 3D Mode

   d. Vector Master

4. Which of the following 3D formats can be imported into Photoshop?

   a. .dae

   b. .3ds

   c. .obj

   d. All of the above

5. U Scale, V Scale, U Offset, and V Offset are all characteristics of:

   a. Free Transform

   b. Options Panel

   c. Texture Properties

   d. None of the above

6. The red handle of the 3D axis control modifies which property of a 3D object?

   a. X

   b. Y

   c. Z

   d. Scale

7. Diffuse, Specular, and Shine are indicative of working with what in the 3D panel?

   a. Transparency

   b. Blending modes

   c. Light source

   d. Warp features

8. What icon is representative of a keyframe in Photoshop's Timeline?

   a. Black circle

   b. Yellow diamond

   c. Red square

   d. Blue triangle

9. Which of the following options is available in the Render Video window?

   a. Format

   b. Range

   c. Field Order

   d. All of the above

10. What is the process called that Photoshop uses to create high-quality renders of 3D images?

   a. Ray tracing

   b. Downsampling

   c. Tweening

   d. None of the above

Project 2	**Adding 3D Text**

Working with 3D text can be a little tricky. Make sure you choose a font that will show up well when creating 3D text. Unfortunately not all fonts translate well in 3D, such as thin, cursive fonts. The extrusion setting is something that has an impact on the effectiveness of the design of the text as it translates into a three-dimensional image. When using thin, curvy fonts this can look a little awkward. You'll try some text out to see the results of using a font that may not be the best choice.

1. With the **pyramid.psd** file still open, select the Type tool and click on your document to create a new type layer. Type out the word **Pyramid**.

2. Set the font size to about **85**. Pick a font that has script in the name, such as Edwardian Script.

3. In the Options bar, click the 3D button so the text is converted into a 3D scene.

4. Start to work with the various settings available through the 3D properties.

5. Rotate and manipulate the text in such a fashion so you can see how the text is looking as a three-dimensional image. Kind of extreme for that style of font isn't it?

6. Repeat the steps above with new text but try a more logical font such as Arial. Try some of the same 3D settings for this type and notice the difference.

7. Choose File > Save As and save the file as **pyramid_3Dtext**.psd. Keep this file open for the next part of the exercise.

Project 3	**Animating in the Z Space**

You can have a lot of fun animating in 3D space because you've got this whole new plane to play with. The Z plane which allows you to travel forward and backward as opposed to just up and down or side to side. You can create some interesting animations when you discover this new space; it's great for creating a sense of distance.

1. With **pyramid_3Dtext.psd** open, choose Window > Timeline. Click the Create Video Timeline button to generate a timeline for your image.

2. Select the pyramid layer and use the Slide the 3D Object tool in the Options bar to move the pyramid image back away from the text.

3. Set a keyframe as you did earlier for the 3D camera position property to set the initial positions of both the pyramid and the text.

4. Move forward in time and adjust the pyramid so it's brought forward again and this time, push the text back so they swap positions in the foreground and the background. Set additional keyframes as needed.

5. Play the animation to see the results in terms of how both objects change their positions in Z-space.

6. Choose File > Save As and name this file **pyramid_animation**.psd.

Photoshop CS6 New Features

Key Terms

- 3D Merge
- 3D widgets
- scripted fill
- user interface

Skill	Objective
Demonstrate knowledge of retouching and blending images	4.5

Business case

So you think you know everything about Photoshop? People saying that are usually the ones that haven't discovered all the little things the program has to offer. The pros know that Photoshop is basically endless and that you can always learn more. With Adobe Photoshop CS6, there's much more to explore.

Starting up

This lesson is an introduction to new features in Photoshop CS6. Some of the features are major, such as the newly-added, content-aware Move and Patch tools, and the options for vector strokes and fills. Other new features may seem minor to new users, but current users will recognize them as important improvements. An example of an important improvement is the Layers panel and its new options for keeping track of complicated layered images. This lesson does not include step-by-step exercises for each feature that is discussed, but you will learn about some of the features that will likely have the most impact on the way you work in Photoshop. Keep in mind that some of the new features that are discussed are existing features that have been renamed or made more prominent and easier to find in the user interface.

Before starting, make sure that your tools and panels are consistent by resetting your preferences. To do this, press and hold the Ctrl+Alt+Shift keys (Windows) or Command+Option+Shift keys (Mac OS). Continue to hold these keys while launching Photoshop. A dialogue box appears verifying that you want to delete the Adobe Photoshop settings file. Release the keys, then click OK.

You will work with several files from the ps14lessons folder in this lesson. Make sure that you have loaded the pslessons folder onto your hard-drive from *http://www.wiley.com/college/sc/adobeseries*. See "Loading lesson files" in the Starting up section of this book.

New Look and Feel

When you open Photoshop CS6, you will immediately notice the new, darker UI (**User Interface**, which is the interface that allows a user to interact with the software). This is a modern look for Photoshop. The new look is easy to get used to, but you can change to a lighter UI by selecting Edit > Preferences > Interface and choosing a lighter Color Theme.

Sketch and paint with new brush tips

There seems to be a resurgence of the pencil. Many designers are rediscovering the benefits and the appeal of a sketch. Now you can achieve that same sketch-look in Photoshop by using one of the new erodible brush tips. These tips actually wear down as you paint with them. Find the Erodible brushes by selecting a painting tool, such as the Brush tool, selecting Windows > Brush, and locating one of the tips that look like a pencil and provide you a tooltip that includes Erodible in the name (Figure 14-1).

Figure 14-1: One of the new Erodible brush tips.

While you are in the Brush panel, look for the new airbrush tools. Airbrush tools are different than regular brushes because you have options that help your brush tool work more like a real-life airbrush. You can also locate the Airbrush tools in the Brush panel by passing the cursor over the brush tips until you see Airbrush appear in the Tooltip. When you click on an Airbrush tip,as you can see in Figure 14-2 the settings at the bottom of the Brushes panel reflect options specific to that brush tip.

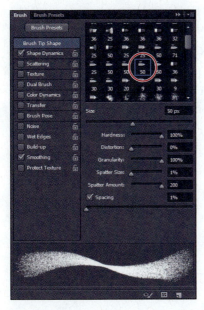

Figure 14-1: The new Airbrush tip offers options that make your brush work more like a real airbrush.

Once you select a brush tip, create a new blank document (using the default Photoshop preset) and use the Brush tool to paint on the canvas. Experiment with the Erodible brush and watch as the strokes become less defined as you continue brushing. To sharpen your tip again, click Sharpen Point in the Brushes panel.

When using the airbrush tip, experiment with some of the settings, such as Granularity, which adjusts how grainy the paint spray is, or Spatter Amount, which can be reduced to create a more definite stroke.

New content-aware tools

In previous versions, you were able to take advantage of two incredible content-aware features, the content-aware scale and content-aware retouching. Now in Photoshop CS6, you have the content-aware Move tool and the improved Patch tool that includes content-aware features. Locate the Patch tool by clicking and holding the Spot Healing Brush tool in the Tools panel, and then selecting the Patch tool.

The Patch tool is helpful when patching (or replacing) large areas of an image. This could be the background of a scratched image, or a section of someone's skin. To use the Patch tool, click and drag the Patch tool over a section of an image that you want to clone (and blend) into another section of your image. After making your selection, click and drag that section to another part of the image. Follow the next steps for hands-on experience of this tool.

Step-by-Step	**Follow these steps to explore the content-aware Patch tool**

1. Choose File > Browse in Bridge, locate the ps14lessons folder, and open the image called **ps1401.psd**. An image of a gentleman in military uniform appears.

2. Choose File Save As and name the file **ps1401_work**. Keep it in the .PSD format and save it into the ps14lessons folder.

3. Use the Zoom tool (🔍) to zoom into the lower-left part of this image. As you can see in Figure 14-3, notice some artifacts in the image: a random dot and a stain. You will use the patch tool to replace those sections.

Figure 14-3: Zoom into the lower-left section of the image.

4. Select the Patch tool (⬡) that is hidden in the Spot Healing Brush tool.

5. In the Options bar, select the Patch drop-down menu and choose Content-Aware.

6. Click and drag around the area of the image that contains the black spot as shown in Figure 14-4.

7. Drag the patch selection to a part of the image that is not marked with artifacts (Figure 14-5). The original selection is not only replaced with the clean section of the image, but it is blended in a manner that makes it difficult to see your original selection as you can see in Figure 14-6.

 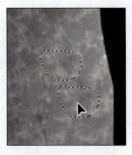 

Figure 14-4: Click to select the area of the image with the black spot.   *Figure 14-5: Drag the patch to replace the selected patch area.*   *Figure 14-6: The result.*

As a default, the options for this tool are to replace the source with the area that you are dragging to.

8. On your own, try replacing the stained section of the wall with a clean section. When you are finished, choose File > Save, and then File > Close.

Investigating the Content-Aware Move tool

This new content-aware tool is likely to become a favorite. Using the Content-Aware Move tool, you can select and relocate a section of your image without leaving a hole in your image. Try it by following the next steps.

Certification Ready 4.5

How can you move an object to a new location using the Content-Aware move tool?

Follow these steps to discover the Content-Aware Move tool

Step-by-Step

1. Choose File > Browse in Bridge and locate the image called **ps1402.psd** in the ps14lessons folder. An image of a bird appears.

2. Choose File Save As and name the image **ps1402_work**. Keep the format as .PSD and choose to save it in the ps14lessons folder.

3. Select the Content-Aware Move tool (✖) located under the Patch tool, and click and drag to select the bird that is sitting on the branch (Figure 14-7).

Figure 14-7: Click and drag to create a selection around the bird.

4. With the Content-Aware Move tool still selected, click and drag the bird selection to the left (Figure 14-8), and then release. The image area behind the bird is replaced with sky image as shown in Figure 14-9.

Figure 14-8: Click and drag using the Content-Aware Move tool.

Figure 14-9: This method leaves no hole in your image.

5. Choose File > Save and then File > Close.

Stroke and fills

Even though you have been able to apply fills and different types of strokes in previous versions of Photoshop, it was not very intuitive, and many options were lacking. In Photoshop CS6, you can now take advantage of features that you would expect in Adobe Illustrator, such as applying a stroke to the inside, middle, or outside of a vector shape, the creation of dashed strokes, and the ability to change the caps and joints of a stroke.

If you want to experiment, try the following steps:

Step-by-Step   **Follow these steps to try out the new stroke and fill features**

1. Choose File > Open and open the image called **ps1403.psd**.

2. Choose File > Save As, name the file **ps1403_work**, and keep the file in .psd format. Choose Save and an image of someone typing appears. Next, you will create a vector shape using the custom shape tools.

3. Click and hold the Vector Shape tool (the default is the Rectangle tool) and select the Custom Shape tool as shown in Figure 14-10.

Figure 14-10: *Select the Custom Shape tool.*

4. From the Shape drop-down menu in the Options bar, select the shape called Arrow 9 as shown in Figure 14-11.

Figure 14-11: *Select Arrow 9 from the custom shape drop-down menu.*

5. Click and drag to create an arrow shape anywhere on the image; any size is fine.

6. Look for Fill and Stroke in the Options bar at the top of the workspace, and then select Fill to see the swatches appear. In this example, you will sample a color from the image, so you will need the Color Picker.

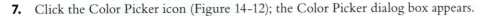
7. Click the Color Picker icon (Figure 14-12); the Color Picker dialog box appears.

Figure 14-12: *Open the Color Picker to select a color.*

8. With the Color Picker open, choose any of the blue tones in the shirt on the right side, and then click OK. The fill of the arrow now matches the blue tone.

9. Now click Stroke in the Options bar and select Black from the Swatches panel that appears.

10. Type **1.33** into the stroke Width textbox, and then click the Set shape stroke type drop-down menu; the Stroke options appear as shown in Figure 14-13.

Figure 14-13: *You now have additional stroke options in Photoshop.*

11. Choose Center from the Align window. The Align feature allows you to align your stroke on the inside, center, or outside of a shape.

Notice that you can also change the caps and corners in the Stroke options window.

12. Take the graphic one step further by applying transparency to the fill only. If you do not see the Layers panel, choose Windows > Layers now. Make sure that the shape layer that you just created is active, and then change the Fill to 50% by clicking and dragging the slider to the left until you reach the 50% mark (Figure 14-14). Note that the fill is semi-transparent, but the stroke is still at 100%. Figure 14-15 shows the result of this change.

Figure 14-14: Change the Fill's transparency.   *Figure 14-15: The result.*

13. Keep this file open for the next section on layers.

Layer panel improvements

Current Photoshop users will like the new layer filters, and new users will find that working with layers is an intuitive feature that will help them produce better, more exciting imagery.

The Photoshop CS6 Layers panel now has added filters that allow users to organize and find layers. The default filter is set to Kind and allows you to choose the type of layer you want to isolate (only show) in the Layers panel. As labeled in Figure 14-16, you can choose a filter for the following types of layers: Pixel layers, Adjustment layers, Type layers, Shape layers, and Smart Objects.

Figure 14-16: You can now filter layers in the Layers panel.

A. Pixel. B. Adjustment. C. Type. D. Shape. E. Smart Objects.

If you want to experiment with this feature and still have **ps1403_work.psd** open, follow these steps.

| Follow these steps to investigate enhancements to the Layers panel | Step-by-Step |

1. Choose the Shape layer filter button from the Kind filter to see that the pixel layer's (Background) visibility is turned off and only the shape layer is visible.

2. Click and hold Kind; you see that a drop-down menu appears with many other filtering options, including Name, Effect, Mode, Attribute, and Color. When you select any of these filters, you can enter additional information to narrow the search results.

3. Click on the the Shape layer filter icon, and then select the Name filter. Type **shape** into the textbox that appears; only the Shape 1 layer appears (Figure 14-17).

Figure 14–17: *Select additonal filters and enter information to give you more accurate results.*

4. You can choose File > Save and File > Close.

More options for creating patterns

Even though Photoshop has offered the ability to include patterns for a long time, options beyond creating your own pattern and scaling the pattern were the limit. Now you can take advantage of filling with a pattern and applying a **scripted fill**. Some of the scripted fills include Cross Weave, Random Fill, Spiral, and Symmetry Fill (Figure 14-18). You will find these new Scripted Patterns in the Edit > Fill dialog box. Unfortunately, they are not in the Adjustment layer option at this point, which means that you will need to scale the pattern source before making the pattern. Follow the steps below to try out this new feature.

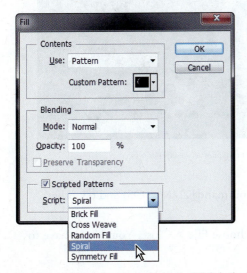

New Scripted Patterns have been added to the Fill dialog box.

Lesson 14

Step-by-Step	Follow these steps to experiment with the new pattern-creation options

1. Choose File > Browse in Bridge, locate and open the image called **ps1404.psd**. Since you will only be using this image to create a pattern, there is no need to save it as a work file.

   This file is relatively small, but if you wanted to make a smaller pattern, you would have to use Image > Image Size at this point to scale it.

   Since you will choose the entire image for the pattern, you do not have to make a selection; typically, you would use the Rectangular Marquee tool (▢) to define the area of an image that you want to define as a pattern.

2. Choose Edit > Define Pattern. The Pattern Name dialog box appears as shown in Figure 14-19. Keep the default pattern name, which is the file name, and click OK.

Figure 14-19: Define a pattern from the ps1404.psd image.

3. Choose File > Browse in Bridge, select the image called **ps1405.psd**, and open it in Photoshop CS6. An image of a girl kicking a soccer ball appears.

4. If the Layers panel is not visible, choose Window > Layers to see that this file contains a Background and two additional layers.

5. Make sure that the second layer, called Put Pattern Here, is active and then choose Edit > Fill. The Fill dialog box appears.

6. Select Pattern from the Content drop-down menu, and then choose your newly created pattern from the Custom Pattern drop-down menu.

7. Check Scripted Patterns, select a Scripted Pattern from the drop-down menu (Figure 14-20), and click OK. As shown in Figure 14-21, the pattern is applied.

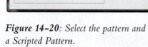

Figure 14-20: Select the pattern and a Scripted Pattern.   *Figure 14-21: The pattern is applied to the layer as a fill.*

8. Experiment by pressing Ctrl+Z (Windows) or Command+Z (Mac OS) and try other scripted patterns.

9. When you are finished experimenting, you can choose File > Close. You do not have to save this file.

New and improved 3D features

The 3D features in Photoshop are extensive enough to write another book, but in this section, you will be introduced to some of the important features that can help you find the tools you need when working in 3D. Keep in mind that Lesson 13 includes a step-by-step exercise to help you get started using this incredibly intense feature.

Some of the new 3D features are described next.

OpenGL is now required

OpenGL is now required in Photoshop CS6. Although OpenGL is the industry's most widely used, supported, and best documented 2D/3D graphics Application Program Interface (API), it could stop some of your experimenting before you begin. Check to see if you have the option available by selecting Edit > Preferences > Performance. If Use Graphics Processor is an option, you can use 3D; if it is grayed out, you may need to update your hardware or software to work in 3D using Photoshop CS6. Find more information about OpenGL and Photoshop at Search for OpenGL Support. On Adobe's site, you find information about preferences that you can change, as well as information on how to check your video card drivers.

Better tool unification

Now in Photoshop CS6, the 3D environment has its own workspace, making it easy to find the tools you need when you want them. Enter this workspace by selecting Window > 3D.

3D Widgets

In Photoshop CS6, **3D widgets** are automatically enabled to help you get a better sense of your 3D environment and perform tasks such as directly manipulating your shadows. Once you have created a 3D object, you can Shift and drag to change the light of the object and also its shadow.

3D Merge improved

In Photoshop CS6, by using **3D Merge** you can now merge more than two 3D layers; the handling is better for 3D layers with different scales and positions.

The best way to find out what works with 3D is to experiment with your files. If 3D is new to you, select a layer and then right-click (Windows) or Control+click (Mac OS) and select Postcard. You are now in the 3D workspace where you can experiment with various Properties in the Properties panel, as well as options in the 3D panel.

As mentioned, this Lesson has been an introduction to some of the new Photoshop CS6 features. If you have skipped to this lesson for a quick peek at "what's new," make sure you start with Lesson 1 of this book to find out how to integrate many of the new features into your workflow.

Skill Summary

In this lesson you learned how to:	Objective
Demonstrate knowledge of retouching and blending images	4.5

Lesson 14

Knowledge Assessment

True/False

Circle **T** if the statement is true or **F** if the statement is false.

T F **1.** The appearance of the Photoshop UI can be modified by choosing Preferences > Interface.

T F **2.** The Erodible brushes actually wear down as you paint with them.

T F **3.** The Patch tool requires the same keyboard combinations for use as the Clone Stamp.

T F **4.** In previous versions of Photoshop, applying fills and strokes have always had advanced features and were easy to work with.

T F **5.** Transparency of strokes and fills are connected to each other and cannot be affected separately.

T F **6.** The Photoshop CS6 Layers panel now has added filters that allow users to organize and find layers.

T F **7.** In Photoshop CS6, 3D layers have improved, but you cannot merge 3D layers at this time.

T F **8.** The 3D workspace environment was first introduced in Photoshop CS2.

T F **9.** You may need to update your hardware or software to work in 3D using Photoshop CS6.

T F **10.** Besides the filter options that the Layer panel now offers, you can enter additional information to narrow layer search results.

Multiple Choice

Select the best response for the following statements.

1. What two new tools have been added to the content-aware features of Photoshop?
   a. Move and Scale
   b. Scale and Retouching
   c. Move and Patch
   d. Patch and Marquee

2. The Patch tool is grouped together with which other tool?
   a. Marquee
   b. Spot Healing Brush
   c. Brush Tool
   d. Lasso

3. Using the Content-Aware Move tool, you can select and relocate a section of your image without leaving what behind?

   a. A hole

   b. Color artifacts

   c. A duplicate image

   d. None of the above

4. Strokes can be aligned to which part of a shape?

   a. Inside

   b. Center

   c. Outside

   d. All of the above

5. Which of the following is not an option when it comes to choosing a filter for organizing layers?

   a. Pixel layers

   b. Vector layers

   c. Shape layers

   d. Smart Objects

6. Cross Weave, Random Fill, Spiral, and Symmetry Fill are all kinds of what?

   a. Patterns

   b. Blending modes

   c. Scripted Patterns

   d. Textures

7. Which feature is automatically enabled to help you get a better sense of your 3D environment?

   a. 3D layers

   b. 3D widgets

   c. 3D objects

   d. OpenGL

8. What is the name of the industry's most widely used, supported and best documented 2D/3D graphics Application Program Interface (API)?

   a. Vector Acceleration

   b. 3D Viewing Enhancement

   c. OpenGL

   d. None of the above

9. Typically, you would choose which tool to define the area of an image that you would want to define as a pattern?

   a. Rectangular Marquee

   b. Pen

   c. Lasso

   d. Magic Wand

10. Once you have created a 3D Object, what do you have to do to change the light and shadow of the object?

   a. Control+drag

   b. Spacebar+drag

   c. Shift+drag

   d. Any of the above

Competency Assessment

Project 14-1	Aligning Strokes on Shapes

There's more to strokes than we've seen so far and sometimes the subtle things can make all the difference.

1. Create a new document in Photoshop that is 8″ × 8″ in size, 150ppi, RGB mode with a white background.

2. Using guides, divide the page into 4 quadrants.

3. Create a new shape on its own layer in Photoshop. Give the shape a fill color of your choice as well as a stroke color of your choice.

4. Duplicate the layer three times and position each shape in one of the quadrants.

5. Adjust the stroke on each shape trying the different Align options – inside, center, or outside. Also adjust the style applied to the stroke.

6. Save the file as **ps14_shapes.psd**.

Project 14-2	Taking Fill all the way

In addition to the new Scripted Patterns, don't forget you have some other options to experiment with...

1. Create a new document in Photoshop that is 8″ × 8″ in size, 150ppi, RGB mode with a white background.

2. Using guides, divide the page into 4 quadrants.

3. Select each quadrant and apply a pattern, pick a different Scripted Pattern for each quadrant.

4. Create four different text layers and position the text on each quadrant indicating the scripted pattern applied to each quadrant.

5. Save the file as **ps14_patterns.psd**.

Proficiency Assessment

| Erodible Brush Tips | Project 14-3 |

Photoshop introduced new erodible brush tips that change in size as you use them as if they were wearing down.

1. Create a new document in Photoshop that is 8″ × 8″ in size, 150ppi, RGB mode with a white background.

2. Select the Brush tool, then select one of the new erodible brush tips (indicated by a charcoal pencil icon) and begin drawing. Be creative and create a drawing to see how the erodible brush tips work.

3. Save the file as **ps14_erodible.psd**.

| Airbrush Tips | Project 14-4 |

Photoshop introduced new Airbrush brush tips that change in size as you use them as if you were using an airbrush to paint.

1. Create a new document in Photoshop that is 8″ × 8″ in size, 150ppi, RGB mode with a white background.

2. Select the Brush tool, then select one of the new Airbrush brush tips (indicated by an airbrush icon) and begin drawing. Be creative and create a drawing to see how the Airbrush brush tips work. If you have access to a Wacom tablet, you'll benefit from the pressure sensitivity options when working with this tool.

3. Save the file as **ps14_airbrush.psd**.

Adobe Visual Communication using Photoshop CS6 Objectives

Skill	Objective	Lesson
Setting Project Requirements	**1**	
Identify the purpose, audience, and audience needs for preparing image(s).	**1.1**	**1**
Demonstrate knowledge of standard copyright rules for images and image use.	**1.2**	**3**
Demonstrate knowledge of project management tasks and responsibilities.	**1.3**	**1, 8**
Communicate with others (such as peers and clients) about design plans.	**1.4**	**1**
Identifying Design Elements When Preparing Images	**2**	
Demonstrate knowledge of image resolution, image size, and image file format for web, video, and print.	**2.1**	**4, 12**
Demonstrate knowledge of design principles, elements, and image composition.	**2.2**	**1, 9**
Demonstrate knowledge of typography.	**2.3**	**4**
Demonstrate knowledge of color correction using Photoshop CS6.	**2.4**	**4, 5, 6, 7**
Demonstrate knowledge of image-generating devices, their resulting image types, and how to access resulting images in Photoshop.	**2.5**	**3, 7, 12**
Understand key terminology of digital images.	**2.6**	**4**
Understanding Adobe Photoshop CS6	**3**	
Identify elements of the Photoshop CS6 user interface and demonstrate knowledge of their functions.	**3.1**	**2, 7, 10**
Demonstrate knowledge of layers and masks.	**3.2**	**5, 7, 8, 9, 11**
Demonstrate knowledge of importing, exporting, organizing, and saving.	**3.3**	**3, 4, 12**
Demonstrate knowledge of producing and reusing images.	**3.4**	**3, 10**
Demonstrate an understanding of and select the appropriate features and options required to implement a color management workflow.	**3.5**	**6, 7**
Manipulating Images by Using Adobe Photoshop CS6	**4**	
Demonstrate knowledge of working with selections	**4.1**	**3, 5, 8**
Use Photoshop guides and rulers.	**4.2**	**12**
Transform images.	**4.3**	**1, 4, 10, 12**
Adjust or correct the tonal range, color, or distortions of an image.	**4.4**	**5, 7, 9**
Demonstrate knowledge of retouching and blending images.	**4.5**	**2, 6, 7, 9, 14**
Demonstrate knowledge of drawing and painting.	**4.6**	**1, 2, 5, 6**
Demonstrate knowledge of type.	**4.7**	**1, 8**
Demonstrate knowledge of filters.	**4.8**	**5, 7, 8, 9, 10, 11**
Publishing Digital Images by Using Adobe Photoshop CS6	**5**	
Demonstrate knowledge of preparing images for web, print, and video.	**5.1**	**3, 4, 12**

Glossary

#

3D images Images presented in a three dimensional environment that can be viewed and modified on an x, y, and z axis.

3D Merge The process of merging two or more 3D layers together in Photoshop.

3D mesh The 3D shape and structure of an object.

3D space The working space or environment in which 3D objects are manipulated and created.

3D widgets Visual elements that assist in viewing and modifying 3D elements.

A

adjustment layer A layer in Photoshop that applies any variety of tonal adjustments to an image.

airbrush A brush tip in Photoshop that simulates the use of an Airbrush.

Align and Distribute features A feature in Photoshop that allows you to align and distribute layers to one another.

animation The process of moving and transforming objects in time to produce an animated scene.

B

Batch Rename A function of the Bridge application that allows you to quickly and accurately rename multiple files.

blending mode Controls how one layer interacts with another layer. A blending mode is applied to the layer that appears above another layer. When using a blending mode, there is a base color (the layer beneath) and a blend color (the layer that the blending mode is applied to), the result of the blending mode depends on the actual mode applied.

Bridge An application that ships with the Creative Suite, Creative Cloud, and many individual Adobe products that allows you to visually browse and open files on your computer.

Bristle brushes Brush tips that simulate traditional Bristle brushes and mimic the behavior in Photoshop.

Brush presets A way of saving the settings defined in a brush tip so that those settings can be recalled and reused when needed.

brush stroke When using the Brush tool, each application of the brush on the canvas is a brush stroke.

brush tip The shape and attributes that are used when using the Brush tool as well as many other tools in Photoshop that use a brush tip as part of its behavior.

C

Camera Raw A file format generated from high-end digital cameras that contains unprocessed image data providing extended editing and adjustment capabilities in Photoshop.

clipping mask A feature in Photoshop that allows you to "clip" the contents of one layer to another, essentially masking one layer using the contents of another.

Glossary

Clone Stamp tool Primarily used for retouching, the Clone Stamp tool copies content from one area of an image and pastes it to another, effectively removing portions of an image with existing areas.

Clouds filter A filter that generates a pattern resembling clouds based on the active foreground and background color.

Collection A virtual folder that can be created in Bridge that allows you to view files in one area even though they are located in various locations on a computer.

composition The placement or arrangement of visual elements in an image.

contour Is a property found in layers that controls how an object is shaded in Photoshop.

Crop tool Used to adjust the framing of an image to make it more aesthetically pleasing. The Crop tool often removes pixels after its use.

Curves Adjustment The Curves Adjustment provides a way to adjust the tonal range of an image by altering the input and output values.

Custom Shape tool Used to draw vector-based shapes or paths in Photoshop. When using this tool, you can select any number of interesting shapes to draw.

CMYK (Cyan, Magenta, Yellow, and Black) The Subtractive primary colors using in the Printing process and is also one of the available color modes in Photoshop.

D

DNG file (Digital Negative) Similar to a Camera Raw image but not a proprietary format. The DNG format is a universal unprocessed format.

E

emboss An effect applied in Photoshop that produces the appearance of a 3D surface.

EPS (Encapsulated PostScript) is a format that is used primarily for print-based projects. A somewhat antiquated format that gained popularity for its ability to include vector-based clipping paths to remove the background of an image and maintain crisp edges.

Eyedropper tool A tool in Photoshop used to pick up the color from an image.

F

Fade command After applying a filter, you can use this command to minimize the application of the filter to varying degrees.

Favorites panel A panel in the Bridge application that provides a shortcut for various locations on a computer.

file formats The format in which a file is saved in Photoshop. Photoshop has the ability to save to a variety of formats, each of which has advantages and disadvantages for various uses.

fill opacity Controls the amount of transparency applied to the pixel fill of an object.

Filter Gallery A feature in Photoshop that displays a gallery of filters that can be applied to an image. Using the Filter Gallery, you can preview filters and apply multiple filters on top of one another.

Filter panel A panel in the Bridge application that allows you to filter the files being viewed based on different properties such as file type, keyword, label, etc.

filters Texture based effects that are applied to layers or selected areas in an image.

Free Transform Provides a method by which you can transform an object in a variety of different ways including scale, rotate, and skew.

G

gamut Defines the range of colors available in a specific color model.

GIF format (Graphic Interchange Format) A common format used in web pages and mainly for graphics that contain areas of solid color such as logos. GIFs are capable of making a certain color of the graphic transparent.

gradient A transition between two or more colors that can be defined in Photoshop.

H

Hand tool Used to change the currently viewed area in a Photoshop document. The Hand tool is a more efficient way to move around in a document than the typical scroll bars that are used.

Healing Brush tool A tool similar to the Clone Stamp tool that adds additional properties that "heal" an area to blend a cloned area into its destination.

HD Video (High definition video) is video that contains a higher resolution picture than traditional SD (Standard Definition) video.

highlight and shadow Describes the lightest tones of an image (highlight) and the darkest tones of an image (shadows).

histogram Visual representation of the tones in a particular image. Similar tones in a specific tonal area of an image are stacked on top of one another to generate a visual representation of an image.

History panel Every action that is performed in Photoshop, is recorded as a state in the History panel. The History panel provides a way that you can selectively undo or go back to specific points in the history of a document.

I

Image Size dialog box A dialog box in Photoshop that allows you to adjust the size of an image using both pixel measurements as well as traditional units such as inches, or millimeters.

J

JPEG (Joint Photographic Experts Group) A common format used in web pages. Used mainly for graphics containing continuous tones such as photographs.

K

keyframe Defines a specific point in the timeline of an animation that indicates a change.

keywords Descriptive metadata about an image that can be used to filter and identify an image.

L

Lasso tool A tool in Photoshop used to draw free-form selections.

layer mask A mask applied to a layer that hides portions of that layer and reveals portions of an image. In a Layer Mask, white reveals the layer, black conceals the layer.

layer styles A way of applying effects to a layer in a non-destructive manner so that the effects can be adjusted at any time.

layers Subcomponents of a Photoshop file that allow users to maximize the editability of a file. Layers work similar to traditional overlays in that they are "layered" on top of one another.

Glossary

light sources When working with an effect or with 3D effects, lighting sources can be adjusted and/or added to change the appearance of an effect and its object.

M

materials Textures and their related appearance settings applied to a 3D object.

Magic Wand A tool in Photoshop used to create selections based on the tonal values of the area that is clicked with the Magic Want tool. A tolerance setting can be used to control the selected area.

Marquee tools Tools in Photoshop that are used to create fundamental geometric selections including rectangles, squares, ovals, and cirlcles.

metadata Embedded information in a file (in the case of Photoshop and Bridge an image) that helps you to filter and find files on a computer.

midtones The tones of an image found between the highlights and the shadows of an image.

Mini Bridge A panel in Photoshop that allows you to view files on a hard drive without the need to manually navigate to a file using Photoshop or the computer's Operating System. Note: The Bridge application needs to be running in order for the Mini Bridge to properly function.

Mixer Brush A brush in Photoshop that mixes color in a file and simulates paint on canvas. This tool allows you to adjust the wetness of the canvas as well as the cleanliness of the brush.

Motion Blur A filter in Photoshop that blurs an image to create the appearance of motion.

Move tool Used to move objects in Photoshop.

N

neutral An area of an image that should be balanced in color; usually an area of white or gray.

O

opacity The measure of transparency of an object in Photoshop.

OpenGL A method used by a computer to accelerate 2D and 3D rendering.

Options bar A contextual bar in Photoshop that provides options for the currently selected tool.

optimizing image slices The process of adjusting the settings for individual slices.

P

panel group In Photoshop, panels can be "grouped" together into a related group of panels.

panels A small window providing specific functionality or controls. Many features are controlled within panels. All panels can be opened from the Window menu.

Patch tool A tool that is used to remove elements of a photo by selecting an area and "patching" it by dragging the selected area to another area of an image.

Paths Vector-based elements used in Photoshop and other Adobe applications to define precise selection areas.

pattern fill An effect applied that fills an area with a pattern.

Pen tool A tool in Photoshop used to draw vector-based paths and shapes.

perspective planes When using the Vanishing Point filter, perspective planes are defined to establish the perspective used within the Vanishing Point filter.

Place By choosing File > Place, you can import a graphic into Photoshop. During this process, the placed object is converted to a Smart Object automatically.

PDF (Portable Document Format) An Adobe format that provides for a versatile vector and raster based format that allows for easy distribution to virtually any computer platform. Using the free Adobe Reader or Adobe Acrobat application, a file can be opened and viewed with confidence that the file will retain its visual appearance on any computer.

PNG (Portable Network Graphic) A format used on web pages that elevates the features of a web graphic in that it can represent a wide range of colors and can contain varied levels of transparency.

Q

Quick Mask A mode in Photoshop used to generate selections using the Brush tool as well as other selection tools.

Quick Selection tool A tool in Photoshop that provides a way to create selections quickly. The Quick Selection tool uses a brush tip to define areas to be selected and detects contrast edges to create the selection.

R

RGB (Red, Green, Blue) The Additive color model used for on-screen viewing and for maximum editing capabilities in Photoshop.

red eye When an image of a person or pet contains red in the pupils of the eye. This is caused by the flash of a camera reflecting light into the eye and back into the camera.

Refine Edge When a selection is active in Photoshop, the Refine Edge feature can be used to refine a selection in a number of different ways to create a more accurate selection.

Render Video The process of generating a video file from raw video and animation data in Photoshop.

resampling The process of scaling an image up or down and adding or removing pixels as needed.

resolution The number of pixels per area of an image. Commonly represented as ppi (pixels per inch).

retouching A term used to describe the process of improving an image in a variety of ways including removing and/or improving areas of an image.

S

Save Selection Allow you to save an active selection so that it can be recalled at any point in the future.

scripted fill A fill option that allows a user to fill an area with a pattern but with random or symmetric fills.

selection An area defined using one of the selection tools in Photoshop that indicates an active "selected" area in the file.

sharpening A process where an image is improved by enhancing the detail in areas of an image to improve clarity.

slices An individual portion of a larger image used to display images on the Web.

Smart Filter When applying a filter to a Smart Object, the filter is applied in a non-destructive way and can be modified at any time.

Smart Object A Photoshop object that embeds an element in Photoshop so that when modified, the original embedded element is referenced to minimize loss of quality.

Glossary

T

Tabbed workspace When multiple files are open at the same time in Photoshop, a tabbed workspace can be used that displays each file as a tab across the top of the Photoshop workspace making it easy to make each file active quickly and easily.

TIFF (Tagged Image File Format) A common file format used in photography and the print industry. Generally used as a high resolution file format capable of compressing an image using LZW compression (a lossless compression algorithm).

text styles When text is formatted in Photoshop, text styles provide a way to record this formatting so that it can be reapplied to other text.

Timeline panel A panel in Photoshop used to animate images over a defined length of time.

tint An attribute of certain effects applied in Photoshop that adds a color tint to the effect being applied.

Tools panel The panel in Photoshop that houses every tool available in the program. The Tools panel has two different views, single-column and double-column.

type layer Whenever type is added in Photoshop, a new layer is created called a Type Layer.

U

User Interface The interface that allows a user to interact with the software.

V

Vanishing Point filter A filter in Photoshop that is used to adjust, transform, and clone images in perspective.

view The current appearance of a document including zoom level and viewing area.

Visibility icon Layers can be hidden or shown at any time by enabling or disabling the Visibility icon found on the left side of every layer in the Layers panel.

W

warp A transformation option that allows you to distort an image using a technique that twists and warps.

Web Photo Gallery A feature in the Bridge application that allows you to create a photo gallery of a group of images and post them to a web site that can be viewed by anyone with an internet connection.

white and black point Areas of an image that should be white or black.

Z

zoom The act of increasing or decreasing the magnification of a document in Photoshop.

Index

Index

Index

Magic Wand tool, 115–117, 123

managing
  blending modes, 163–164
  color
    with adjustment layers, 252–254
    settings, 99–100
  fill opacity in layer styles, 273
  folders in Adobe Bridge, 56–59
  Hue-Saturation layer, 258
  image size, 100–101
  layers, 218
  lighting, 377–380
  midtones, 195–196
  multiple Smart Object layers, 292–293
  opacity of brush strokes, 156–157
  selections into layers, 114–115
  shading in layer styles, 272–273
  Smart Filters, 300–301
  units of measurement, 335–336
  views in Adobe Bridge, 78–79
  visibility of layers, 226

Marquee tool (M), 30, 108–110, 113

masks
  adding to vector layer, 8
  adjustment layer, 254–257
  clipping, 243–245
  layer, 121–122, 227, 233–236
  refining Black & White, 254–257
  Smart Filter filter effects, 319–322

Material picker thumbnail, 387

maximizing productivity with screen modes, 46–48

measuring tools, 30

Media Encoder, 363

menu (Tween), 357

metadata
  creating, 61–65

locating, 61–63

templates, 64–65

midtones, adjusting, 195–196

Mixer Brush tool, 40

modes
  blending, 163–164
  CMYK
    overview, 145–146
    previewing, 186
  Frame, 354–358
  RGB
    overview, 145
    reasons for using, 186
    working in, 146–147
  Timeline, 359–362

modifying
  blending modes, 163–164
  color
    with adjustment layers, 252–254
    settings, 99–100
  fill opacity in layer styles, 273
  folders in Adobe Bridge, 56–59
  Hue/Saturation layer, 258
  image size, 100–101
  layers, 218
  lighting, 377–380
  midtones, 195–196
  multiple Smart Object layers, 292–293
  opacity of brush strokes, 156–157
  selections into layers, 114–115
  shading in layer styles, 272–273
  Smart Filters, 300–301
  units of measurement, 335–336
  views in Adobe Bridge, 78–79
  visibility of layers, 226

Motion Blur dialog box, 114, 239, 296, 300, 320

Move tool (V), 30, 267
  content-aware, 397–399
  overview, 13, 21
  setting layer opacity with, 239–240

moving

images from other documents, 231–232

layers, 225

Mpeg4, 382

N

name, searching files by, 65–66

naming layers, 220–222

navigating
  Adobe Bridge
    automation tools, 69–78
    changing views, 78–79
    creating and locating metadata, 61–63
    creating metadata templates, 64–65
    Favorites, 59–60
    folders, 56–59
    keywords, 63
    opening files from, 65
    overview, 55–56
    review, 79–83
    saving collections, 68
    searching for files using, 65–67
  image area
    Hand tool, 44–45
    overview, 42–43
    screen modes, 46–48
    tabbed windows, 45–46
    Zoom tool, 43–44
  shortcuts, 45

navigation tools, 31

neutral colors
  overview, 197
  setting, 198–200

New dialog box, 152, 218

new features
  3D, 405
  3D Merge, 405
  3D widgets, 405
  brush tips, 8–10, 158, 396–397
  content-aware tools, 397–399
  fills, 400–402
  Layers panel improvements, 402–403

Move tool, content-aware, 397–399

OpenGL, 370, 405

overview of, 395–396

patterns, creating, 403–404

stroke, 400–402

New Guide dialog box, 359

New icon, 10

New Layer dialog box, 9, 220–221, 323

New Style dialog box, 273

O

O (Dodge tool), 30, 34, 289

objects, 3D
  adjusting lighting, 377–380
  animating soda cans, 380–381
  creating objects, 369–377
  overview, 369
  positioning in 3D space, 375–377
  review, 390–393

opacity
  changing brush stroke, 156–157
  fill, 273
  layer, 239–240

Open dialog box, 334

OpenGL, 370, 405

opening
  Contour Editor, 270
  documents
    in Adobe Bridge Mini Bridge, 28–29
    overview, 86–87
  files
    from Adobe Bridge, 65
    overview, 185
  images as Smart Objects, 282–285
  preferences dialog box, 206

optimizing, 347

optimizing image slices, 351–352

options
  Smart Filters, 317–318
  transform, 91–93

Index

Index

All the photos in this book were printed with permission—including those credited below—or were created by the authors of this book:

Front Matter

Page vii (Figure 1): Boy & skateboard silhouette (@ John Rawsterne/iStockphoto); Flip it (@ Stephen Keable/iStockphoto); Skate park (@ Ju-Lee/iStockphoto); Nose Grab - Red Sky Silhouette (@ Christian Carroll/iStockphoto); Skateboarder - Frontside Disaster (@ Christian Carroll/iStockphoto); Frontside Air over the Hip (@ Christian Carroll/iStockphoto); Young Girl - Skateboard Practice (@ Christian Carroll/iStockphoto); Young Girl - Skateboard Fun (@ Christian Carroll/iStockphoto); Skateboarder - Frontside 5-0 Grind (@ Christian Carroll/iStockphoto); Skateboarder - Frontside Air (@ Christian Carroll/iStockphoto); Skateboarder - Frontside Grind (@ Christian Carroll/iStockphoto); Skateboarder - Sunset Rail Slide (@ Christian Carroll/iStockphoto); Skateboarding - Tail Slide (@ Christian Carroll/iStockphoto); Camera on top of the skateboard (@ Nejc Slatner/iStockphoto)

Page viii (Figure 1): Colorful Rooster (@ narvikk/iStockphoto), Brown and White Cow (@ narvikk/iStockphoto); Red Barn (@ Stephan Hoerold/iStockphoto)

Page viii (Figure 2): Red car in Havana sunset (@ Roxana Gonzalez/iStockphoto)

Page ix (Figure 1): Hot_Air_Balloons4 (@ Curtis J. Morley/iStockphoto)

Page ix (Figure 2) Skateboarder - Frontside Disaster (@ Christian Carroll/iStockphoto); Frontside Air over the Hip (@ Christian Carroll/iStockphoto); Young Girl - Skateboard Practice (@ Christian Carroll/iStockphoto)

Page xxv (Figure 1): Skier with sun and mountains (@ Jeannette Meier Kamer/iStockphoto)

Page xxvi (Figure 1): Red car in Havana sunset (@ Roxana Gonzalez/iStockphoto)

Page xxvi (Figure 2): Boy & skateboard silhouette (@ John Rawsterne/iStockphoto); Flip it (@ Stephen Keable/iStockphoto); Skate park (@ Ju-Lee/iStockphoto); Nose Grab - Red Sky Silhouette (@ Christian Carroll/iStockphoto); Skateboarder - Frontside Disaster (@ Christian Carroll/iStockphoto); Frontside Air over the Hip (@ Christian Carroll/iStockphoto); Young Girl - Skateboard Practice (@ Christian Carroll/iStockphoto); Young Girl - Skateboard Fun (@ Christian Carroll/iStockphoto); Skateboarder - Frontside 5-0 Grind (@ Christian Carroll/iStockphoto); Skateboarder - Frontside Air (@ Christian Carroll/iStockphoto); Skateboarder - Frontside Grind (@ Christian Carroll/iStockphoto); Skateboarder - Sunset Rail Slide

(@ Christian Carroll/iStockphoto); Skateboarding - Tail Slide (@ Christian Carroll/iStockphoto); Camera on top of the skateboard (@ Nejc Slatner/iStockphoto)

Page xxvii (Figure 1): Colorful Rooster (@ narvikk/iStockphoto), Brown and White Cow (@ narvikk/iStockphoto); Red Barn (@ Stephan Hoerold/iStockphoto)

Page xxviii (Figure 1): Jump (@ Yulia Popkova/iStockphoto), Funny Duck (@ George Clerk/iStockphoto), King Penguins (@ Mlenny Photography/iStockphoto)

Page xxix (Figure 1): Portait of young boy (@ Dimo Popcev/iStockphoto), Antique photograph (@ Duncan Walker/iStockphoto)

Page xxxi (Figure 1): Boy jumping (@ Galina Barskaya/iStockphoto)

Page xxxii (Figure 1): Isolated Portraits-Young Hispanic Businesswoman (@ Jacom Stephens/iStockphoto), LA Skyline at Twilight (@ ekash/iStockphoto)

Page xxxii (Figure 2): Monarch butterfly (@ Shirell Delaney/iStockphoto)

Page xxxiv (Figure 1): kiteboard - starting (@ Lukasz Gumowski/iStockphoto); Hot_Air_Balloons4 (@ Curtis J. Morley/iStockphoto); Cumulus Clouds over Lake (@ AVTG/iStockphoto)

Page xxxv (Figure 1): Guitarist (@ Niko Guido/iStockphoto)

Page xxxv (Figure 2): Bird on a limb (@ Jupiterimages/Getty Images, Inc.)

Lesson 1

Skier with sun and mountains (@ Jeannette Meier Kamer/iStockphoto): Lesson opener (Page 1), Figure 1-1 (Page 3), Figure 1-2 (Page 4), Figure 1-5 (Page 5), Figure 1-7 (Page 6), Figure 1-9 (Page 7), Figure 1-10 (Page 8), Figure 1-14 (Page 11), Figure 1-19 (Page 14), Figure 1-20 (Page 14), Figure 1-21 (Page 15), Figure 1-30 (Page 21)

Lesson 2

Red car in Havana sunset (@ Roxana Gonzalez/iStockphoto): Lesson opener (Page 27), Figure 2-2 (Page 28), Figure 2-3 (Page 29), Figure 2-10 (Page 34), Figure 2-11 (Page 35), Figure 2-15 (Page 37), Figure 2-17 (Page 38), Figure 2-18 (Page 38), Figure 2-19 (Page 39), Figure 2-28 (Page 42), Figure 2-30 (Page 44), Figure 2-32 (Page 47), Figure 2-33 (Page 48)

Street of Trinidad, Cuba (@ Maria Pavlova/iStockphoto): Figure 2-2 (Page 28), Figure 2-31 (Page 45)

Credits

Lesson 3

Boy & skateboard silhouette (@ John Rawsterne/iStockphoto): Lesson opener (Page 53), Figure 3-1 (Page 55), Figure 3-4 (Page 58), Figure 3-5 (Page 59), Figure 3-6 (Page 60)

Flip it (@ Stephen Keable/iStockphoto): Lesson opener (Page 53), Figure 3-1 (Page 55), Figure 3-4 (Page 58), Figure 3-5 (Page 59), Figure 3-19 (Page 70), Figure 3-23 (Page 74), Figure 3-27 (Page 78)

Skate park (@ Ju-Lee/iStockphoto): Lesson opener (Page 53), Figure 3-1 (Page 55), Figure 3-4 (Page 58), Figure 3-19 (Page 70), Figure 3-23 (Page 74), Figure 3-27 (Page 78)

Nose Grab - Red Sky Silhouette (@ Christian Carroll/iStockphoto): Lesson opener (Page 53), Figure 3-1 (Page 55), Figure 3-4 (Page 58), Figure 3-13 (Page 66), Figure 3-19 (Page 70), Figure 3-21 (Page 71), Figure 3-23 (Page 74), Figure 3-27 (Page 78)

Skateboarder - Frontside Disaster (@ Christian Carroll/iStockphoto): Lesson opener (Page 53), Figure 3-1 (Page 55), Figure 3-4 (Page 58), Figure 3-19 (Page 70), Figure 3-21 (Page 71), Figure 3-23 (Page 74), Figure 3-27 (Page 78), Figure 3-28 (Page 79)

Frontside Air over the Hip (@ Christian Carroll/iStockphoto): Lesson opener (Page 53), Figure 3-1 (Page 55), Figure 3-4 (Page 58), Figure 3-5 (Page 59), Figure 3-6 (Page 60), Figure 3-19 (Page 70), Figure 3-21 (Page 71), Figure 3-23 (Page 74), Figure 3-27 (Page 78), Figure 3-28 (Page 79)

Young Girl - Skateboard Practice (@ Christian Carroll/iStockphoto): Lesson opener (Page 53), Figure 3-1 (Page 55) Figure 3-4 (Page 58), Figure 3-5 (Page 59), Figure 3-6 (Page 60), Figure 3-19 (Page 70), Figure 3-23 (Page 74), Figure 3-27 (Page 78), Figure 3-28 (Page 79)

Young Girl - Skateboard Fun (@ Christian Carroll/iStockphoto): Lesson opener (Page 53), Figure 3-1 (Page 55), Figure 3-4 (Page 58), Figure 3-5 (Page 59), Figure 3-19 (Page 70), Figure 3-23 (Page 74), Figure 3-27 (Page 78)

Skateboarder - Frontside 5-0 Grind (@ Christian Carroll/iStockphoto): Lesson opener (Page 53), Figure 3-1 (Page 55), Figure 3-4 (Page 58), Figure 3-5 (Page 59), Figure 3-13 (Page 66), Figure 3-14 (Page 67), Figure 3-19 (Page 70), Figure 3-23 (Page 74), Figure 3-27 (Page 78)

Skateboarder - Frontside Air (@ Christian Carroll/iStockphoto): Lesson opener (Page 53), Figure 3-1 (Page 55), Figure 3-4 (Page 58), Figure 3-13 (Page 66), Figure 3-14 (Page 67), Figure 3-17 (Page 68), Figure 3-19 (Page 70), Figure 3-23 (Page 74), Figure 3-27 (Page 78)

Skateboarder - Frontside Grind (@ Christian Carroll/iStockphoto): Lesson opener (Page 53), Figure 3-1 (Page 55), Figure 3-4 (Page 58), Figure 3-13 (Page 66), Figure 3-14 (Page 67), Figure 3-17 (Page 68), Figure 3-19 (Page 70), Figure 3-27 (Page 78)

Skateboarder - Sunset Rail Slide (@ Christian Carroll/iStockphoto): Lesson opener (Page 53), Figure 3-1 (Page 55), Figure 3-4 (Page 58), Figure 3-19 (Page 70), Figure 3-27 (Page 78)

Skateboarding - Tail Slide (@ Christian Carroll/iStockphoto): Lesson opener (Page 53), Figure 3-1 (Page 55), Figure 3-4 (Page 58), Figure 3-6 (Page 60), Figure 3-19 (Page 70), Figure 3-27 (Page 78)

Camera on top of the skateboard (@ Nejc Slatner/iStockphoto): Lesson opener (Page 53), Figure 3-1 (Page 55), Figure 3-4 (Page 58), Figure 3-6 (Page 60), Figure 3-15 (Page 67), Figure 3-19 (Page 70), Figure 3-27 (Page 78)

green field and blue sky (@ Iakov Kalinin/iStockphoto): Figure 3-1 (Page 55), Figure 3-4 (Page 58), Figure 3-19 (Page 70), Figure 3-27 (Page 78)

Lesson 4

Colorful Rooster (@ narvikk/iStockphoto): Lesson opener (Page 85), Figure 4-1 (Page 86), Figure 4-4 (Page 89), Figure 4-5 (Page 90), Figure 4-7 (Page 91), Figure 4-8 (Page 92), Figure 4-9 (Page 93), Figure 4-10 (Page 94), Figure 4-11 (Page 94)

Brown and White Cow (@ narvikk/iStockphoto): Lesson opener (Page 85), Figure 4-1 (Page 86), Figure 4-5 (Page 90), Figure 4-7 (Page 91), Figure 4-8 (Page 92), Figure 4-9 (Page 93), Figure 4-10 (Page 94), Figure 4-11 (Page 94), Figure 4-12 (Page 95), Figure 4-13 (Page 95)

Red Barn (@ Stephan Hoerold/iStockphoto): Lesson opener (Page 85), Figure 4-1 (Page 86), Figure 4-4 (Page 89), Figure 4-5 (Page 90), Figure 4-7 (Page 91), Figure 4-8 (Page 92), Figure 4-9 (Page 93), Figure 4-10 (Page 94), Figure 4-11 (Page 94), Figure 4-12 (Page 95), Figure 4-13 (Page 95)

Lesson 5

Jump (@ Yulia Popkova/iStockphoto): Lesson opener (Page 107), Figure 5-18 (Page 118), Figure 5-19 (Page 119), Figure 5-20 (Page 119), Figure 5-24 (Page 121), Figure 5-25 (Page 122), Figure 5-26 (Page 123)

Funny Duck (@ George Clerk/iStockphoto): Lesson opener (Page 107), Figure 5-33 (Page 126), Figure 5-34 (Page 126), Figure 5-35 (Page 126), Figure 5-36 (Page 127), Figure 5-38 (Page 128), Figure 5-39 (Page 129), Figure 5-40 (Page 129)

King Penguins (@ Mlenny Photography/iStockphoto): Lesson opener (Page 107), Figure 5-33 (Page 126), Figure 5-39 (Page 129), Figure 5-40 (Page 129)

smiling woman (@ Marcin Bania/iStockphoto): Figure 5-27 (Page 124), Figure 5-28 (Page 124), Figure 5-29 (Page 125), Figure 5-30 (Page 125), Figure 5-31 (Page 125), Figure 5-32 (Page 125)

Red apple explosion (@ Gustaf Brundin/iStockphoto): Figure 5-44 (Page 133), Figure 5-45 (Page 133), Figure 5-48 (Page 134), Figure 5-49 (Page 134)

Lesson 6

Portait of young boy (@ Dimo Popcev/iStockphoto): Lesson opener (Page 143), Figure 6-26 (Page 161), Figure 6-28 (Page 162), Figure 6-29 (Page 163), Figure 6-30 (Page 165), Figure 6-31 (Page 166)

Antique photograph (@ Duncan Walker/iStockphoto): Lesson opener (Page 143), Figure 6-32 (Page 167), Figure 6-33 (Page 168), Figure 6-34 (Page 168), Figure 6-36 (Page 169), Figure 6-37 (Page 170), Figure 6-38 (Page 171), Figure 6-39 (Page 172), Figure 6-40 (Page 172), Figure 6-41 (Page 173), Figure 6-42 (Page 173), Figure 6-43 (Page 173), Figure 6-44 (Page 173), Figure 6-47 (Page 175), Figure 6-49 (Page 175), Figure 6-51 (Page 176), Figure 6-52 (Page 176), Figure 6-53 (Page 176), Figure 6-56 (Page 178), Figure 6-57 (Page 178)

Colorful Body Painted Woman Posing Against Pink Wall (@ eva serrabassa/iStockphoto): Figure 6-4 (Page 147), Figure 6-9 (Page 152)

Powerful music (@ Anja Koppitsch/iStockphoto): Figure 6-19 (Page 157), Figure 6-21 (Page 158), Figure 6-23 (Page 159), Figure 6-24 (Page 160), Figure 6-25 (Page 160)

Innocent Perception (@ Dimo Popcev/iStockphoto): Figure 6-30 (Page 165)

Grunge background (© Duncan Walker/iStockphoto): Figure 6-55 (Page 177), Figure 6-56 (Page 178), Figure 6-57 (Page 178)

Lesson 8

Boy jumping (@ Galina Barskaya/iStockphoto): Lesson opener (Page 217), Figure 8-24 (Page 231), Figure 8-27 (Page 233), Figure 8-28 (Page 234), Figure 8-29 (Page 234), Figure 8-30 (Page 234), Figure 8-31 (Page 235), Figure 8-32 (Page 236), Figure 8-33 (Page 236), Figure 8-34 (Page 237), Figure 8-35 (Page 237), Figure 8-36 (Page 237), Figure 8-39 (Page 239), Figure 8-40 (Page 239), Figure 8-41 (Page 240), Figure 8-43 (Page 241), Figure 8-44 (Page 241), Figure 8-45 (Page 242), Figure 8-46 (Page 243), Figure 8-48 (Page 244), Figure 8-49 (Page 244), Figure 8-50 (Page 244)

Lesson 9

Isolated Portraits-Young Hispanic Businesswoman (@ Jacom Stephens/iStockphoto): Lesson Opener (Page 251), Figure 9-1 (Page 252), Figure 9-2 (Page 252), Figure 9-3 (Page 252), Figure 9-4 (Page 253), Figure 9-6 (Page 255), Figure 9-7 (Page 255), Figure 9-8 (Page 256), Figure 9-9 (Page 257), Figure 9-10 (Page 258), Figure 9-14 (Page 260), Figure 9-16 (Page 260), Figure 9-18 (Page 261)

LA Skyline at Twilight (@ ekash/iStockphoto): Lesson Opener (Page 251), Figure 9-19 (Page 262), Figure 9-20 (Page 263), Figure 9-22 (Page 263), Figure 9-25 (Page 264), Figure 9-26 (Page 265), Figure 9-27 (Page 265), Figure 9-28 (Page 267), Figure 9-29 (Page 267), Figure 9-30 (Page 268), Figure 9-31 (Page 269), Figure 9-32 (Page 269), Figure 9-33 (Page 269), Figure 9-37 (Page 271), Figure 9-39 (Page 271), Figure 9-43 (Page 272), Figure 9-45 (Page 273)

Lesson 10

Monarch butterfly (@ Shirell Delaney/iStockphoto): Lesson Opener (Page 281), Figure 10-1 (page 282), Figure 10-3 (Page 283), Figure 10-4 (Page 284), Figure 10-6 (Page 285), Figure 10-9 (Page 288), Figure 10-13 (Page 291), Figure 10-16 (Page 294), Figure 10-17 (Page 294), Figure 10-18 (Page 295), Figure 10-20 (Page 297), Figure 10-23 (Page 299), Figure 10-25 (Page 299), Figure 10-27 (Page 301)

Lesson 12

kiteboard - starting (@ Lukasz Gumowski/iStockphoto): Lesson Opener (Page 333), Figure 12-1 (Page 334), Figure 12-4 (Page 336), Figure 12-7 (Page 338), Figure 12-9 (Page 339), Figure 12-11 (Page 340), Figure 12-12 (Page 341), Figure 12-13 (Page 342), Figure 12-14 (Page 343), Figure 12-15 (Page 344), Figure 12-16 (Page 345), Figure 12-17 (Page 345), Figure 12-18 (Page 345), Figure 12-20 (Page 348), Figure 12-25 (Page 350), Figure 12-26 (Page 350), Figure 12-27 (Page 352)

Hot_Air_Balloons4 (@ Curtis J. Morley/iStockphoto): Lesson Opener (Page 333), Figure 12-21 (Page 349), Figure 12-22 (Page 349), Figure 12-23 (Page 349), Figure 12-24 (Page 349), Figure 12-28 (Page 353), Figure 12-29 (Page 353), Figure 12-30 (Page 354), Figure 12-31 (Page 355), Figure 12-32 (Page 355), Figure 12-33 (Page 356), Figure 12-35 (Page 357)

Cumulus Clouds over Lake (@ AVTG/iStockphoto): Lesson Opener (Page 333), Figure 12-31 (Page 355), Figure 12-32 (Page 355), Figure 12-33 (Page 356), Figure 12-35 (Page 357)

Lesson 13

Guitarist (@ Niko Guido/iStockphoto): Lesson Opener (Page 369), Figure 13-1 (Page 371), Figure 13-2 (Page 371), Figure 13-7 (Page 375), Figure 13-8 (Page 375), Figure 13-9 (Page 376), Figure 13-10 (Page 377), Figure 13-11 (Page 377)

Lesson 14

Bird on a limb (@ Jupiterimages/Getty Images, Inc.): Lesson Opener (Page 395), Figure 14-7 (Page 399), Figure 14-8 (Page 399), Figure 14-9 (Page 399)

Female hands typing (@ Dmitriy Shironosov/iStockphoto): Figure 14-14 (Page 402), Figure 14-15 (Page 402), Figure 14-16 (Page 402)

Soccer Player (@ Bob Thomas/iStockphoto): Figure 14-21 (Page 404)